RENEGADE FOR JUSTICE

Renegade for Justice

Defending the Defenseless
in an Outlaw World

Stephen Lee Saltonstall

Foreword by Michael Meltsner

University Press of Kansas

© 2022 by the University Press of Kansas
All rights reserved

Published by the University Press of Kansas (Lawrence, Kansas 66045),
which was organized by the Kansas Board of Regents and is operated and
funded by Emporia State University, Fort Hays State University, Kansas
State University, Pittsburg State University, the University of Kansas, and
Wichita State University.

Library of Congress Cataloging-in-Publication Data

Names: Saltonstall, Stephen Lee, author. | Meltsner, Michael, 1937–,
writer of foreword.
Title: Renegade for justice : defending the defenseless in an outlaw world
/ Stephen Lee Saltonstall ; foreword by Michael Meltsner.
Description: Lawrence : University Press of Kansas, 2022. | Includes index.
Identifiers: LCCN 2022000496
ISBN 9780700633678 (paperback)
ISBN 9780700633685 (ebook)
Subjects: LCSH: Saltonstall, Stephen Lee. | Criminal defense
Lawyers—United States—Biography. | Defense (Criminal
procedure)—United States.
Classification: LCC KF373.S175 A3 2022 | DDC 340.092 [B]—dc23/eng/20220630
LC record available at https://lccn.loc.gov/2022000496.

British Library Cataloguing-in-Publication Data is available.

Printed in the United States of America

10 9 8 7 6 5 4 3 2 1

The paper used in this publication is acid free and meets the minimum
requirements of the American National Standard for Permanence of Paper
for Printed Library Materials Z39.48–1992.

For my wife, lover, and best friend,
Ellen Claire Bosinoff Saltonstall

Your Honor, years ago I recognized my kinship with all
living beings, and I made up my mind that I was not
one bit better than the meanest on earth. I said then,
and I say now, that: while there is a lower class, I am in it;
while there is a criminal element, I am of it; and while
there is a soul in prison, I am not free.

—Socialist Party leader Eugene Victor Debs, addressing the
United States District Court at his sentencing hearing on
September 18, 1918, after his conviction under the Sedition Act
for the "crime" of making a speech against America's entry
into World War I.

Contents

Foreword

One is wise to approach most lawyer memoirs with a healthy skepticism. Any memoir faces the challenge of avoiding narcissism, selective memory, and exaggeration. The lawyer version of the form famously runs into an additional set of problems: The my-life-in-court syndrome leads to constructing a narrative confined to the corners of this case or that; the depiction of human elements is often distorted as it bends to the demands of legal claims; and, of course, there is the perennial problem of converting legalese into language the common reader can comprehend.

As the author of two memoirs of my own lawyer life, I know the risks of writing one all too well and can only hope I more or less avoided them.

But certainly Stephen Lee Saltonstall has. The reader is immediately engaged by the compelling origin story of his years at the exclusive Phillips Exeter Academy, a brilliant takedown of a rigid, humorless, class-bound institution that paradoxically helped to form the identity and resilience of the advocate he became, one who easily makes the case that he deserves his claimed identity—"Defender of the Defenseless." While he says relatively little about the influence of his legal education, Saltonstall attended Northeastern at a time when it was widely thought to have the most radically innovative law school program in the nation. (Full disclosure: some years after his graduation I became the school's dean; I still teach there.)

Saltonstall has some wonderful stories to tell, mostly from a remarkable career in the criminal court trenches—litigation of the sort that test stamina and commitment. But just as notable is the wide range of relationships with friends, foes, celebrities, malefactors, and officials he encounters in an unusually diverse series of lawyer roles and workplaces. Saltonstall takes us into the world of insurgent legal practice in a fashion that should engage any reader interested in the topic, but also law students and especially those considering the profession who want to know what happens behind the arras.

But no matter how full of moment—regardless of the challenging caseload, the memorable clients, the injustices addressed—a good book requires writing that takes the reader in and keeps her in for the long haul. Here the author exceeds all expectations, in part because of the no-nonsense way he deals with his own struggles. The text is also aided by his facility with short paragraphs and a plethora of signposts telling the reader what to expect. Saltonstall has produced one of the finest first-person books about legal practice I have read.

A particular strength of *Renegade for Justice* is a multitude of cameo descriptions of public figures (from Barney Frank to Ram Dass), unrepentant criminals, the wrongly accused, judges, and prosecutors and police—some dishonest, some impartial, some paragons of justice, and others who are reprehensible hacks—as well as fellow lawyers who make the grade and others who should have gone into a different profession. Saltonstall never blinks at calling out his opinion of the folks he works with, for and against, but he does so briefly in a persuasive and plain-spoken manner—at times with forgiveness; sometimes even sweetness emerges.

What I'm trying to say is that the reader will tend to trust the author, an estimable trait in a lawyer memoirist. Some specifics: He injects legal principles concisely, accurately, readably, and in a manner unlikely to engender criticism from other professionals or confusion from the laity; he also writes about cases involving a range of concerns—criminal defense, of course, but also protection of civil liberties, care and protection of children, assertion of First Amendment rights, and environmental depredation.

He totally lacks sentimentality in assessing those who pass through his office—clients who can be innocent or violent or merely reprehensible. Often broken by the circumstances of their lives, they can be poor (whom he represents for nothing) or even occasionally well-to-do, and either might be capable of refusing to pay the lawyer's fee even when he has won a money judgment on their behalf.

Finally, he is gracious to those he has worked for or with. At the same time, he has a talent for spotting the pompous judge, the lying police officer, the overreaching DA. Often the irony of winning against injustice but knowing the system of punitiveness and inequality has been largely left untouched by his victory . . . and still grinds on.

In short, Saltonstall provides the reader with a unique perspective and a richly experienced life that comes alive on the page.

Michael Meltsner
February 2022

⚖️

Preface

This is a book of courtroom war stories, drawn from my forty years of experience as an obscure lawyer for the underdog and the downtrodden. Like that familiar Bob Dylan persona, I'm a "complete unknown," and that's a plus. With nothing to lose, I'm free to tell the whole truth, and I'm accountable to nobody but you and my conscience. My cases will entertain you, but they have value beyond that, as an insider look at the American justice system, which is rigged against the poor and people of color and tolerates police perjury.

Here are my most memorable trials and appeals, gritty and heartfelt accounts of my work, for people who were guilty of terrible crimes, for powerless victims of injustice, and for clients who fit both descriptions. I begin with an account of my devolution, one might say, from a privileged birth, to near-death (twice), to an emotional crackup and life on the minimum wage, a fall from grace that educated me and led me to summon the inner strength needed to work for and among the despised and downtrodden.

Then come my stories of actual courtroom battles, arranged in emotional order as I remembered and wrote them. I've put you directly into the pit, the space right below the judge's bench, assigned by custom and rule to lawyers and clients. The pit is a place where whirlpools of surprise evidence, or the riptides of karma in the guise of chance, can sweep you away into uncharted, rogue-waved seas without benefit of life jacket.

This book is meant for everyone, but my hope is that law students and others thinking about becoming a lawyer will read it, because values-based lawyering is something that's out there and worth considering. I hope my stories will challenge those of you—you know who you are, you who dream of soft landings in the glittering halls of boring, soul-free law firms doing the bidding of the uber-rich and powerful—to visualize the alternative, a career that's built on cases and causes that further the public interest, human rights, and care of the natural world.

I know from experience that you can succeed as a lawyer working for the public good, even if no one will hire you. I was happiest and most productive when I worked privately and flew solo, with no support staff, relying instead on my telephone, my computer, Westlaw legal research, and paying Google to prioritize me in response to searches for criminal defense lawyers. By keeping my overhead low, I was able to work on righteous cases like those described here, for the benefit of working people, the indigent, people of color, abused and neglected children, and on behalf of wildlife. So, if after reading this you want to be a Renegade for Justice, whether as a lawyer or in some other helping profession, feel free and go for it; it's a wide-open field. All you have to do is begin.

Stephen Lee Saltonstall
February 2022

Acknowledgments

I'm grateful for the ongoing, generous help and guidance of my editor, David Congdon, PhD, and for the enthusiasm and expertise of the rest of the University Press of Kansas team. The early editorial suggestions of lawyer and writer Ronald Goldfarb were invaluable.

My thanks for their support go to retired criminal court judge and sometime horologist Charles Russell Peck of Sussex, England, a childhood neighbor and my close friend and mentor since the age of four, and to my friends for sixty years, Ted and Nancy Hammett.

I salute my friend and copilot on Humane Borders water runs too numerous to count, Guillermo Francisco Raphael Jones, as well as Humane Borders fellow-travelers Doug Ruopp, Rebecca Fowler, Poncho Chavez, John and Diane Hoelter, Laurie Cantillo, Tracey Ristow and Tony Lozano, Brad Jones, Phil Hunger, and Joel Smith. I'm grateful for the advice of my friend, adviser, and former law partner, Robert Woolmington and for the friendship and support of Mitch Epstein, whose photos of me appear in his book *Property Rights* (2021), and I owe thanks to David Overmeyer for designing my blog, www.renegadeforjustice.com.

My siblings Sarah Bonnell Saltonstall, RN, and Thomas Lee Saltonstall (along with his wife, Maggie) have always been there for me. I owe everything to my wife, Ellen Claire Bosinoff Saltonstall, the most beautiful woman in the world, who provided me with sage advice on changes to this book.

Here's a tip of my Thelonious Monk porkpie hat to friends old and new who have enriched my life, including Jon Block, Charles "Buddy" Karelis, James Kaplan, Charles Deknatel, Jesse Kornbluth, Andrew Weil, MD, Richard "Leroy" Odom, Steve and Joe O'Donnell, Tom Fels, Donna Lam, Doug and Shirley Dechant, Jim and Ruth Friedman, Jay and Judi Feldstein, John and Laurie Camelio, Jackie and Skip Sargood, Marshall and Elaine Witten, Susan and Dan McManus, George and Marina Hatch, Dona Ann McAdams and Brad Kessler, Stephen Daedalus Lerner, Charles Wyzanski, Weslie Rosen, Deborah Bancroft, Patrick and Bliss Bernal, Pat and Terry Waterman, Brad Myerson and Pauline DeLazlo, Mike Addis and Maddalena Fiorillo, Hedy Feuer and Mike Perlman, Barbara and Peter Danes, and to my San Domingo neighbors Chris and Christy Sorbe, Lynne and Steve Raspet, and Don VandeGriff.

The loving kindness and advice of my mother, Margaret Bonnell Saltonstall, who died too soon at age 70 in June 1991, guide my thoughts and behavior every day.

CHAPTER I

⚖

Prelude

Suicide Notes and Golden Hits
on the Way to the Bar

There once existed parents who, in accordance with a venerable upper-class New England tradition, happily rid themselves of their adolescent male offspring by sending them to boarding schools.

Kicked Out as the Way In

At age 14, I was packed off to the Phillips Exeter Academy, located in Exeter, New Hampshire. The school's pretentious Latin motto, *Huc Venite Pueri, ut Viri Sitis*, was inscribed in marble over the main building's entrance: "Come hither, boys, that you may become men."

At Exeter, becoming a man meant getting a ticket of admission into one of the only three colleges considered of any consequence: Harvard, Yale, or Princeton, in that order of preference. My father made it clear that Harvard was my only acceptable destination (he was class of 1938; his father was class of 1900). As Captain Ahab put it, "The path to my fixed purpose is laid with iron rails, whereon my soul is grooved to run." Like it or not, Harvard was my White Whale. This was an historical imperative as well. Henry Saltonstall was a member of Harvard's first graduating class, and there has been an unbroken chain of Saltonstalls at Harvard in every generation thereafter.

This all began when a member of my family, Richard Saltonstall, arrived in America in 1630 with John Winthrop and the other original members of the Massachusetts Bay Colony, on a ship called the *Arbella*, to build "A City Upon a Hill." Saltonstall was Winthrop's first assistant. After the initial landing in Salem, Saltonstall sailed up the Charles River and founded Watertown, Massachusetts, on the border of what is now Cambridge.

My direct ancestor Nathaniel Saltonstall fought in our first civil war (1675–1677) against aggrieved Native peoples in an uprising led by Metacomet (known to the English as King Philip), a Wampanoag sachem and son of Massasoit. This was a ghastly conflict of attrition, during which both sides committed unspeakable atrocities, including the murder of women and children, and entire towns were burned to the ground. Nathaniel was later appointed a judge on the Salem witch trials, but he resigned in protest after the first proceeding, which culminated in the execution of Bridget Bishop in 1692. Judge Saltonstall opposed the introduction of "spectral evidence," which allowed witnesses to testify that they saw apparitions of the accused engaged in witchcraft at times and places where they were not physically present, thereby making the defense of alibi impossible. For his heresy, Nathaniel was accused of being a witch himself, though he was never arrested.

Exeter's headmaster was my cousin William Gurdon Saltonstall, whom I had never met. He was a tall, slim, silver-haired, pipe-smoking image of gangly rectitude, strolling about the campus with a perpetual, superficially warm smile suggestive of ice floes not far beneath. Gurdon Saltonstall, for whom Cousin Bill was partially named, was the head of the breakaway Connecticut branch of the family, and he was that state's governor from 1708–1724. Gurdon was heavily involved in the slave trade, a perpetual stain on the family so terrible that I wonder why Cousin Bill never dropped or changed his middle name, especially given that, after retiring as Exeter's headmaster, he served for two years as director of the Peace Corps in Nigeria.

At the beginning of each academic year, Cousin Bill read the school rules aloud to the 800 students assembled in the academy chapel. The only two that I remember were, first, that possession of a radio was a serious disciplinary offense, resulting in confiscation of the item and a period of suspension, and, second, that "reprehensible conduct with girls" was punishable by dismissal. But where was the red line between the acceptable and the "reprehensible"? In an all-boys school, that didn't matter much.

Exeter was a tryout terrarium of the Social Darwinist universe for which we were being "prepped," and the mainstay of a secret curriculum—known to alumni but not listed in the school catalogue—was hazing. I discovered this immediately. My assigned roommate, Bill Dietrich, was a junior varsity wrestler and a devoted acolyte of the school's star grappler, faculty brat, and writer-in-waiting: John Irving. Bill's idea of fun was to practice various painful wrestling "holds" on my unwilling five-foot, 85-pound body. He allowed his buddies to come into our room when I was in class and enjoy themselves by short-sheeting my bed and filling my shoes with shaving cream and toothpaste. Once a group of "Lower Middlers" (Exeterese for sophomores) held me by my legs headfirst over a fifth-floor dorm stairwell and threatened to drop me all the way down. Looking back on this, I believe that I was singled out for the worst hazing because of my last name, which made me a fun target for casual cruelty because I was related to the headmaster.

For me the most depressing compulsory duty at Exeter was attendance at religious services, called "chapel," every weekday morning after breakfast, and Phillips Church on Sundays. In chapel, we had to sing the same dreadful, tired hymns (like "Onward Christian Soldiers") over and over and listen to a boring, pompous sermon from a faculty member or the school minister, Frederick Buechner, whose devoutness, though sincere, verged on a Christ complex. This six-days-per-week cough-syrup dose of required religion extinguished any positive feelings I had about Christianity and made me an atheist. I felt badly for the Jewish kids, who had to endure this awful indoctrination five days a week, although, in what the administration must have thought of as an act of "Christian charity," Jews were permitted to attend an out-of-town synagogue on Saturdays (there were none in Exeter) instead of Phillips Church on Sundays.

The one time I remember having fun at Exeter occurred in chapel. One evening, a few others recruited me to help remove a row of benches from the auditorium. We carried the long, heavy benches into a closet, stacked them on top of one another in pickup-stick piles so high they would be difficult to undo without causing an earthquake, and rearranged the remaining ones to make it appear that nothing was amiss. Student seats in chapel were assigned, and you found your place every morning by counting the rows as you walked down the aisle. The rows were arranged in alphabetical order, but they had no identifying marks or numbers on them.

On the morning after removal of that one row, all was well for the students whose last names began with the letters A through R, but in the back, beginning around the S row, confusion and anarchy reigned. There were loud arguments about who was supposed to sit where, and students were milling around aimlessly throughout the service. The sermon was ruined by the ringing of alarm clocks that a student had hidden in the podium.

There was a different sort of anarchy at Phillips Church, where Sunday attendance was required. A faculty toady checked everyone off on a list;

skipping the service was a serious disciplinary offense. The church organist was our music teacher, Arthur Landers, whom some students disrespectfully called "Artie," talented and emotional on his chosen instrument. In Music Appreciation class, an elective that I took and enjoyed, he played records of all the great Western composers, from Buxtehude to Bartok, and at the end of the year by listening to a piece of music we could identify who wrote it and in what era (pre-Classical, Classical, Romantic, and Modern) it was written.

Mr. Landers's speech and mannerisms made it obvious to all that he was gay—the only person at Exeter with that orientation who didn't try to hide it—which made his life difficult in a time when being queer was socially isolating and dangerous.

Mr. Landers was seriously ill from alcoholism. One Sunday, during a sermon delivered by Reverend Buechner at Phillips Church, Mr. Landers, seemingly out of nowhere and without warning, punctuated the homily with an organ chord, delivered in a minor key and loud as a horn blast from a cruise ship heading out to sea.

There was something genuinely funny about this daring form of improv. It was as if Mr. Landers were disagreeing with the sermon's content and expressing an alternate, atonal view. But because Mr. Landers was in his cups, it was the strong drink talking as well, and the extent of Mr. Landers's disease-fueled rebellion was troubling.

Knowing that Mr. Landers was blotto and a tragedy in progress, Reverend Buechner's reaction to the unscheduled chord was a study in WASP culture, Exeter-style. Reverend Buechner couldn't bring himself to deal with Landers's embarrassing organ fragment by leaving the sanctuary behind and climbing the stairs to the organ loft to bring aid to his sodden colleague. Instead, the Reverend pretended that nothing was amiss, and he soldiered on with his New Testament exegesis, as dry as a San Berdoo wind and as irrelevant to the *res gestae* as a random paragraph from an obscure Henry James novel. Arthur Landers was in dire need of help, and neither the learned Reverend, nor I, nor anyone else did anything about it.

I confronted the hazing I endured at Exeter by becoming what was uncharitably termed a "nego" (pronounced "naygo"), signifying a "negative" attitude, one of a very small number of Exeter students who walked hunched over, staring at the ground, a way of saying that we weren't buying into this school's elitist, "aren't we all superior beings" mantra. Instead of going to pep rallies and football games and dances with the ruling rah-rah "posso" (i.e., "positive," pronounced "pozzo") faction, I stayed in the library, or in Dunbar Hall when I was assigned a single room, studying and reading and listening to my favorite jazz album, *Kind of Blue* by Miles Davis. (Phonographs, as they were called then, were permitted.)

In addition to the assigned work in American literature, which didn't go beyond 1939 and Steinbeck's *The Grapes of Wrath*, I read the work of the Beat Generation, including Jack Kerouac's *On the Road* (1957).

There is a passage from chapter 3 of *On the Road* that forms the essence and the heart of the novel, which captures the way I was feeling at Exeter, and which still rings true now in my old age. The book's narrator, Sal Paradise, recalls

> the one distinct time in my life, the strangest moment of all, when I didn't know who I was—I was far away from home, haunted and tired with travel, in a cheap hotel room I'd never seen, hearing the hiss of steam outside, and the creak of the old wood of the hotel, and footsteps upstairs, and all the sad sounds, and I looked up at the cracked high ceiling and really didn't know who I was for about fifteen strange seconds. I wasn't scared; I was just someone else, some stranger, and my whole life was a haunted life, the life of a ghost.

Ancient Greek was my favorite subject at Exeter, taught with great skill by Dr. William Earnest Gillespie, a man who stuttered terribly, with grimaces and eyeblinks that conveyed extreme, unnamable suffering, except when he was reading aloud from *The Iliad* or *The Odyssey* in the original, when his diction was perfect, his facial muscles became relaxed, and he radiated joy. Homer is music when read aloud, and Dr. Gillespie's renderings gave me chills.

The need for social change and a desire to become a part of the politics of resistance to authority were constants in my thoughts. I admired the Montgomery bus boycott, triggered by Rosa Parks and led by Rev. Martin Luther King Jr. I read and reread a comic book published by the pacifist group Fellowship of Reconciliation, *Martin Luther King and the Montgomery Story*. I fantasized becoming a crewmember on the *Golden Rule*, the 30-foot ketch skippered by Albert Bigelow, who attempted to sail into the nuclear test zones near the Marshall Islands, in a daring albeit unsuccessful effort to stop the hydrogen bomb atmospheric tests that were irradiating native communities and spreading atomic fallout throughout the earth.

In 1961, my junior (or "Upper Middler") year, I became a radical, at least by Exeter's standards, which were derived primarily from the Republican Party playbook. I joined the Student Peace Union and the Young People's Socialist League, which sent me a red membership card. I became one of the handful of members of the Student Peace Group at Exeter.

These were the days when official Civil Defense short films showed how students could survive thermonuclear war merely by "taking shelter" under their desks. I considered this a ridiculous lie and government propaganda of the worst sort, though studies of Japanese atomic bomb survivors later showed that those in shadow during the explosion were more likely to avoid being vaporized. On April 28, 1961, I deliberately violated New Hampshire law by refusing to take shelter when the town fire siren sounded the alert, and instead I sat in the middle of the academy lawn. Fourteen students from the University of New Hampshire were arrested in Durham that day for doing the same thing. The New Hampshire Supreme Court upheld their criminal convictions in the case *State v. Pinsince* (1963).

Mr. Galt, my 6'5" Latin teacher, pulled me indoors by an ear as I tried without success to explain to him my motivation. The tale of my Galt-interrupted act of civil disobedience spread through campus, on the strength of which I was elected president of the Student Peace Group. I proposed, and we agreed unanimously, to construct peace signs opposed to nuclear war and stand while holding them silently on the edge of the academy lawn as the 1961 Memorial Day parade marched past. I argued that Exeter's version of this parade was more of a militaristic display of super-patriotic fervor than an appropriate memorial for the fallen. Even the Boy Scouts in that annual ceremony marched in lockstep in full dress-brown uniforms, festooned with scarves, buckles, and merit badge sashes, shouldering real M-1 rifles.

I spent a lot of time on my sign. I found a piece of two-by-three-foot particle board and stapled to it pieces of white cardboard that the laundry used as inserts to the button-down shirts we were required to wear. My sign read "End the Arms Race. Ban the Bomb," with the peace sign drawn in the middle of those two sentences.

On Memorial Day I was the only Student Peace Group member to show up with a sign. It turned out that someone had snitched about our demonstration, and half the student body had signed up to join the "Student War Council," an act which doubtless chilled the enthusiasm of our Peace Group membership. Stu Russell, a day-student, member of the Student War Council, and local "townie," which at snob-rule Exeter was a synonym for "nitwit," joined the parade, marching next to a car filled with Gold Star Mothers with a sign advocating for the "Complete Destruction of the World." The school disciplined Stu with a warning and ordered him to write a letter of apology to the local newspaper.

The administration treated me differently. A day or two after the parade, I was summoned to the headmaster's office. This was the first time in my three years there that I had ever had a conversation or been alone with this man, my cousin William Gurdon Saltonstall. He told me that I was being expelled from Exeter for holding my peace sign, then added, with solemn finality that precluded any further discussion: "I'm sorry, Steve, but there is nothing I can do about this."

The faculty vote wasn't unanimous. The lone dissenter was my Ancient Greek teacher, Dr. Gillespie. My father drove up from Boston to get me. On the way home, he said of my being kicked out of Exeter that "this will be a black mark on your record for the rest of your life."

A "black mark" forever on my "record"—an offense engraved in the Book of Life that would follow me everywhere. In other words, I was out of it. Henceforth, I would be a permanent alien. I had been expelled, indeed expunged, not simply from Phillips Exeter Academy but from the New England "elect." No longer would I be entitled by birth, breeding, and blood to be a part of the divinely blessed "City Upon a Hill" mission of John Winthrop and Richard Saltonstall.

Like Sal Paradise in Kerouac's *On the Road*, for a moment I didn't know who I was. Then it came to me: I am a stranger, a ghost, a fleeting image projected on an empty wall, not some captive of history bound to a family tree. My expulsion was something I had wanted, something that I had brought about on my own. The "elect" can repudiate their election, and in doing that, I freed myself to choose a destiny that opposes the elitist and authoritarian system symbolized and perpetuated by the Phillips Exeter Academy. After years of confusion and wandering, I found my place: I became a criminal defense lawyer and a renegade for justice.

My path to becoming a lawyer was overgrown with brambles and riddled with deep, dangerous potholes, primarily of my own making, but I arrived there after years of struggle, years often marked by failure, depression, and long days and nights bereft of self-esteem, after finally coming to terms with what I was meant to do with my life.

I'm grateful for my hard times, which helped me overcome ingrained assumptions of entitlement, opened me to the lives and feelings of people on the bottom, and gave me the empathy and strength to defend the defenseless. Lost at night in a dark forest, I stumbled onto a road less traveled, and as Robert Frost tells us, this made all the difference.

From Exeter to Cairo

Finding a school that would admit me after being bounced from Exeter wasn't easy. Exeter had refused to give me academic credit for my junior year, even though I'd been there through the end of May. My summer of '61 was a series of verbal stress tests at other academic institutions, whose admissions officers were mostly bent on hammering me about my bad behavior and telling me how shameful it was that I had embarrassed and disgraced my parents—the "black mark" lecture again.

In late August, with no prospects, I visited Buxton, a private coeducational boarding school in Williamstown, Massachusetts. This was a "progressive" institution with only seventy students, originally opened in 1928 in Short Hills, New Jersey, for the benefit of the children of the "One Big Union" Industrial Workers of the World, or "Wobblies," founded by the labor leaders Eugene Debs and Big Bill Haywood.

The director was Benjamin Fincke, who had been a conscientious objector during World War II and had spent the duration in a kind of concentration camp, felling trees with manual crosscut saws and building dirt roads. Ben (we called the teachers by their first names) was delighted by my expulsion from Exeter for peace movement activity, and he accepted me on the spot. Ellen Geer Sangster, the school's founder, codirector, and perennial funder, populated Buxton with American Black kids from places in the Deep South like Mobile, Alabama, and with foreign students of color from Ghana, Liberia, and Thailand. What a change from Exeter: the school was both coed and racially diverse.

Ben Fincke required me to play on our soccer team, which was ranked number one in the country in our small school division, thanks to the ability of our center-forward, Seth Dei of Accra, Nigeria, a member of that country's national team who went on to become an All-American at Cornell, and strikers Dovi Afesi, also of Accra, and Nathan Barnes Jr. of Liberia. My award for "most improved" (meaning I was the worst player on the team) was a book of short stories by Chekhov. Our female cheerleaders had fun confusing the opposing players and their supporters with loud Shakespearean chants from the sidelines, such as this one from *The Tempest*: "Flout 'em and scout 'em and scout 'em and flout 'em! Thought is free!"

In the summer of 1962, after my first year at Buxton, I signed on with the American Friends Service Committee (Quakers) as a workcamp volunteer in a place called Circle City, in Missouri's Bootheel, a distinctly Southern part of the state that juts down into Arkansas and Tennessee. Circle City wasn't a city; with a hundred people or so, it wasn't even a town, but rather just a bunch of poverty-row shacks packed in a circle around a small community center building in the midst of cotton fields that stretched to the vanishing point in all directions. The town was segregated: all-white. Our work camp of a dozen or so kids was nominally integrated, with one African American girl. The boys roughed it in tents, and the girls slept on cots in the clapboarded community center, which had a kitchen and a bathroom and an outdoor shower.

Our mission in Circle City was to clear scores of large trees that had grown up in the town's mile-long drainage ditch, clogging it and causing all the homes to flood every year when the rains came. We were given crummy hand tools—dull axes and rakes—to do this job in 90- to 100-degree weather. The citizens of Circle City shunned us—with one notable exception, an elderly woman who thanked us and invited us to her church one Sunday—because we were outsiders and do-gooders, most likely Communists, and, worse, one of us was Black. They were able to see what we were doing. Their homes literally surrounded our tents and the community center, and the drainage ditch was a short walk away. We knew we were being watched, but so what? We were being good citizens with nothing to hide, clearing the trees to stop flooding and performing another task that we hadn't been asked to do: scraping and painting the community center.

Soon, however, we had a visit from a bunch of scary night riders in pickup trucks, armed with clubs and shotguns. We camper-kids withdrew to the community center kitchen and decided collectively that, if the mob came inside, the boys would lie on top of the girls to protect them from beatings or worse violence. Luckily, our head camp counselor, Mick Micklem, was from Virginia and blessed with a Southern accent, and with Quakerly soft words he managed to get the night riders to leave. But our one Black camper was so terrorized that she left shortly thereafter and returned to her home in New York City.

My best female friend in Circle City was the late Priscilla Pace, the daughter of Frank Pace, a former secretary of the army, CEO of General Dynamics, and chairperson of the Corporation for Public Broadcasting. Priscilla took a different path. She joined the Peace Corps in Tanzania, became fluent in Swahili, earned an MA in early child development and a PhD in philosophy, became president of the writer's workshop at her alma mater, Antioch College, and spent her selfless, compassionate life in charitable pursuits in the areas of domestic violence, animal rights, environmental and public health planning, and teaching illiterate adults how to read.

We managed to finish our flood prevention task in about six weeks and capped it by sitting in the now-cleared drainage ditch, holding a silent Quaker service while surrounded by beautiful red cotton flowers as far as we could see.

During our time in Circle City, Chuck Neblett, one of the founding members of the Freedom Singers and a resident of Cairo, Illinois, paid us a visit, taught us civil rights songs, and recruited us to join the struggle there. Cairo, pronounced like "KAY-ro" syrup, is located at the southern tip of Illinois, on the spot where the Ohio and Mississippi Rivers converge. It was a Ku Klux Klan stronghold in the 1960s and early 1970s. A favorite evening sport of some whites was to shoot guns randomly into public housing populated by Black people. Cairo's one public library was open to "whites only" until 1973, after the filing of a federal civil rights lawsuit. In 1962, Black residents of Cairo were denied the right to vote.

After the Quaker workcamp ended, I decided to answer Chuck Neblett's call, and I rode to Cairo in a white Ford Falcon convertible owned and driven by one of my work camp counselors, Jerry DeMuth, a social activist and journalist.

The Student Nonviolent Coordinating Committee (SNCC) project that Jerry and I joined in Cairo late in the summer of 1962 was directed by the great John Lewis. This was before Lewis became president of SNCC, before he gave his stirring, militant speech in front of the Lincoln Memorial to the crowd at the March on Washington, before his walk across the Edmund Pettus Bridge in Selma, Alabama, and long before he achieved well-deserved prominence as a member of Congress from Atlanta.

It isn't that well-known that John Lewis was an ordained Baptist minister, and his speech was a beautiful, authentic mixture of pulpit eloquence with the down-home accent of the sharecropper. Reverend Lewis was the bravest person I ever met. At a voting rights demonstration in a corridor of the Cairo city hall, just outside the open city clerk's office, he led an impromptu prayer, asking God to bring wisdom and enlightenment to the hearts of the benighted segregationists working there, who were refusing to register Black people to vote. The Cairo clerks were grumbling and fuming to the point that I feared they would rise from their desks and beat us or kill us. But there was an aura about John Lewis, a righteous and saintly one, that kept them fumbling with their paperwork and glued to their chairs.

One of the aims of the Cairo project was to integrate public facilities, including the officially segregated municipal swimming pool, which had been built with federal funds. Integrating the municipal pool was an especially important SNCC goal, because the only place where Black citizens of Cairo were permitted to swim was a tiny, rocky beach at the junction of those two great rivers, the Ohio and the Mississippi. The river currents are so strong and unpredictable that drownings, especially of Black kids, were a common summer occurrence. To prevent Black people from swimming in the only safe place in town, the white political establishment converted the municipal pool into a private club (a typical segregationist dodge), requiring an application and purchase of a membership card.

John Lewis sent me on a long walk from the African Methodist Episcopalian Church that served as SNCC headquarters to the municipal swimming pool to try to get a membership card. If I could become a pool member, a group of Black SNCC activists would then seek admittance with me as my "guests."

Lewis picked me for this task because I was the only white boy in the movement at the time, and I looked like a little kid. I felt vulnerable and frightened as I walked out of the Black neighborhood, all alone, into Klan-bossed territory, where the pool was located and where I tried to join the "club." But the racist guardians of the pool knew I was from SNCC, and with death threats they denied my application and told me to get the hell out of there.

In response, we marched to the pool in a group and tried to get in, blocking the entrance. John Lewis recalled in his autobiography *Walking with the Wind* (1998), and I vividly remember watching in horror, as a white man drove a pickup truck into our line, injuring a Black girl who was no more than eight years old. One night, just before I left Cairo to begin my senior year at Buxton, we marched to the segregated Roller Bowl, the only skating rink in town. We went up to the door, and someone had stuck a sign on it with an ice pick, with the scrawled message "No Niggers Here!" Inside the rink a Ku Klux Klan recruitment meeting was going on. The day after I left for school, the Klan attacked and injured Black SNCC demonstrators, including Reverend Lewis, with chains and tire irons.

SNCC's efforts failed to integrate the pool. Instead of opening the facility to all, the city fathers defiantly filled the pool with cement, and it became a car wash. Now even the car wash is gone, and the site is a vacant lot. When integration finally became a legal imperative in Cairo, the white community fled, and the business owners among them abandoned the former bustling downtown commercial area, turning it into a ghost town.

Cairo is run now by folks elected by the 80 percent Black citizenry, many of whom are descended from runaway slaves who came to Cairo during the Civil War, seeking protection from the large contingent of Union soldiers who were camped there at Fort Defiance. In 2008, I returned to Cairo with my wife, Ellen, went to the city offices, and shook hands with its first African American mayor, Judson Childs. We met for an hour with the city treasurer, Preston Ewing Jr., who was head of the local NAACP chapter during the worst years of white violence in Cairo, 1967–1973, which began with the murder by hanging of Army private Robert L. Hunt in the Cairo police station on July 15, 1967, whom the cops had arrested for the "crime" of riding in a car while Black. Six years of terrorism followed, led by a racist group called the "White Hats," who were supplied with guns and CB radios by the all-white Cairo police force. Mr. Ewing has written a photo essay book about that era, *Let My People Go* (1996), which documents the institutional racism and violence that gripped Cairo through the 1960s and into the mid-1970s.

Harvard, Selma, and Mack the Knife

After Buxton I returned to my hometown of Cambridge, Massachusetts, to attend Harvard, continuing my political activism.

In the spring of 1964, during my freshman year, the Metropolitan District Commission (MDC) finalized plans to "improve" the parklike banks of the Charles River in Cambridge and to clear space for an underpass by cutting down all of its ancient sycamore trees, which provided shade and beauty for everyone. Otherwise decent public officials, including Governor Endicott Peabody and Secretary of the Interior Stuart Udall, refused to stop the project. One balmy night in May, a thousand Harvard and Radcliffe students, including me, held an impromptu "Save the Sycamores" rally at the river. Six years before the founding of Earth Day, this gathering may well rank as the first mass environmentalist demonstration in U.S. history, and we blocked traffic on Memorial Drive for about an hour.

The MDC cops dispersed us with growling, barking, and yes, snarling and biting German Shepherds, despite the friendly chant with which we greeted the canines and their handlers:

"Dogs need trees!"

Overnight, the political establishment became appropriately embarrassed. They abruptly changed their tune, and the underpass project was cancelled and the sycamores were saved. These beautiful trees still live by the Charles River at this writing.

My academic career in college reflected my commitment to the cause of civil rights. I majored in U.S. history and literature, concentrating on the era of antislavery agitation, the Civil War, and the failure of Reconstruction and the rise of the Ku Klux Klan. I wrote my honors thesis on Colonel Robert Gould Shaw of Boston, who led the first Black regiment in the Civil War, the Massachusetts 54th Regiment, whose soldiers included Lewis Douglass, the son of abolitionist Frederick Douglass.

As they marched through downtown Boston, racist white malcontents stoned the soldiers, and the Social Register denizens of the Somerset Club lowered the curtains so as not to have to witness what they considered to be an atrocity of race-mixing. In their first battle, the storming of Fort Wagner in South Carolina, nearly half the regiment, including Shaw, were killed in what I believe was a suicide mission deliberately designed to see whether African Americans would stand and fight in hopeless circumstances. The late U.S. army general and secretary of state Colin Powell agrees with this assessment: the 54th Regiment's assault on Fort Wagner, almost a mile across an open beach, through a trench and then over a parapet, "was a race to death. Colonel Shaw knew it and his men knew it, and yet they surged forward with a courage that we wish that all of us possessed."

After the battle, a Confederate officer sent a message to the Union side, saying of Shaw: "We have buried him with his niggers." In the words of General Powell, this was a "gesture of contempt" by the Confederates, who thought that by doing this they were "disgracing his memory." They were wrong. Shaw's family and their Unionist and abolitionist allies considered his dumping into a common trench with his fellow soldiers an honor. This mass burial was a kind of racial integration, which became a rallying point for those who believed in equal rights for all. As William James put it in 1897: "In death and in life . . . the 54th bore witness to the brotherhood of Man."

When the war ended, Augustus St. Gaudens spent twelve years crafting a stunningly beautiful, life-sized bronze bas-relief sculpture of Shaw on horseback leading the African American soldiers of the Massachusetts 54th Regiment, and many consider it the finest work of public art in the country. It's set at the northeast corner of Boston Common on Beacon Street, facing the State House. During the summer of 2020, a few misguided Black Lives Matter demonstrators, apparently offended by the sight of a white officer leading Black troops (the only politically feasible option in 1863), defaced the monument. It's since been restored.

In 1964, I would see Robert Lowell, a Cambridge fixture whose life was marred by mental illness, writing alone on a greasy spoon table at Tommy's Lunch on lower Mount Auburn Street, a block or two up from Club 47, the coffeehouse where Joan Baez got her start. Lowell published a poem that year exploring the legacy of Robert Gould Shaw, the 54th Massachusetts Regiment, and their monument, titled "For the Union Dead." In this, his best work, Lowell contrasts the idealism and sacrifice of the soldiers of the 54th Massachusetts regiment with our country's reflexive commercialism and racism a century later. Of Shaw, Lowell writes: "He is out of bounds now. He rejoices in man's lovely, peculiar power to choose life and die— when he leads his black soldiers to death, he cannot bend his back."

If Colonel Shaw and his regiment were ready to make the ultimate sacrifice, the least I could do was to continue as a part-time foot soldier for civil rights. I volunteered for and was accepted into SNCC's "Mississippi Summer" in 1964, but I was unable to go because of an illness that required me to finish my freshman year at Harvard's summer school. Then, during Spring Break in March 1965, I drove with a friend, John Ballard, and two local middle-aged Black women I had never met before and whose names unfortunately escape me, to Selma, Alabama.

That year was a violent time down South. On February 26, Alabama State Police trooper Bonard Fowler shot and killed the Black activist Jimmie Lee Jackson after a voting rights march, when Jackson tried to protect his mother, whom Fowler was in the process of savagely beating. March 7 was "Bloody Sunday" in Selma, when Alabama State Troopers on horseback attacked and mercilessly and severely injured peaceful marchers, led by John Lewis, whose skull was fractured. On March 11, three white racists murdered James Reeb, a Unitarian minister from Boston, as he emerged from a restaurant. John Ballard and I left for Selma the next day.

One muggy March afternoon in Selma, I took part in a demonstration in an all-white neighborhood, the purpose of which was to assert the right of integrated groups simply to walk together on the public sidewalk. I was scared about what might happen to me and felt sick to my stomach, and I drank a bottle of Pepto-Bismol to prepare. It didn't help.

To get to the demonstration, I imprudently rode with John Ballard in his Mercury Comet, which had New York license plates. We passed a police vehicle that was pulled off the road onto the shoulder. The officers were standing outside, surveying the traffic. They saw us, and one of the officers took out his billy club, stared at me, and whacked the club onto his outstretched palm, signaling that my head was the next place his weapon was going to land. The policemen piled into their squad car and chased us, with lights and siren going, but in what seemed like divine intervention, it overheated, whooshing a cloud of steam as its radiator boiled over, and we were gone.

We arrived at a tree-lined segregated neighborhood whose sidewalk led to Mayor Joe Smitherman's house. We walked quietly in pairs, I with a middle-aged Black man I didn't know; there was no time for introductions. I heard a screen door slam, looked to my right, and saw a white woman running out of her house to confront us. She put a revolver a few inches from my head, bullets visible in the chambers. Overwhelmed by anger and hatred, she screamed, "I'm going to shoot you, nigger-loving white boy!"

I thought my life was over. I kept walking, staring straight ahead, waiting for the end. When the woman didn't fire, I looked back, and she was still standing by her house, talking with some neighbors, and gesticulating toward us with her gun. The Black man with whom I was walking met my

gaze, but we were silent. There was nothing to say. We had survived. Together. I don't know why. This is always on the edges of my mind. I think
about it every day. I wonder what became of the woman who wanted to
shoot me and whether, in that moment of hesitation, index finger on the trigger, her inner light had blessed her with a saving grace and change of heart.

Selma police chief Wilson Baker, with his violent, helmeted cohort Sheriff
Jim Clark, had school buses ready for us in front of Mayor Smitherman's
home. They took us to a high school gym because the jails were full. The
police ordered the male prisoners to stand in a parking lot behind the main
drag and out of the sight of news reporters. They had painted lines on the
asphalt, and Chief Baker made us toe those lines for several hours. It was
hot, and we were thirsty. I never moved. The one demonstrator who did
got a clubbing. Baker told the press that we were in "protective custody,"
though it was he and Sheriff Clark and their vigilante followers from whom
we needed protection.

Chief Baker unlocked the gym doors and let us go at dawn, following a
night spent on the floor. We had never been formally arrested or booked.

The next day, my mother, who had come to Selma against my advice because she was frail and handicapped with breathing problems from COPD,
told me shakily that Chief Baker had warned her that the Klan had marked
her for death and that she was going to be next. She asked me if I would
please take her home to Boston, and of course I did.

The day we left, March 25, the Klan shot and killed a fellow activist,
Viola Liuzzo of Detroit, a 39-year-old mother of five children, as she drove
back to Selma after shuttling other volunteers to the Montgomery airport.
My mother and I were headed to that airport, and it's quite possible that our
cars passed one another going in opposite directions.

After my mother died, I learned from my brother Tom that she'd lied to
protect me. Chief Baker had told her that the Klan had decided that I was
the one who was going to be their next victim, not she.

When I reflect on Selma, I wish my mother hadn't persuaded me to leave.
Probably I would have survived, but if the Klan had killed me, my death
would have furthered the civil rights cause. The murders of white-skinned
movement foot soldiers triggered popular and official uproars. The killing
of Reverend Reeb, who became the centerpiece of President Lyndon B. Johnson's electrifying "We Shall Overcome" voting rights bill speech to Congress
while I was in Selma, is one example. LBJ never mentioned the police assassination of Jimmie Lee Jackson or any other Black victim of racist violence by
name. But his emotional paean to Reverend Reeb was a factor in the passage
of the Civil Rights Act.

After Selma, I continued with antiwar activity—the very thing that had gotten me into trouble at Exeter.

By late 1966, when I was a junior at Harvard, there were 385,000 U.S. soldiers on the ground in Vietnam, plus an additional 60,000 U.S. Navy troops offshore. More than 6,000 of these were killed that year and 30,000 wounded. In October, the Department of Defense, led by Robert Strange McNamara, President Johnson's Vietnam War head honcho, started a program he called "Project 100,000."

McNamara's object was to draft more young men into the conflict by deliberately targeting people of color. As a result, 41 percent of subsequent draftees were Black, though they comprised only 11 percent of the population. McNamara justified this race-based policy by paternalistically claiming that it would provide those he apparently deemed to be ignorant members of an underprivileged class with much-needed skills, discipline, and training.

The Vietnam War still had much popular support; it would take another year for mass antiwar protests to be organized and held. Campus opposition to the war was just beginning to percolate.

It was in this gung-ho, prowar atmosphere that, in November 1966, Robert McNamara came to Harvard to hobnob with some of its intellectual stars. McNamara was to be the first speaker at the newly minted Kennedy School of Government, run by Professor Richard Neustadt, whose academic focus was the presidency and an adviser to presidents Harry Truman, John Kennedy, and Johnson. When members (including me) of the college chapter of Students for a Democratic Society (SDS) learned of McNamara's visit, we tried to arrange a campus debate on the Vietnam War between him and Robert Scheer.

Scheer was the editor of the Catholic magazine *Ramparts*, which had denounced the war, especially the use of napalm, a form of jellied gasoline that stuck to the skin, burning and inflicting horrible trauma, pain, scarring, and death, on Vietnamese civilians as well as soldiers. (This evil substance was invented at Harvard in 1942 in a top-secret lab by the chemist Louis Feiser.)

More than 1,600 students and faculty signed a petition in favor of the proposed debate between Scheer and McNamara.

From his Olympian Pentagon heights, McNamara, via a thoroughly annoyed Neustadt, gave us the bum's rush. Neustadt told the SDS chapter president, Michael Ansara, that it would be beneath a man of McNamara's stature to force him to debate and that such a requirement would discourage other important personages from gracing the halls of the Kennedy School.

Ansara told Neustadt that SDS would try to confront McNamara and stage an impromptu debate with Scheer on the street. But we learned that

Scheer would not go along with this plan. So physical confrontation was all we had left. On November 7, Harvard students, some 800 strong and dressed in the de rigeur garb of sport coats and ties, waited for him to emerge from Quincy House onto Mill Street in Cambridge.

The afternoon was oddly festive. McNamara fans draped silly signs made of bedsheets from dorm windows, with slogans like "Back Mack" and "Napalm SDS" while one of our antiwar allies used his portable KLH stereo to fog Kurt Weil's Threepenny Opera song, "Mack the Knife" softly, over and over through the crowd.

A black limousine zoomed out of a garage. I and a couple of others intercepted and tried to surround it, but it was a diversionary dummy limo, with only a glum, black-suited government security guy at the wheel. I looked behind me and saw that a few students were sitting down on the pavement, blocking a second car—the one that held McNamara. Confusion reigned temporarily as the crowd pressed forward, and a few people began rocking McNamara's car in the hope that he would emerge, which he soon did.

The secretary of defense climbed onto his limo's roof, and he addressed us using a microphone and battery-operated speaker that the redoubtable Michael Ansara had brought.

McNamara, in his crocodile-tear book on Vietnam In Retrospect (1995), inaccurately described this incident as a "mob" action and an "ugly demonstration" that threatened violence.

Harvard University President Nathan Pusey compared the SDS demonstrators to Nazi "Brown Shirts" in a letter of apology to the secretary. Dean John U. Munro also apologized in writing, stating that "such rudeness and physical confrontation have no place in the university world, and we are appalled that it should happen here at Harvard."

But a photograph snapped by Peter Simon just as the microphone was being handed up to Secretary McNamara belies any rational reason for the unseemly bowing and scraping of the Harvard administration. This was far from an ugly, violent mob; in fact, many of the students are smiling, and McNamara himself appears bemused and hardly threatened.

Bob McNamara, the former Ford Motor Company executive and by now an experienced pol with a reputation for brilliance and for skill in dealing with others, could have turned on the charm, but instead he elected to adopt the persona of a know-it-all daddy dealing with a bunch of recalcitrant children.

"I went to Berkeley, a university every bit as good as this one, where I spent some of my happiest years. The difference between us is, I was tougher than you are then, and I'm tougher than you are now!

"I'll take two questions."

At first, silence.

I forget what the first question was, or who asked it, or what the response was. Then I raised my hand and Mike Ansara called on me. I was nervous, but I managed to ask McNamara: "How many civilian casualties have our armed forces inflicted on the Vietnamese people?"

As far as I know, no one had ever asked McNamara this before. I think it was an important question, a question deserving an honest answer.

If anyone knew the answer, it was Secretary of Defense Robert Strange McNamara, a noted numbers-cruncher who took pride in his complete command of military stats, including the latest Vietcong and North Vietnamese soldier body counts. But he couldn't tell the truth because the truth would have been damning.

We know now from *L.A. Times* reporter Nick Turse and his definitive book on Vietnam War civilian casualties, *Kill Anything That Moves* (2013), that the best estimate is that 2 million noncombatants were killed and 5.3 million wounded. Of the civilian wounded, one-third were women and one-quarter were children under the age of thirteen.

These figures do not include the environmental damage to the country caused by spraying it with the defoliant Agent Orange and the continuing impact of that poison on humans (both Vietnamese and American) and other living creatures and things.

McNamara had to lie. He gave the only answer he could give.

"I don't know."

This did not go over well. People in the crowd yelled "Why don't you know?" "Don't you care?" and "War criminal!" On cue, probably from McNamara himself, a phalanx of Harvard and Cambridge cops, batons menacingly held forward, rushed the secretary 10 yards or so into the Leverett House dormitory.

This "tougher than you are" icon of the powerful and privileged, who couldn't be bothered to defend his administration's position on the war to a bunch of undergraduate students in a debate, made a pathetic, cowardly escape through Harvard's network of underground steam tunnels, and he arrived on time for his next meeting.

Fittingly, that meeting was with Henry Kissinger, the Harvard éminence grise who would later persuade President Richard Nixon to carpet-bomb Cambodia, a policy that killed tens of thousands of civilians and triggered the rise of Pol Pot, the Khmer Rouge, and that country's Holocaust. To my knowledge, there is no record of the McNamara–Kissinger confab, but my guess is that it had nothing to do with Lord Acton's maxim, something that the Kennedy School ought to teach every one of its students: "Power tends to corrupt, and absolute power corrupts absolutely. Great men are almost always bad men."

This was not the end of McNamara's day having to endure the annoying presence of SDS members. Three or four of us were also members of an entertaining if grandiose club called the Signet Society, whose membership is limited to those with literary ambitions or pretensions. The Signet owns a building on Dunster Street in Cambridge, a five-minute walk from Mill Street.

In our day, the club had two dining tables. One was in the darker, dingier "Lowbrow Room" for the likes of my roommate Jesse Kornbluth and me and the other rebels and cynics who wanted no truck with the self-adoring Harvard student elite. In the adjoining, fancier, and well-lit "Highbrow Room," those aiming for Fulbrights and Rhodes scholarships and guaranteed glittering futures, gathered reverently around their faculty mentor and patron, Marty Peretz, later the owner and publisher of *The New Republic*, to chit-chat over toasts and tinkling glasses of Harvey's Bristol Cream.

We Lowbrow sherry-hating backbenchers learned that the Kennedy School had somehow received permission—no doubt from some officious club Highbrow—to use our building to host a wingding for McNamara. We decided to camp out at the entrance to wait for him.

Kornbluth and I wrote a brief statement that Jesse agreed to read to McNamara, standing with a few other Signet Society members off to one side. The plan was that I would stand in front of the door, blocking it so that McNamara would have to listen to what we had to say. After the other guests had arrived, including a couple students, one of whom was my classmate Richard Blumenthal, now a U.S. senator, the secretary of defense confidently strolled up. He was squired by a young, puffed-up Kennedy School administrator who had managed to snag the plum job of McNamara Factotum and Harvard Steam-Tunnel Docent.

I blocked the entrance as planned, and McNamara, who must have remembered me and the impertinent question I'd asked him on Mill Street, stared blowgun darts at me. Jesse read our statement aloud. It concluded:

"Harvard stands for free and open debate. If you had come to Harvard and agreed to debate the war, we would have welcomed you. But as you refused to debate, we condemn you."

McNamara's face turned the color of the medium-rare roast beef that he was about to be served. "You *boys* have your facts wrong. I am leaving this gentleman here (gesturing to his Kennedy School minion) to tell you what the facts are and to set you *boys* straight."

For some reason I stepped aside and allowed McNamara to enter our club, leaving behind his furious guide who paused, then said: "I'm not going to tell you little bastards anything!"

And that man was Barney Frank.

Barney wrote of the McNamara debacle in his 2015 autobiography, *Frank, a Life in Politics*: "[T]he spectacle of the U.S. Secretary of Defense being temporarily captured by a mob of Harvard students reverberated around the world. That it happened just before the mid-term congressional elections magnified the embarrassment—to the Johnson administration, Harvard, the institute, and me."

Years later, I sought out Barney Frank, by now an ultra-lionized liberal and the first openly gay member of Congress, after one of his typically witty, erudite speeches, this to the understandably enthralled members of the local Democratic Club at the Paradise Motel in Bennington, Vermont. Cornering Barney at the sinks in the men's room, I introduced myself, reminded him of the Signet Society ending to McNamara's bummer of a Harvard experience, and asked him whether in the light of subsequent historical events he still considered us "little bastards."

As he dried his hands hurriedly with a paper towel while gazing down at his shoes instead of meeting my eyes (one of the classic "tells" of a fib to come), Congressman Frank replied that he had no recollection of the incident, no memory of it at all.

After Harvard, the Deluge

College was exhausting. I graduated on schedule during the "Summer of Love" in June 1967, but I ignored the good advice of my honors program tutor and academic mentor, the American history professor Joseph Kett (now emeritus at the University of Virginia), who urged me to become a lawyer.

Instead, after a summer job working as a junior fellow at the Center for the Study for Democratic Institutions in Santa Barbara, California, with coworkers who ran the gamut from the comedian and jazz musician Steve Allen to the Nobel Prize–winning chemist Linus Pauling, I enrolled in the American Studies PhD program at Yale, with the idea of becoming a teacher at the college level. But I couldn't hack it. With no break after college, the academic pressure was too great for me, and I dropped out at the end of the first semester and returned to Cambridge, moving into a beat Green Street walk-up apartment owned by the notorious slum landlady Anna Ciccarelli. The bedroom roof leaked, and after she wouldn't fix it, I moved into the living room with my girlfriend, Cameron, a Boston University dropout who was on the rebound from a failed relationship with the singer James Taylor when we met and fell in love.

I found work, first as a store clerk in Harvard Square, then later as the "boy producer" in the news department of a Boston television station, where I enjoyed the company of veteran reporters whose humorous and cynical worldviews were alluring.

On April 3, 1968, the day before the assassination of the Reverend Martin Luther King Jr., I was on my TV news job, helping to cover an antiwar demonstration on the Boston Common, where a crowd of young men had gathered to turn in their draft cards. Not carrying a draft card was then a felony punishable by up to five years in federal prison. Burning one's draft card—which had become a bit of a fad often seen on TV news—wasn't considered by dedicated movement people to be a genuine "witness" against the war, because the government was unlikely to find out you'd done it. Burning your card was little more than a no-risk publicity ploy.

The April 3 demo plan for those gathered on Boston Common was to make a real stand, by handing over their draft cards to some antiwar celebrities, including the baby-book author Dr. Benjamin Spock the antiwar activist Michael Ferber (both of whom would go on trial the following month for counseling kids to resist the draft), as well as Professors Staughton Lynd of Columbia, Howard Zinn of Boston University, and Noam Chomsky of MIT and the Quaker activist Homer Jack, founder of the Congress of Racial Equality and the Committee for a Sane Nuclear Policy (SANE).

The idea was for Professor Chomsky, academia's leading scholar in the field of linguistics and a persistent critic of the Vietnam War, to take the draft cards to the Selective Service headquarters in Washington, D.C., and politely dump the pile on the desk of the agency head, General Lewis B. Hershey.

General Hershey was a stern super-patriot, and the April 3 demo organizers were sure that he would come down hard on the guys who turned in their draft cards that day. Hershey was so militant that he issued an administrative order in 1967 directing that anyone mutilating or failing to carry his draft card be reclassified forthwith as eligible for military service.

After some speeches that I was able to hear well in the comfortable, climate-controlled confines of my TV station trailer, the call came for young men to turn in their draft cards. On impulse I left my news producer post, walked up the hill and gave my card to Homer Jack, then ran back and returned to my job. I was one of 235 guys to turn in their draft cards in Boston that day. No one in the TV trailer seemed to notice my brief absence.

The following evening, I was stationed in the teletype-machine room of my television station while our nightly news show was on the air, which was one of my cub producer duties in the event of a late-breaking story. The teletype printed out the terrible news of Martin Luther King's assassination, and I ripped the paper off the machine, ran into the studio, and handed it to our newscaster. As a result, we scooped the other Boston stations, and our program director heaped praise on me and gave me a raise, telling the other producers in a meeting that I had succeeded in becoming "plugged into the system"—an unwelcome compliment in that countercultural era of youth revolt against nearly everything even vaguely corporate. I felt guilty, confused, and upset for being rewarded in connection with the King assassination tragedy, and I quit the TV station soon afterward. In any event, I was certain that I was headed for arrest, prosecution, and incarceration for turning in my draft card.

I told myself that I was ready to go to prison. In a naïve way I was looking forward to a federal court trial where I could get on the witness stand, tell the jury why I was against the Vietnam War, and then inform the judge at sentencing that I wasn't sorry about breaking the law. Encouraging me to do that was my enthusiastic draft counselor, Roger Baldwin, then in his eighties, the impish and very cool cofounder of the American Civil Liberties Union, who had done time in prison for refusing to fight in World War I.

I fancied myself emulating the cheerful old rebel Roger and his close associate, the late Socialist Party leader Eugene Victor Debs. In 1918, the U.S. Justice Department had prosecuted Debs for the crime of sedition for opposing World War One. Debs's conviction, which was based on a Canton, Ohio, speech, at which he said: "The master class has always declared the wars; the subject class has always fought them." At his sentencing, Debs told the court: "Your Honor, years ago I recognized my kinship with all living beings, and I made up my mind that I was not one bit better than the meanest on earth. I said then and I say now, that while there is a lower class I am in it, while there is a criminal element I am of it, and while there is a soul in prison, I am not free." The judge sentenced Debs to 10 years. In 1920, Debs ran for president on the Socialist Party ticket from his cell in the Atlanta Federal Penitentiary and received almost a million votes. To his opponent, President Woodrow Wilson, Debs was a "traitor to America," but for me in 1968, he was a hero and an inspiration, and I was ready to follow in his footsteps.

Soon I received a form letter from the Selective Service signed by General Hershey. It said that it had come to the agency's attention that I no longer had my draft card, and it directed me to check a box to the effect that my card had either been "lost, destroyed, mutilated, or stolen." Were I to complete and mail in the form as ordered, the Selective Service would then issue me a brand-new, duplicate draft card. But failing that, arrest and a federal criminal prosecution would follow.

I wrote on the form, in language I wouldn't use now: "You know perfectly well what happened to my draft card. You have it. Fuck you and your imperialist war." I mailed it back. I thought that the FBI would be on my doorstep in short order. But nothing happened. Absolutely nothing.

And nothing made sense in this crazy time, when jazz musician Les McCann sang of the epic confusion he felt while "trying to make it real compared to what." Beginning in 1966, I sought refuge in LSD-25, available for a dollar a hit from a courier sent by my "connection," Richard Alpert, later known as Baba Ram Dass. The Alpert Rule was that you had to ingest the tablet in front of the courier so it couldn't be resold to someone else. This was pure Sandoz lab acid, obtained from the drug's inventor, the Swiss chemist Albert Hofmann, author of the memoir *LSD: My Problem Child* (1979). Hofmann came to believe that LSD is a "sacred" drug, and he used it often until his death in 2008 at age 102.

LSD opened a spiritual door for me; on a good trip with pure acid, taken during the day, outside in Nature, you can actually see the unity of all things, flowing together in a liquid yet airy, paisley-patterned, moving, living mass. The drug dissolves ordinary concepts of reality and makes available otherwise unseen and more profound dimensions of space, time, and connectedness. The problem with LSD, at least for me, is that it can become all-encompassing and demanding of loyalty. I became far more focused on opening the doors of perception than in discovering and pursuing the career that was waiting for me: the law.

Still hoping that my place was in academia, I applied for and was accepted into the American History PhD program at the University of California, Berkeley. I left Boston in June 1969 to stay temporarily with friends in a commune on San Francisco's Bush Street. The commune was set in a two-family dwelling, with a group of sailors and dockworkers on one side, and a family from rural West Virginia on the other. There was a shared backyard, but that yard was the subject of a strictly enforced hippie-house rule: you had to take off all of your clothes to go outside and use it. I complied reluctantly with this bit of Stalinist foolishness, but mostly I was looking forward to the arrival of my friend and lover Cameron, with whom I'd been living for a year in Cambridge, so we could find a place across the Oakland Bay Bridge in Berkeley to continue to be together. Cameron had decided to drive across the country separately to meet me after taking care of some family business. I had won a fellowship from the university; Cameron was going to look for a job.

Berkeley, California—my choice for a new home and an entrée into the world of college teaching—had in 1969 become the epicenter of scary radical student politics. In May, before I arrived, a community effort to turn a 2.8-acre piece of city land owned by the University of California into a "People's Park" was greeted by violent government resistance. Ed Meese, Governor Ronald Reagan's chief of staff, who would become Attorney General during Reagan's presidency, unleashed a force of 800 police officers on the students. The cops beat with nightsticks and pepper-gassed the 6,000 demonstrators assembled peacefully in the park. The police chased the crowd out of the park and down Telegraph Avenue, Berkeley's main street, firing on the retreating mass of people and spectators on rooftops with semiautomatic shotguns. They killed a bystander, James Rector, with a round of buckshot that lodged in his aorta. They also gunned down a local carpenter, Alan Blanchard, shooting him directly in the face, permanently blinding him. By the time I arrived in San Francisco the university had fenced off its property and occupied it with up to 2,700 National Guard troops to prevent it from reverting to the role of a park, and these soldiers patrolled the streets of Berkeley at will.

July 20, 1969—the day that Neil Armstrong set foot on the moon—was also the appointed time for Cameron's arrival. But she didn't show up. She didn't call. She was on the road, or so I thought, and in those days before cell phones I wasn't able to get in touch with her. Her sisters and her mother either couldn't or wouldn't tell me where she was or what had happened to her. I was worried for Cameron's safety and for our future together. I flew back to Boston to look for her. I went to the apartment of one of her sisters, who told me that Cameron, on her drive to San Francisco, had picked up a hitchhiker, whom she then married at a drive-in wedding chapel in Las Vegas.

Had I been thinking rationally, I would have understood that Cameron was a sweet but troubled soul and that ending our relationship in such an impulsive and insensitive fashion was a by-product of her own mixed-up state of mind. But instead I interpreted her extreme way of rejecting me and her impromptu marriage to a stranger as proof that I must be a worthless and horrible person, and this precipitated what used to be called a "nervous breakdown." Included therein was an overdose of a deadly downer, Doriden, which put me in a coma for a week at Massachusetts General Hospital.

My sister Sarah wrote me a letter about this:

I saw you lying on your bed with tubes up your nose and in your arms and all the machines around you, lying so still and pale and beautiful. The only sound in the room was the whir of the machines. I went over to your bedside and looked at your hand, and after awhile I saw your fingertips tremble. That was the only sign of life you showed. You were me and I was you. Our hands. Our common lives.

When I awoke from this mammoth mistake, I had lost every last bit of confidence in myself and my ability to lead a useful and productive existence.

And that is when I got the education that saved me, living among the wretched of the earth whom I was meant to serve. After stays in a couple of hospitals, one of them mental, where I made friends with a middle-aged woman who had lost an arm when she jumped in front of a subway train, I moved to a $75-per-month heated apartment in Bennington, Vermont, at the suggestion of a friend. One afternoon I was driving downhill from my place on McCall Street, and the brakes of my classic Vermont "beater" of a car (a high-mileage 1963 white Plymouth station wagon with push-button drive) utterly failed to work. Pedal to the floor, I saw that I was headed for a likely fatal T-bone collision with a Vermont Transit bus that was speeding toward me on Main Street.

In a moment of lucidity, I pushed the Plymouth's transmission button for reverse, and the car stopped, and I was still alive, and I was happy to be alive. Somehow I nursed the wagon to a local Gulf station without crashing, where the mechanic, Don Conley, found that someone had cut my brake lines with a razor. (I never learned who did this or why.) The slashes in the brake lines were hard to detect, but the brake fluid had found them and dripped gradually to the pavement whenever I put pressure on the brake pedal, eventually emptying the master cylinder.

Don is legally blind, and he is able to see objects only out of the corners of his eyes, but he was able to diagnose and fix the problem and get me back on the road. We talked for a bit about cars and my Plymouth's venerable 318 V-8 engine, with Don's head facing 45 degrees away from where I was standing so he could see me, and he told me the station needed an attendant to pump gas on the graveyard shift, from 2:00 to 10:00 p.m. The pay was minimum wage—$1.25 an hour, in cash and under the table—but the job came with the exalted title of night manager.

This was something I knew I could do. I mean, how hard is pumping gas? I started the next afternoon. I was able to make ends meet, with enough money for rent and food, but sometimes I was forced to forego the laundromat and do my laundry in the bathtub and hang it outside on a clothesline to dry. My trash went into a burn barrel, a hard-core Vermonter custom that is no longer allowed. I bought my clothes used at a thrift store. The Gulf station supplied me with work shirts.

My new workplace was a magnet for low-income people, because Don didn't charge very much; when his stepfather, Bart Toftness, the owner of the station, wasn't around, he would do work at cost or for free.

In the winter, families with kids would keep warm by sitting for hours in the office waiting for Don to finish working on their cars. Not once did one of these needy folks steal from the cash register that was only a few feet away. Homeless people knew that they could use our bathrooms (part of my job was to clean them); we never refused to give anyone the key. I would help Don work on the front ends and brakes of the cars, and I learned how to change engine and differential oil on cars that were barely drivable but were indispensable lifelines for the poor in rural Vermont.

Outside at the pumps, the affluent drivers in late-model vehicles would order me to fill their gas tanks and check their oil level and tire pressure without ever looking me in the eye; as far as they were concerned, I was so low on the totem pole as to be unworthy of notice or human contact.

During slack times when there were no cars to work on and there was little gas traffic, Don would lecture me about how I was wasting my time at his station, and he insisted that I go back to school and get an advanced degree that would enable me to do something better with my life than being a pump jockey. "Yes, Don, you're probably right," I would respond, "but for now this is my world, and I'm honored to be in it with you." I admired Don's work ethic, which propelled him to do dirty, difficult, physical jobs, like removing tires off their metal rims, with heart and soul, even though he could barely see what he was doing, always looking sideways, a disability that he never ever complained about.

My neighbors on McCall Street in Bennington were a mixed bag. Some were friendly, but for a time there was a bad man named Jeremiah who lived with his wife and two kids in the other half of my two-family apartment house. His anger was his kryptonite. Jeremiah got a puppy that he left outdoors on a chain, loveless and without food or water, while the family left on a two-week vacation.

I fed and watered the dog for a couple of days, and then I called the Humane Society, which took custody of her. When Jeremiah returned and found the puppy gone (she would have been dead!) and he was charged with animal cruelty, he learned that I was the creep who notified the authorities. I became a magnet for his car, though he never hit me with it, and he made nasty threats to the effect that effeminate hippies like me (I'd grown my hair down to my shoulders) don't deserve to live.

Then came a Thanksgiving Day when my next-door neighbor George King was arrested for murdering one of his children. My impression of George was that he was a kind person and a good father, whereas his wife, who testified against him at his trial and fingered him as the killer, was notoriously abusive, constantly screaming at the kids out in the street. But the cops never interviewed me.

When George was arrested (he was later convicted and sentenced to life), I knew that I should get a law degree and that defending the downtrodden was going to be my destiny. I broke the news to Don, saying that he had been right and that I was quitting Southgate Gulf to go to law school. We shook greasy hands and parted ways.

In the spring of 1972, I drove Whiteman (my name for my Plymouth wagon) back to Cambridge, gave him away, and scrounged a Fuji ten-speed bike to commute to a job as an operating room orderly at Mount Auburn Hospital, a few miles away from another in my series of communal houses, this one on River Street, north of Central Square. My new roommates included a pregnant astrologer, a leather belt maker, and an inseparable duo: Richie, a refugee from New Jersey, and Macicle, a Native American from Mashpee, who were room-service stewards at the Parker House, a hotel in Boston where Ho Chi Minh worked briefly as a pastry chef before he became president of Vietnam.

Richie and Macicle did well with tips, and they had a complex racket going, the details of which I never understood, involving phony hotel receipts. At the end of each work week, they would happily sort and divide great piles of change and crumpled bills on their bedroom floor. This was a time when "burns" were considered by many a righteous blow to the establishment. The most popular burn was to buy a bunch of traveler's checks, cash them in, then report them stolen and get another set, compliments of "the man," as represented by that evil corporation, American Express.

At "The Mount," I learned the satisfying technique of washing its floors properly, swirling the mophead as I worked the cracks, so that the space where the wall meets the floor got perfectly clean. (When I go to a medical office now, I check that area out and will show a nurse if it's dirty, which it often is.) I wheeled surgery candidates on their beds down to the OR, and once I had the rattling experience of a patient dying in the elevator; the doctors couldn't revive her in the hallway when we emerged. I sanitized surgical instruments in a heating device called an "autoclave." With stiff brushes and disinfectant, I cleaned the sinks used by the doctors to wash their hands.

One of my major responsibilities was to shave the male patients for open-heart operations from neck to toe, and so many of them died at the hands of a famous-long-ago, over-the-hill surgeon that the nurses joked that there should be a chute leading from his operating room to Ward X—the morgue. I was often the last person to talk to these heart patients, and after their surgery I cleaned their blood off the ceilings on a stepladder.

While working at The Mount, I applied to four local law schools and was accepted by Boston University, Boston College, and Northeastern. Harvard turned me down even though I'd graduated Phi Beta Kappa from the college.

I chose Northeastern, a humble place, formerly a night school, whose aim is to train public interest lawyers. The law school building was new and poorly constructed, and during my first year its HVAC system stopped working; because the windows didn't open, it was brutally hot and stuffy in our classrooms.

The school's utter lack of pull or prestige meant that I could never get a job at a top law firm or as a United States Supreme Court law clerk. That was fine with me; I preferred to create my own world. Lawyering never made me wealthy in money. The law is supposed to be a helping profession, not some sterile, self-centered commercial business enterprise, and I was better off going to a non–prestige school, given that I wanted to be a street lawyer for people of color and the poor who'd been charged with serious crimes. Northeastern had the advantage of being the least expensive of the three schools that accepted me (I would be paying for it myself with a ten-year student loan), and the grading was pass/fail, which appealed to me because I wasn't confident about my ability to succeed after six years out of the classroom.

I was never a great law student, though I did well in the academic subjects that I cared most about: Constitutional Law, Equal Protection of the Laws, Federal Jurisdiction, and Criminal Law. The best of the professors there was Dan Schaffer, whose subjects were Federal Taxation, which was required, and an elective, Equal Protection of the Laws, which was my favorite course of all, as it dealt mostly with race discrimination. Professor Schaffer was loveable because he was in outer space much of the time. He would stand for minutes in the middle of the law library, apparently unaware of what was going on around him, his body frozen in time, his eyes on a prize somewhere, way off in the ozone, his mind trapped happily in the intricacies of a Fourteenth Amendment labyrinth.

I liked it when outside speakers visited our classes. I won't forget Robert

Meeropol, who was only six years old when his parents, Julius and Ethel Rosenberg, died in New York's electric chair for allegedly passing atomic bomb secrets to the Russians. Robert believed in their innocence, and he described the emotional trauma he suffered as his parents were tried, convicted (in the court of public opinion as well as federal court), and executed while he and his brother, Michael, were shuttled between relatives, family friends, and an orphanage. Robert's talk convinced me that the impact on children of capital punishment (which I suppose some supporters of the death penalty consider mere "collateral damage") is reason enough to abolish execution.

Thankfully, my world wasn't limited to the law school campus the whole time I was at Northeastern. The law school uses a "co-op plan," requiring students to forego vacations and work three years straight, split equally between the classroom and in law offices for pay. I clerked for criminal defense lawyers in Anchorage, Alaska, and in Boston. I was offered permanent jobs in both places I clerked, one of the advantages of the Northeastern program.

The frontier atmosphere of Anchorage was exciting in 1974, but the ratio of women to men was prohibitive, though my boss, the grizzled, white-haired Wendell P. Kay, was one of the great ones. He was the only lawyer I ever saw who'd mastered the risky lost art of exploratory cross-examination, ignoring the cardinal rule that you should ask witnesses only leading questions to which you already know the answers.

Seated at the defense table with Wendell during one of his trials, I watched as he patiently conducted an improvised, discursive cross-examination, slowly and sweetly eliciting unflattering information from the prosecution's key witness while never treating her with disrespect. Wendell's coup came at the end of her testimony, when he persuaded her to pull from her pocketbook, and hold up in the air for every member of the jury to see, a bottle of a heavy-duty antipsychotic medication she was taking, prescribed by her psychiatrist.

Her credibility was no more, and only the extrasensory "Silver Fox" Wendell P. Kay could pull off something like this. Despite (or perhaps because of) his talent, Wendell was an alcoholic, and when the trial was over, he escorted me to a local watering hole, got stinking drunk, berated me, and fired me. After I left the bar, wondering what the hell to do next, Wendell went on a three-day bender that ended with unconsciousness in the street and an ambulance ride to intensive care.

Wendell's law partners and family were disgusted by his backsliding, and I was his only hospital visitor. Wendell managed to remember firing me, apologized, and asked me to return to his law firm. (I'd taken his sacking of me at face value and hadn't reported for work.) I thanked him and accepted.

I had some success working for Wendell. Motions I'd briefed—attacking the use of prohibited hearsay testimony in a series of grand jury proceedings—resulted in three successive dismissals of murder indictments against our client, a man in his twenties named Larry Ghete. The *Anchorage Daily Times* reacted to the court-ordered dumping of the indictments I'd requested with a sarcastic editorial, titled "Something Wrong," highlighting the dismissals as evidence of the purported collapse of Alaska's criminal justice system. I was proud to be a part of that something. In the wake of the dismissals, the public defender's office offered me a job.

I was tempted to return to live and practice law in beautiful Anchorage by the sea, with its shimmering views of the 20,000-foot mountain Denali during the day, Northern Lights at night, and parks filled with ravens, but the lack of women and a hyper-macho culture, characterized by widespread alcohol abuse and fistfights, were stoppers, along with the depressing sight of fur-coated sex workers on almost every corner and the barroom dumpsters filled with trash that insulated the bodies of freezing homeless Native people with no other place to sleep.

After I left Anchorage to return to classes in Boston, a jury convicted Larry Ghete of murder for stabbing his girlfriend, Patricia Townsend, forty-eight times. An Alaskan trial judge with the wonderful name Seaborn J. "Bucky" Buckalew handed Larry a sentence of 99 years, with no chance for parole until he had served at least 33 years. This was a case that even the great Wendell P. Kay couldn't win.

With Alaska by the wayside, after graduation I joined Zalkind & Zalkind, a small firm on Atlantic Avenue in Boston's North End, facing the harbor. The firm concentrated on criminal defense. Its leader, Norman Zalkind, had been involved in some exciting high-profile cases, including as a member of the legal team fighting federal charges against Meir "Never Again!" Kahane, the militant founder of the Jewish Defense League, for conspiring to manufacture explosives. (Kahane was convicted, but the judge suspended his five-year prison sentence, an amazingly lenient result.)

Whenever Norman won a particularly difficult jury trial or a constitutionally based motion that sprung one of our clients from prison, he would wander about the office, cackling at himself and the mischief for which he was responsible. This was Norman's nervous way of expressing his conviction that beating the all-powerful state because prosecutors cannot prove their case beyond a reasonable doubt, or when police are caught in unlawful behavior that trashes the Bill of Rights, furthers the cause of justice. In the opinion of many, of course, the opposite had occurred: thanks to the unprincipled efforts of some shyster lawyer, another scumbag, guilty-as-hell defendant had been cut loose, ready to prey on the law-abiding.

Criminal defense is honorable work, but many consider it morally suspect or even reprehensible, thanks in part to yellow journalism and the sleazy behavior of the likes of Roy Cohn and F. Lee Bailey, dishonest lawyers who wound up disbarred and disgraced, though Cohn lives on ghoulishly and postmortem as Donald Trump's role model.

Nonetheless, the choice to represent people charged with crimes, most of whom are guilty of something—even though their offenses usually aren't as bad as the prosecution's charges would suggest—requires honest explanation.

CHAPTER 2

$$\text{⚖}$$

The Outlaw Road and Its Challenges

Being a bad boy may be fun some of the time, but it isn't always easy, especially when it's your profession. Friends and family are likely to view the job of criminal defense as ethically suspect, and they will pose polite but pointed questions, the perennial favorite being:

"How Can You Defend Guilty People?"

Lawyers like me will recite reflexive stock responses, including, "Everyone is entitled to a defense and a fair trial," or "I am defending the Constitution and the Bill of Rights, not just a person."

Those rote explanations are inadequate. I know from spending forty years in the criminal court pit that the truth is more complicated. Except for those rare "cause lawyers" equally adept in self-promotion and courtroom skills (like Clarence Darrow or, in my generation, William Kunstler, Gerry Spence, and Alan Dershowitz), criminal defense lawyers reside in the low-rent area of the bar, near the trash-strewn neighborhoods of the bottom dogs they represent.

The negative attitudes toward defense lawyers of some (but not all) of the other players in the system are illustrative of its emotional challenges.

Though most criminal defense lawyers will deny that they have masochistic tendencies, the work requires the ability to take a sucker punch and keep smiling.

First, the judges. There are some excellent robed ones who are bright and impartial. But in the state courts, at least, many of them are political operatives, big money contributors or bundlers, or hacks and hangers-on whose appointment or election has little to do with merit and everything to do with political connections. Martin Erdmann, a veteran New York City public defender, once characterized some of the judges there as "whores who became madams." (The judiciary censured Erdmann for this politically incorrect remark; his double revenge was to get that censure revoked by New York state's highest court and to get himself elected as a criminal court judge in Manhattan.)

Those judges whose inflated egos dwarf their legal judgment love to project from the bench an avuncular "we're all part of this great American system" image while emitting vibes of condescension toward defense lawyers, those pitiable, unwashed creatures in need of a long, cold shower from the judiciary's collective font of wisdom. On the far side of the spectrum, there are the truly mean judges who hate defense lawyers and don't bother to try concealing their disdain as they sentence your clients to unfair prison terms.

Underneath whatever mask they don, too many judges consider it their public duty—more pronounced and all too obvious when it comes to the poor and people of color—to screw your client and you personally if the opportunity arises. Especially if you've managed to get one of their decisions reversed on appeal to a higher court, a humiliation that some will never ever forget and for which they will exact payback in the form of unfavorable decisions in future cases.

There are some decent and thoughtful prosecutors, the ones who take seriously their ethical duty "affirmatively to seek justice, not merely to convict." But many of them are young, on their first job, who ride into court with state power certitude on pretend palominos, as erect in the saddle as Randolph Scott on Stardust but without the life experience or maturity to understand or relate to human frailty or the impact of poverty and institutional racism on the defendants they seek to punish. Such prosecutors will treat defense lawyers with a thin veneer of courtesy. But scratch the surface and you will encounter a wellspring of contempt for the schmucks, turkeys, lamebrains, and Willy Loman losers on the other side (i.e., *you*). The defense lawyer must never take that attitude personally and instead struggle to find a way to advocate for the client that pierces through the prosecutor's armor and appeals to a heart made cold and cynical by the endless daily parade of the damaged and deranged who are processed and excreted by the criminal justice industry.

What about fellow members of the private bar, the ones who do the clean stuff, like estate plans and real estate closings and contracts and maybe an occasional bit of gentlefolk civil litigation on the interpretation of commercial leases or resolution of land survey errors? Their view of counselors who dare to tread on the shady side of the street is exemplified by a partner in a prestigious "white shoe" Boston firm when I asked him why they never did any criminal defense work. His smiling answer: "We'd have to build a separate waiting room." I think he was blissfully unaware of the racism and class bias underlying that unfunny joke.

The cops will kid you and pay you faux deference, but then many of them will lie like rugs, the deep-pile, wall-to-wall shag variety, both on the witness stand and in their written reports if they think they need to do that to ensure a conviction. They are self-righteous about this behavior; lying is a well-known (to criminal defense lawyers) axis of cop culture. I used to half-wonder whether the police academies include perjury classes in their curricula. Prosecutors and judges will pretend to believe the lies of witnesses with badges, and with the help of obedient hireling law clerks, they craft tortured legal arguments designed to stamp their imprimatur on unconstitutional police misconduct.

I came to have deep respect for those officers who rely on hard work to make their cases and who as a matter of honor refuse to lie or stretch the truth. I went out of my way to let them know that I admired their dedication to the rule of law, even when we disagreed on whether the law had been broken or on an appropriate sentence for the guilty.

The public? They may pay lip service to the concept of innocent until proven guilty, but I've had threats to burn down my house, discovered racoons shot dead and posed arm in arm on my driveway, and found antisemitic literature in my rural mailbox (my wife, Ellen, is a Jew). I've been punched in the face in open court, the assault evoking only a mild tut-tut from the judge, Ellen Maloney. The assailant was the father of my clients, young children whose money he'd squandered on trips to Disney World.

On one otherwise relaxing Sunday, I received a series of phone calls from a woman with whom I'd never previously spoken, met, or even heard of. She falsely accused me of making obscene phone calls to her, in an amateurish effort to establish a predicate for a shakedown. I told her I was going to drop the dime on her, which I immediately did, but the Vermont State Trooper on duty in the Shaftsbury barracks that day just laughed and did nothing.

Kevin O'Toole, a Dorset, Vermont, real estate lawyer, once told me the following "wrong man" horror story. Kevin and I look a little bit alike. He was out jogging on an otherwise deserted rural road, and a passing motorist veered as if to hit him but narrowly missed. The driver yelled back to the frightened O'Toole, "I'll get you yet, Saltonstall!"

The lot of the criminal defense lawyer is to make scores of unknown enemies and dodge the not always metaphorical slings and arrows of the citizenry—that is, until one of them gets busted and needs your help. Whenever I go to a restaurant, even in retirement, I sit at a table where I can see who's coming through the front door and spot my nearest safe exit. My former Alaska boss Wendell P. Kay, who was viewed as the best lawyer in the "Upper One" for those charged with serious crimes, always kept three pistols in strategic locations in his small office because he'd had so many death threats. He showed me where he'd hidden the guns, in the event that I might need them myself.

Which brings us to the question, Why would any sane person consider becoming a criminal defense lawyer?

The David and Goliath syndrome is part of it. For the hard core, there is nothing more energizing and exciting than standing up in court and facing down official antagonism and prejudice, daring to expose a stacked deck, fighting a racist, class-biased system that's propped up by the enormous wealth and power of The State. You're the champion of the downtrodden and despised, you speak truth to power, you're the voice crying out in the wilderness, and you do this without showing the fear you feel, knowing that the fix is in. You can't let the self-satisfied members of the fraternity of injustice have their way. Instead, you must always work harder and with more imagination and commitment than the other side, and you can't *ever* make a serious mistake, because if you do, your client will pay for it in years, or even a life sentence without possibility of parole, in a terrifying, loveless cage. Screwing up a case is something that a criminal defense lawyer simply cannot do.

If you choose this exacting path, how does it affect you?

Well, for one thing, you will wake up in the middle of many a night thinking about one of your cases and how to limit the badness and destruction that the system is geared to wreak. You will experience joy in the fact that some of your best ideas jar you into consciousness while the rest of the world is asleep. Given the high stakes for the clients, though, the practice of criminal defense will always place you under stress. Your job requires total attention and dedication, long hours (the equivalent of a six-day workweek or more), very little in the way of vacations (only once in four decades did

I take off more than two weeks a year), and the strength to endure, with lawyerly equanimity, daily stomach-churning and mind-searing doses of a reality soap opera tape-looping through your brain titled *There but for The Grace of God Go I.*

But who's complaining? As that hoary Boston-accented maxim goes, in this world it's either "love it or shove it," and for years I felt very much at home dog-paddling through the bewitchingly roiled, muddy, and stinky waters of the criminal courtroom pit.

The defense lawyer's faith isn't in the here and now, a place that constantly disappoints because kindness and compassion are so hard to find, but rather in the grand scheme of things and in the greater good. Our mission is to help those lost in anger, distress, and confusion and to guide and steer them to a better path, in the conviction that nearly all beings, even those who have done very bad things, are capable of goodness and redemption.

In law school I naively believed that the legal profession could bring about positive social change. I was wrong. The courts, especially the United States Supreme Court, are hostile to human rights; their essential role is to make the prison buses run on time, to prop up a system that's programmed for the wealthy, and to relegate the poor and people of color to the bottom and keep them there. Chiseled into the Vermont marble above the Supreme Court building's entrance is the slogan "Equal Justice Under Law." But this grand-looking edifice is no more than a Potemkin village, a Hollywood backdrop designed to disguise a shameful tradition of inequality and injustice.

I did my best to make equal justice under law a reality on a micro level, in the cases that came my way and as chronicled here, but unequal justice is still the system's whispered mantra and daily driver. In the end, that is why criminal defense is worth doing. One can make a difference in a small way, client by client, life by life, even as the big picture remains the same.

CHAPTER 3

⚖

My First Case

Representing a Serial Killer

I had the good fortune to have as my first boss a Boston street-lawyer whose specialty is court-appointed murder cases. Norman Zalkind is known at the New Courthouse ("new" by Boston standards because it was built in the 1940s) by the nickname "Big Bird," the loveable Muppet he really does resemble. Norman is fabulous on his feet, and he knows the law and what the law should be if it were fair and just, and he is a master of the obscure tactic of salting the trial record with innovative motions and objections that he knows the judge will deny. So that if he loses the trial there will be a decent basis for winning the case on appeal.

Norman's strongest point is his ability to perform in the courtroom, rather than in legal research and writing, and doing live, real-time advocacy before judges and juries is the area of law practice that he enjoys the most. He hires young lawyers who are energetic and ambitious and have a modicum of talent for legal research and writing to do that academic work for him.

In order to be appointed to represent an indigent client in a murder case, a Massachusetts lawyer had to be placed on an all-star list, compiled by the administrative judge, of those with superior qualifications to do that type of work based on prior experience and case outcomes. Norman was proud to be on that list. He and everyone else on the staff worked at least as hard on these low-paying murder cases for poor people as we did on serious criminal cases for clients who could pay high fees.

This was a matter of professionalism for us. We wanted to achieve the best possible outcome under the circumstances, even with the most horrible of homicides committed for no discernible reason by sick or sociopathic people. By approaching murder cases in that fashion, and by showing care and compassion for the worst among us, we were doing the job of criminal defense in the way it should be performed. That is, with total commitment, in the hope that in the end justice will be done and that, when justice prevails, the world will be a little bit better for it.

My salary was only $100 a week in 1976, but I didn't mind, because I would be working on murder cases right out of the box, and I was able to survive by living in communal houses in Cambridge's low-income neighborhoods (none of which have survived the gentrification spawned by Harvard and MIT; our former working-class and student streets are now filled with 900 square-foot, low-ceilinged, roached and flyblown condos costing as much as a million bucks).

My first assignment was to write an appellate brief to the Massachusetts Supreme Judicial Court (the shorthand for which is "SJC"; this is not the "Great and General Court," which is the name for the legislature) on behalf of a client named Thomas McInerney. Thomas had been convicted of the first-degree murder of Cynthia Hartford, a young woman he'd met one night at The Point After, a pickup joint just off Boston's Copley Square. After he'd imbibed six beers and she the same number of wine coolers, they went to her apartment and drank some more. When they tried to have sex, McInerney was impotent, a chronic problem of his, and Ms. Hartford mocked him and laughed and slapped his flaccid penis back and forth. McInerney flew into a rage and grabbed a nearby piece of twine and strangled her to death.

In Massachusetts, first-degree murder carries an automatic life sentence with no chance for parole. Complicating the appeal from the defense standpoint was the fact that this was McInerney's second murder. Only twelve years before, he beat a 29-year-old woman to death by hitting her over the head with a bottle. He'd been convicted of first-degree murder in that matter, but based on McInerney's good behavior in prison, the governor had commuted his sentence to second-degree, thereby making him eligible for parole.

McInerney was in fact on parole when he killed Cynthia Hartford, the first time in Massachusetts history that a defendant with a commuted no-parole sentence had gotten out of prison and murdered again. As a result, McInerney was dangerously unpopular in the joint with all the other lifers hoping for a commutation someday; and to say the least, the Massachusetts judiciary was understandably leery of doing anything that might possibly be construed by the citizenry as giving this Bozo a break.

Hopeless case, right? Maybe that's why, after reading my brief, Norman assigned me the task of orally arguing the appeal in the Massachusetts Supreme Judicial Court.

This was going to be my first case as a lawyer in any courtroom. I had passed the bar exam with a couple of hundred others. But none of the successful applicants had been "sworn in" to the bar, an event that had been scheduled after the date of Thomas McInerney's appellate hearing.

A week before the oral argument, Norman told me that he'd arranged for me to be one of the few lucky ones (a group that included the future senator, presidential candidate, and secretary of state John Kerry) chosen for a special Bicentennial swearing-in ceremony in Boston's Old State House. Built in 1713, at the top of State Street (not to be confused with the more modern, golden-domed State House, which is located on Beacon Street), the Old State House is a beautiful piece of history surrounded by dreary high-rise nonentities. All I remember about my swearing-in was watching a group of newspaper reporters swarm over John Kerry after it was done. We were all nobodies except for Kerry, who as head of the organization Vietnam Veterans Against the War had already attracted much media attention, and his entry into the legal world as a prosecutor in Middlesex County, Massachusetts, likely as a prelude to running for political office, was big news.

After reading the McInerney trial transcript several times, I decided that the only potentially winning legal issue to bring on appeal before the SJC was the distinction between first- and second-degree murder.

In Massachusetts, first-degree murder requires proof beyond a reasonable doubt of the element of "deliberate premeditation" by the defendant. Second-degree murder is a killing committed without premeditation but with malice.

Malice is an elusive legal concept, different from that word's ordinary meaning, colorfully defined by Chief Justice Lemuel Shaw (Herman Melville's father-in-law) in the 1850 case *Commonwealth v. Webster* as a state of mind evincing "a heart regardless of social duty, and fatally bent on mischief."

Given the circumstances of the Cynthia Hartford murder, it seemed to me that the SJC Justices might view it, assuming they were able to be objective despite the notoriety of the case, as a sudden crime of passion not involving premeditation. The difficulty I faced was Massachusetts case law, first set forth in 1905 in *Commonwealth v. Tucker*, to the effect that premeditation can occur in the briefest of moments before a homicide. In the words of the SJC's decision, "while it must be shown that there must be a plan to murder formed after the matter had been made a subject of deliberation and reflection, yet, in view of the quickness with which the mind may act, the law cannot set any limit to the time. It may be a matter of days, hours, or even seconds."

This "in a matter of seconds" doctrine, which I understand is still good law and used as part of the standard homicide jury instruction, essentially conflates the distinction between first- and second-degree murder. That is so because almost everything a person does, except for involuntary actions like sneezing, involves deliberation for at least a passing moment. Despite *Tucker*, I did the best I could drafting the legal brief, stressing the victim's unkind laughter and mocking of the defendant's inability to perform sexually, and that the string he used to strangle her was handily in reach on a bedside table, contrasting that with cases where the killer brings a weapon to the crime scene.

The Massachusetts Supreme Judicial Courtroom is large, with generous spaces for an audience and the press. The lawyers' tables and the podium are set beneath a long bench behind which the seven Justices are seated, looking down on the mere mortals in the pit giving their arguments. Before the proceedings begin, a court officer stands, bangs a gavel, and announces in stentorian tones and with seventeenth century–style solemnity: "Hear ye, hear ye, hear ye. All persons now having business before this, the Supreme Judicial Court, draw near . . . give your attendance . . . and you shall be heard. God Save the Commonwealth of Massachusetts."

Mostly I recall the nervousness, verging on terror, that I felt when my turn came. Here I was, a total rookie, patently unqualified to argue such a serious case in the highest court in the state. Litigators are supposed to banish nervousness by always keeping in mind that their cases aren't about them but rather about their clients and their fate. But I'm afraid that I was too green to follow this teaching to the extent that I should have.

I know that I broke another convention in appellate cases, which is that the judges are familiar with the facts, so one should confine oral presentations to legal analysis. While tipping my hat and paying required homage to the *Commonwealth v. Tucker* precedent, I spent my fifteen minutes of hell going over the facts of the case in as much detail as possible, stressing the crime of passion angle, the handy nearby ligature that belonged to the victim, and my client's spontaneity and lack of deliberate premeditation. I asked the Justices to reduce the degree of guilt from first- to second-degree murder.

Appellate Judges usually interrupt the arguments of counsel with questions designed to poke holes in their reasoning or logic, but there were none during my presentation, which is considered a bad sign. Afterward, my button-down blue shirt was soaked with sweat. I was happy to be out of there.

The court issued its decision seven months later, and to my shock we won. The Justices agreed by a 6–1 vote that this was a murder in the second degree and that a reduction in the degree of guilt was legally required.

> The evidence shows that the defendant went to the victim's apartment at her invitation, that they engaged in consensual conduct without discord until the point where the victim laughed at him. The defendant had not gone there with any plan or purpose to inflict harm on the victim, and he had gone there unarmed. The cord with which he brought about her death was fortuitously within reach. . . . In short, the circumstances of this homicide would not support an inference or finding of deliberate premeditation on the part of the defendant.

I drove to the Bridgewater Correctional Center, then reserved for the mentally ill and those deemed to be targets for murder by other inmates, and informed Mr. McInerney of the court's decision.

Thomas was a mousy little fellow who behaved like the "excuse me for everything" Arnold Stang, the 1950s TV comedian who once described his schtick as "a frightened chipmunk who's been out in the rain too long." There was no clue when interacting with the mild-mannered, self-effacing McInerney that he was capable of murder. Tom seemed pleased, because now that the first-degree conviction had been stricken from his record, he might be eligible again for parole at some point down the road.

This was an unlikely scenario. McInerney would next appear in the trial court for resentencing, at which the issue would be whether the penalty for his second murder conviction would run concurrently with the first sentence or "on and after" it.

In order to become eligible for release with "on and after" (i.e., consecutive) murder sentences, McInerney would have to be paroled from the first conviction—a parole that he'd already violated by killing again—onto the Cynthia Hartford sentence. It was obvious that no Massachusetts judge would sentence McInerney to concurrent life terms on both murder convictions. Such a ruling would mean there would be no additional punishment for killing Ms. Hartford, making that homicide a "freebie," and arguably it would make McInerney eligible, at least technically, for immediate parole.

When we appeared in the Norfolk County Superior Court in Dedham for resentencing (in the same courtroom where Sacco and Vanzetti were

tried in 1921), I was bummed out to learn that, instead of Judge John Mc-
Naught, whose professionalism and political acumen would eventually earn
him a promotion to the federal bench, the case had been assigned to Henry
Chmielinski. This creature was a notorious bully of a judge, often criticized
by other courts for his rudeness and unfairness. For example, in *Oses v.
Commonwealth of Massachusetts*, a 1991 federal court postconviction decision, Judge Douglas P. Woodlock, a conservative Republican and Ronald
Reagan appointee, granted the petitioner a rare new trial based on judicial
misconduct, holding that Chmielinski had evinced "an ostentatiously de-
monstrative undermining of the basic attributes of a fair and orderly proceeding. The record of trial conduct presented to me for review is suffused
with an atmosphere of unfairness and deprecation of the defendant. . . .
Judge Chmielinski acted out what was at best a grudging and sardonic adherence to the formalities of proper trial procedure without implementing
the substance of fair practice."

With Chmielinski at the helm, and McInerney's resentencing conveniently
providing this guy with another opportunity to be his abusive self, I knew we
were going be throttled, dumped overboard, and keelhauled.

I had filed a motion to dismiss the indictment based on a forgetful court
clerk's failure for 16 months to schedule the sentencing hearing. The clerk
finally got it together only after McInerney himself wrote a letter asking to
be sentenced. I argued in part that such a delay violated my client's rights
under a Massachusetts statute mandating that all criminal sentences be imposed within seven days of verdict. I wrote that, because the court had failed
in that regard, it was now without power to impose a sentence and so must
dismiss the indictment.

The existence of the seven-day rule meant that the dismissal motion
wasn't frivolous, but the problem with the argument was that McInerney
was incarcerated, so he hadn't suffered any prejudice from the delay, and
the statute provided no remedy for violation of the seven-day rule. Judge
Chmielinski summarily refused to dismiss the case. This wasn't a surprise.
What shocked me was the tone of the SJC's decision on appeal, holding in
a stinging, over-the-top opinion that my motion was "totally without legal
foundation," an "extreme claim of entitlement," and "equally without merit
on any other consideration."

Please, O Learned Ones of the Supremes, give me a break. Okay, so the
argument wasn't a winner. But it had a legal basis, in the form of a sentencing statute that had been duly enacted by the legislature, approved by the
governor, and published in a volume of the Massachusetts General Laws. I
regret that Mr. McInerney's motion to dismiss offended your sensibilities,

but you of all people must be aware that the job of a defense lawyer is to explore every possible avenue to freedom, however remote, and that, as times change, today's "good law" can become tomorrow's reversible error.

Anyway, with Judge Chmielinski I did my level best to make the argument for concurrent life sentences with the possibility of parole, based on all I could come up with: Mr. McInerney's good behavior while incarcerated, which included his many years of dutiful counseling and teaching of other inmates, and his lack of any prison disciplinary record.

Chmielinski's clever rejoinder, directed at me personally, with joyous venom and with obvious intent to demean me and to crush into nothingness my star-crossed but sincere effort at advocacy:

"Yah mean he was a kind murderah?"

Silence. There could be no lawyerly response, and the barroom retort that came to mind would have meant big trouble. Judge Chmielinski ordered my client to stand and receive his preordained consecutive life sentences. I stood with him.

The sheriff took away the defendant in chains and back to Bridgewater. I gathered up my papers and walked out, passing by the historic, mean little cell in the back of the courtroom where Sacco and Vanzetti were held during their farce of a trial presided over by Judge Webster Thayer, who called the defendants "anarchist bastards," and ended with death sentences and, after unsuccessful appeals, electrocution.

My first case was done—a win on paper only, the product of many weeks of work that changed Thomas McInerney's bleak future not a whit. Though the reduction of his second murder conviction to second degree meant that eventual release was theoretically possible, perhaps on humanitarian grounds in the event of a terminal illness in old age, to me this seemed like cold comfort. Rookie though I was, I had done my absolute best for Thomas; but having done the crime, and having done it more than once, now he'd have to do the time, most likely doing it for the rest of his life. Although McInerney was paroled from his first murder up to the Cynthia Hartford conviction in 1983, would a parole board ever take the chance of releasing him again, possibly to kill a third time? I don't think so.

According to a decision available on the internet, the Massachusetts Parole Board refused to release McInerney in 2015 (at age 72), finding that, based on his record of violence against women, including two nonfatal stabbings as a juvenile (at ages 12 and 13) and two murders (the first when he was 19), he was a continuing danger to the community.

We don't know why people like Thomas McInerney, who came from a law-abiding, middle-class family (his father was a fire department lieutenant in Springfield and his older brother was a dentist), repeatedly commit violent crimes beginning when they are very young.

At his 2015 parole board hearing, McInerney self-diagnosed his violent proclivities as the product of "the adversity he faced growing up." He told the board: "He was not athletically inclined and referred to himself as a day-dreamer and reader. He recalled his father referring to him as a 'sissy,' which intensified his self-hatred. He said he was petrified of his father and perceived himself as a disappointment in his father's eyes. He described being bullied and spoke of his feelings of inadequacy and inferiority that plagued him throughout his life."

I don't doubt the truth of this, and I'm sympathetic to Tom McInerney's difficulties growing up, but they don't explain fully why Tom stabbed two women as a child and killed two as a young adult. Many people suffer from "feelings of inadequacy" due to overbearing or abusive parenting, but that doesn't necessarily compel them to commit stabbings and murders.

In a 2020 parole board hearing, Mr. McInerney (now 77) changed course and declared that the underlying motivation behind his violence toward women wasn't his father's bullying but rather the fact that his mother had been "mean" to him, and he told the board that *she* was the person he'd really wanted to kill.

Maybe so. In 1942, in his pioneering book *Love Against Hate*, the psychiatrist Karl Menninger theorized that, because of institutional prejudice and society's general lack of respect for femininity, mothers are often resentful of the sexist behavior of adult men, and in unconscious retaliation they impose their deep-seated anger on their male offspring. Dr. Menninger believed that this culturally spawned "mother hate" is the root cause of much antisocial and criminal behavior by men. But Menninger's theory has never been tested clinically or scientifically, and few people who have mean mothers stab and kill other women as a result.

If serious, in-depth medical, psychiatric, and genetic studies were done on a large, representative number of violent prison lifers to determine the origins of extreme antisocial behaviors, it is possible that effective early interventions could be developed to stop them. We already know that there are some common denominators among serial killers; the physical and sexual abuse of animals in childhood is a well-known predictor of later, similar violent crimes against humans. But the reasons why young children torture animals and later go on to kill human beings are obscure.

Our criminal justice system is geared to reaction and punishment, not prevention. Serial killers whose record is far worse than that of Tom McInerney—such as Ted Bundy, who sexually assaulted and killed college coeds;

John Wayne Gacy, who raped and murdered young men and buried them in his basement; or Dr. Harold Shipman, a British physician who dispatched as many as 250 of his patients—have never been studied, at least not in any depth. Bundy and Gacy were executed by judicial order, and Dr. Shipman committed suicide.

We should recognize that people such as this have potential value as keys to the enduring mystery of why human beings are capable of horrible crimes.

CHAPTER 4

⚖

Representing a Cop-Killer

One of my other murder cases working with Norman Zalkind was unusual because its treatment in the state court system was overshadowed and haunted by the specter of an earlier homicide.

In separate incidents during the early 1970s, two brothers who were Boston Police officers, Walter Schroeder and John Schroeder, were gunned down in the line of duty, murders so traumatic for members of local law enforcement that they live on in the minds of police even now.

The place where Boston Police Department headquarters is located is named One Schroeder Plaza in honor of Walter and John, and the Schroeder Brothers Memorial Medal is the department's highest award for valor.

The first crime, the murder of Walter Schroeder, was hatched in September 1970, when a group of white revolutionaries, including three Brandeis University students (Susan Saxe, Kathy Power, and a Vietnam veteran on parole named Stanley R. Bond) together with two professional criminals (Robert J. Valeri and William "Lefty" Gilday), broke into a National Guard armory in Newburyport, Massachusetts, stealing guns and ammunition and setting the facility on fire. This action, considered "right on" by some on the far left, thankfully involved no injury to human beings.

A few days later, the same five robbed the State Street Bank in the Brighton neighborhood of Boston, stealing $26,000. They claimed they intended to use the money to help the Black Panther Party and to finance a war against the United States government—which was at best an imaginary revolution, at worst a sociopathic delusion. During the robbery, Lefty Gilday shot and killed Officer Walter Schroeder in the back with a submachine gun. Walter Schroeder died despite four hours of surgery during which he received seventy-seven pints of blood. He left behind a wife and nine children, at least four of whom later became police officers.

Lefty Gilday was arrested, tried, and given a death sentence that eventually was reduced to life without parole. He became a skilled jailhouse lawyer, respected and admired among inmates and some licensed lawyers for his occasional success. However, when Robert Valeri testified against Gilday in exchange for a lesser sentence, he claimed that, when he'd asked Lefty why he'd killed Schroeder, Gilday boasted that he'd "always wanted to shoot a cop." Lefty Gilday died in prison in 2011 from Parkinson's Disease.

Robert Valeri pled to reduced charges of manslaughter and armed robbery, and he was later released. In 1998, he was arrested for distributing a small amount of cocaine and unlawful gun possession. After a federal court trial, he was convicted and sentenced to 17.5 years. He was released from custody in 2004 and died in 2014.

Stanley Bond's case was never tried. Bond blew himself up while awaiting trial when a bomb that he was making as part of an effort to escape from Walpole Prison accidentally exploded.

Susan Saxe and Kathy Power successfully fled and were placed on the FBI's Ten Most Wanted list, thereby achieving celebrity status in many revolutionary and radical feminist quarters. Saxe was captured in 1975 and went to prison for five years. (Her lawyer, Nancy Gertner, became a federal judge.) Power married and gave birth to a son while on the lam, and she was living and working as a chef and cooking teacher in Oregon when she decided, after twenty-three years of freedom, to turn herself in. She then made a plea deal that resulted in her incarceration for six years.

The second Schroeder murder occurred during the armed robbery of a Boston pawnshop in November 1973. Three young Black men, including 17-year-old Terrell Walker (who lived with his mother in the racially segregated Columbia Point housing project, built on top of the former city dump), robbed the Suffolk Loan Company in the predominantly Black neighborhood of Roxbury, stealing cash and jewelry.

During the robbery, John Schroeder, a Boston police detective, suddenly emerged from a closet, where he had been ensconced for reasons unknown. A struggle ensued, during which Terrell Walker shot the detective to death in the neck and stole his gun. Boston cops apprehended Walker and his accomplices, Anthony Irving, age 18, and Nathaniel Williams, age 21, in a Columbia Point apartment later the same day.

The martyred John Schroeder was survived by his wife and four children and another brother, Barney Schroeder, also a Boston police officer.

Terrell Walker's murder prosecution became a law enforcement rallying point and righteous cause in Boston, evoking overwhelming public sympathy for the police.

Because of the importance of the case, the aggressive Assistant District Attorney, Newman Flanagan, whom the voters would soon elevate to the post of District Attorney, appeared as lead counsel for the Commonwealth of Massachusetts. The Superior Court appointed my boss Norman Zalkind to represent the indigent teenager Terrell Walker.

At the trial there was no dispute that Walker was the triggerman. With no other available port in this legal storm, Norman presented a respectable albeit unsuccessful insanity defense. In addition to the supporting opinions of two psychiatrists, Terrell's family members testified to the youth's bizarre behavior at home, which included his having extended one-way conversations with his deceased grandmother. When confronted about them, Terrell had calmly insisted that his grandmother "is still with me."

The prosecution didn't present any expert medical testimony, choosing to rely on the circumstances of the crime itself and something called the "presumption of sanity." This is a judicial instruction given to the jury to the effect that they may consider, as a piece of evidence, that, because most people in the world are sane, the defendant is presumed sane. Which is highly debatable in this context: one proposition doesn't necessarily follow from the other, especially when evidence of a person's insanity is adduced. Logically, then, any presumptive bubble of sanity, which is based on the mental health of the population as a whole, should burst.

The jury returned a guilty first-degree murder verdict, and the veteran Superior Court Judge August "Gus" Taveira immediately imposed on Walker the legally required sentence of life without possibility of parole.

I became part of the case as a third-year law student working for Norman, helping to prepare the Walker appeal to the Massachusetts Supreme Judicial Court. Under the guidance of Suffolk University law professor Eric Blumenson, I wrote portions of the legal brief. I also visited Terrell at Walpole Prison (since poetically renamed Cedar Junction, as if it were a vacation spot) every few weeks, sparing Norman that time-consuming responsibility.

Visiting an incarcerated client at this maximum-security joint is for a criminal defense lawyer a necessary but depressing and enervating exercise that always gave me what I called The Walpole Blues, and as I write this, I feel those blues.

After going through a magnetometer and pat-down search, you must cross a prison yard and then stand for an unnerving minute while locked in the "Trap," a tiny hallway with impenetrable metal doors on either end, with guards scrutinizing you from a balcony above, shotguns at the ready, pointing downward at your head.

Walpole Prison sows nagging thoughts of suicide into the brains of all who enter. You are transported into an alternative, Dante-esque universe: an enormous echo chamber of loud noises, roiled into a horrible, distorted, endless din—the blasting of radios and televisions, the shouts and screams of inmates, the constant slamming of cell bars and heavy prison doors. There is no visual relief from the bare, shiny, gloss-painted concrete walls, and the calming force of Nature is nowhere to be found. The smells of unwashed and undeodorized bodies, flushed and unflushed toilets, and the remnants of the disgusting food fed to the inmates permeate the hot, thick atmosphere. On the narrow floor, below tiers of cells stacked above one another, lies a mishmash of garbage and sometimes urine and shit that the prisoners hurl at the sometimes cruel and violent guards, who, according to prisoners with whom I spoke, are the main source of illegal drugs in the institution.

On my first visit with Terrell, I represented him in a prison disciplinary matter. A Walpole guard's disciplinary report (or "D-report") accused Terrell of throwing an empty plastic peanut butter jar at a guard from one of the upper tiers. As a matter of due process, prison inmates are entitled to a hearing when they are accused of offenses in the joint because they may suffer loss of good time; at Walpole, they may be stashed for months in total isolation in the disciplinary Block Ten, in eight-by-ten foot "boxcar" or "steel tomb" cells with no windows, reading material, or media. For one hour a day, five days a week, inmates in Block Ten are permitted to go outdoors, but in small, narrow cages known as "dog kennels."

Terrell had become a member of the Nation of Islam, which gave him a powerful group of friends to protect him from neo-Nazi skinheads, members of the Aryan Brotherhood gang, and others who might want to make a name for themselves by "shanking" him (stabbing him with an improvised blade) or beating this notorious cop-killer to death.

In accordance with Nation of Islam discipline, Terrell was overly polite, with a formal, pseudo-military bearing and way of speaking. But even so, he was still a youngster, and despite the seriousness of his crime and the grievous harm to others that he had caused, there was a kind of naïve sweetness about Terrell that motivated me to help him without the cool, objective, scrimlike barrier of professionalism that as a law student I was just beginning to learn to adopt.

Our defense at the hearing, with two guards sitting as "judges" protected from us behind a heavy metal mesh screen, was that because of his religion, Terrell couldn't have been the one who threw the peanut butter jar at the guard. As Terrell testified: "The Honorable Elijah Muhammad forbids us from eating peanut butter because he tells us it is the same as putting cement into the temple of our bodies. The Honorable Elijah Muhammad also commands us never to touch peanut butter or to come anywhere near it."

The corrections officer who was the alleged victim of this incident didn't show up to testify. Either he wasn't on duty that day or he blew off the case because he figured that, given the composition of the "court," the outcome of the hearing was rigged in his favor.

To my surprise, the guards knew about Nation of Islam's ban on peanut butter and found Terrell not guilty of the offense. Terrell was happy with his exoneration and with me as well. He now trusted me as a sincere helper, rather than viewing me as a "white devil" out to mess him up. After the hearing, we discussed at some length his pending appeal to the Massachusetts Supreme Judicial Court. If the appeal were successful, it would result in a new trial, not in any sort of exoneration that would set him free.

But as Emily Dickinson taught us, "hope is the thing with feathers / that perches in the soul." For a prison lifer, hope, however tenuous, is what keeps you going.

Terrell Walker's SJC appeal went nowhere, an outcome that wasn't a surprise given that in murder cases it matters who you kill, and it's no exaggeration to say that John Schroeder had achieved the status of near sainthood in Boston.

We filed a habeas corpus petition in federal district court. This is a specialized kind of postconviction review that is limited to cases involving serious violations of federal constitutional law; garden-variety errors under state law aren't considered. We struck out there as well, so we appealed to the United States Court of Appeals for the First Circuit, which sits in Boston and is one step below the United States Supreme Court. At the time, the First Circuit had the reputation of relative fairness in criminal cases. In 1969, for example, the court overturned the convictions of famed pediatrician Dr. Benjamin Spock and several others who had been convicted of conspiracy to interfere with the Vietnam War draft by condemning the war and advocating resistance to it.

Eric Blumenson and I divided the briefing and oral argument, focusing on two main points that we thought were the strongest. My baby, the "prisoner's dock," was a systemic criminal justice issue for us affecting felony jury trials in Massachusetts. This was both a daunting and exciting assignment on which I was honored to be the point person.

Under Massachusetts practice at the time, defendants on trial for felonies were confined in a three-foot-high box located ten or twelve feet behind defense counsel's table. The "dock" made it difficult for defense counsel to communicate with the client. Any defendant on trial would first have to somehow get the attention of his lawyer, who would then have to seek leave of court to leave counsel table and walk back to the dock to converse with the client.

Even more important, we were certain that confinement of a defendant in the dock suggests to the jury that the person on trial is already in prison custody, almost certainly dangerous, and very probably guilty. Use of the prisoner's dock was an antiquated Massachusetts legal tradition, dating back to the beginning of its criminal justice system. A tradition likely derived from the roomier, classier, and less prejudicial British dock, such as the one in London's "Old Bailey" courtroom, depicted in the 1957 Billy Wilder film *Witness for the Prosecution*, starring Charles Laughton and Tyrone Power. I understand from Charles Russell Peck, an old friend who is a retired criminal court judge in Britain, that the "prejudice of the dock," as he puts it, is still a part of the system there.

The federal constitutional right implicated by use of the dock is the presumption of innocence, a rule that is not specifically mentioned in the text of the Constitution. But it is an ancient legal principle that is found in the Talmud and in Roman law. It has become so engrained in jurisprudence throughout the world that the Universal Declaration of Human Rights (adopted in 1948 by a 48–2 vote of the General Assembly of the United Nations) requires in Article 11 that every defendant in a criminal trial "has the right to be presumed innocent until proven guilty."

At the time of Terrell Walker's trial, however, federal constitutional law on the presumption of innocence was surprisingly sparse.

In the 1895 decision *Coffin v. United States*, the Supreme Court declared: "The principle that there is a presumption of innocence in favor of the accused is the undoubted law, axiomatic and elementary, and its enforcement lies at the foundation of the administration of our criminal law." But the court's opinion didn't point to the Constitution as the legal basis for the presumption of innocence. The only constitutional argument available in such a circumstance is that which the judiciary calls "fundamental fairness," a concept grounded in the spirit of the Fourteenth Amendment, which contains the prohibition "nor shall any State deprive any person of life, liberty, or property without due process of law."

Another hurdle we had to leap over somehow was the absence of any case law outside of the Massachusetts Supreme Judicial Court decisions on the prisoner's dock. Massachusetts cases simply declared, without any historical discussion or legal analysis, that the dock doesn't erode the presumption of innocence and that its use is "within the sound discretion" of the trial judge.

The lawyer's job in this situation is to search for an apt analogy. The only one I could think of, and for which I could find any legal support, was a somewhat obscure doctrine to the effect that it is fundamentally unfair, and therefore an error of constitutional magnitude, to require a defendant to appear in a prison uniform during a trial by jury.

There existed a smattering of favorable federal cases on this point, but they were from other federal judicial circuits. Under the abstruse rules governing federal jurisdiction, a federal court of appeals decision is legally binding only within that court's circuit. We could cite the existing jail clothing cases as persuasive outside authority, but they didn't have the force of law in any court, either state or federal, within the First Circuit, which includes only Massachusetts, New Hampshire, Maine, Rhode Island, and Puerto Rico. Terrell Walker's prospects for relief changed after his appeal in the Massachusetts Supreme Judicial Court had been briefed and argued.

In May 1976, in *Estelle v. Williams*, the United States Supreme Court ruled for the first time in our history that "the presumption of innocence, although not articulated in the constitution, is a basic component of a fair trial" and a right protected under the Due Process Clause of the Fourteenth Amendment. The Court went on to hold that forcing a criminal defendant to wear prison clothing violates due process because the "constant reminder of the accused's condition implicit in such distinctive, identifiable attire may affect a juror's judgment . . . and [is] so likely to be a continuing influence throughout the trial, that . . . an unacceptable risk is presented of impermissible factors coming into play."

The Court's opinion was written by Chief Justice Warren Burger, an extremely conservative Nixon appointee, and every one of the Justices agreed with the legal principle it articulates. The Justices split only on whether the defendant's trial lawyer had waived the prison garb issue. A majority found such a waiver because, even though a jail guard had refused the defendant's request to wear civilian clothing at the trial, his clueless defense lawyer had failed to raise the issue with the trial judge and object.

The Nixonian ideological views of the decision's author and the unanimity of the Supreme Court's holding—that it is unconstitutional to require a defendant to wear a prison uniform at trial if the lawyer objects—endowed the case with decent analytical and emotional force for application in other contexts, even in jurisdictions where the presiding judges might have philosophies on the far right of the spectrum.

Norman Zalkind had for years as a matter of routine filed written motions to allow his clients to sit with him at counsel table, which is allowed everywhere else in America. Norman knew based on experience that Judge Taveira would deny the motion in Terrell's case. Norman was personally committed to the dock's abolition. He believed that someday an appellate court would agree and change the system, and the opportunity to help make new law fell to me.

The First Circuit's courtroom in the 1970s was the antithesis of the gritty, hurly-burly atmosphere in Massachusetts state courts. It had dark oak-paneled walls, red velvet curtains, metal-mullioned windows, and spotless carpeting, and there was total quiet, without the distraction of litigants and their families whispering among themselves and running in and out. Legal arguments there were a bit like amicable debates on matters of history or literature between fellow intellectuals at the Harvard Club over snifters of Rémy Martin cognac. And I must confess, with some embarrassment, that based on my rarified life experience at the time I felt more at home and considerably less nervous in the First Circuit than in other venues.

By the time of the oral argument, I no longer worked at the Zalkind firm. But I was still a part of Terrell's legal team, and on the day of the appeal, I was the first lawyer up in the pit.

I argued that the cell-like appearance of the prisoner's dock, with its door locked and court officers nearby, must suggest to any jury that a defendant thus confined must already be in jail, dangerous, and probably guilty. The prisoner's dock erodes the presumption of innocence in a way closely analogous, if not perfectly so, to being forced to appear in a prison uniform.

Professor Blumenson was up next for the team, and he blasted the legal equivalent of a home run over Fenway Park's Green Monster.

Despite Norman's objection in what was an insanity defense case, Judge Taveira arbitrarily had ordered that Terrell Walker, in violation of his right to remain silent, personally announce in open court the defense decisions on whether to agree or object to the seating of each prospective juror during the selection process. To make matters worse, the prosecutor Newman Flanagan in his summation argued to the jury that they should consider these forced communications as evidence of Walker's sanity.

In Flanagan's words, quoted verbatim from the trial transcript: "Ask yourself about this particular defendant. What do you think? Do you think he knew what he was doing when he stood up there and said, 'I am content with this juror? I am content with this juror? I am content with this juror?' Do you think he knew what he was doing then?"

Blumenson stressed that forcing Walker to communicate substantive, strategic decisions violated the defendant's Fifth Amendment privilege against self-incrimination. Newman Flanagan's characterization of the forced communications as evidence of sanity, and his exhortation to the jury that they should use them as a reason to convict, made this constitutional violation even more egregious.

None of the three judges on the court of appeals panel were from Massachusetts. Judge Frank Coffin, a Lyndon Johnson appointee, was from Maine. Judge Hugh Bownes, also nominated by President Johnson, was a New Hampshire resident. Judge Raymond Pettine, whom Jimmy Carter had put on the federal bench, lived in Rhode Island. I hoped that our panel members, because they were from outside Massachusetts, would be less likely to be constrained by local backlash and more likely to decide in our favor.

Judges like those who sat on Terrell Walker's case, especially those appointed by Democratic presidents, are often lambasted as result-oriented "liberal" activists who substitute their left-wing political views for principled decisions based on law, particularly in the criminal sphere. That perception is incorrect. They are in fact traditionalists who follow in the footsteps of Chief Justice John Marshall, a Federalist and an appointee of the Federalist President John Adams.

John Marshall was the first Justice to articulate and establish the Supreme Court's power and duty to review and determine the constitutionality of congressional legislation, and he is universally viewed as the high court's greatest legal mind. More than 200 years ago, in an 1819 decision, Marshall wrote that "we must never forget that it is a *constitution* we are expounding" and that the judiciary must interpret that document with fidelity to its "letter and spirit," not simply with a one-dimensional adherence to textualism, the narrow view currently favored by the wrongly named Federalist Society when it furthers its political agenda. (Justice Antonin Scalia and his followers had no problem with ignoring the precatory Second Amendment language, "A well-regulated militia, being necessary to the security of a free state," in order to hold that there is a personal right to bear arms in a purely civilian context.)

Chief Justice Marshall's insistence that courts must consider the spirit of the Constitution as well as its literal text is at the root of essential modern Supreme Court decisions, running the gamut from the requirement that government provide lawyers for indigent defendants to ensuring the freedom of Americans to use birth control devices without fear of arrest and imprisonment.

The Constitution doesn't mention a right to free legal assistance for the poor. But it's obvious that the Sixth Amendment guarantee of the assistance of counsel "in all criminal prosecutions" would be useless and hollow unless read expansively enough to require government to pay for defense lawyers for impoverished defendants.

In a similar vein, it was until very recently a criminal offense in many states, including Massachusetts and Connecticut, to buy and use condoms and other birth control devices. The Constitution makes no mention of birth control, but the Supreme Court has ruled that its use is lawful under the freedom of speech and association provisions of the First Amendment. Writing for the court in a 1965 decision, Associate Justice William O. Douglas said that the First Amendment casts a long, protective shadow that stretches beyond the narrow confines of its text, in the form of "a penumbra where privacy is protected from government intrusion."

The traditionalist judges of the First Circuit decided in Terrell Walker's favor. The court of appeals rested its ruling to issue a writ of habeas corpus on the Fifth Amendment. The prosecution had maintained that there was no constitutional violation, citing Supreme Court decisions that upheld the legality of instances where an accused is forced to talk—such as in police lineups, at which the participants may be required, for the limited purpose of identification, to repeat aloud something that the victim has overheard the perpetrator say.

The Constitution makes no mention of procedural safeguards for jury selection. But the First Circuit held that the words that Judge Taveira required Terrell to speak were used for their substantive content; they revealed the defendant's thought processes. Terrell's words were the equivalent of testimony, thereby subject to Fifth Amendment protection.

The court's decision also ended further routine use of the prisoner's dock in Massachusetts criminal trials, even though there is nothing in the Constitution specifically to prohibit it. As Judge Pettine put it: "The right to a fair trial is simply too delicate and valuable a right to be impeded by an anachronistic practice. Because confinement in the prisoner dock is unnecessary to accomplish any important state interest and may well dilute the presumption of innocence, the Massachusetts prisoner dock must be considered, as a general matter, to be an unconstitutional practice."

The court's decision, though heavily criticized by police, prosecutors, and the press, was well within the bounds of Chief Justice John Marshall's traditionalist approach to constitutional jurisprudence.

Norman Zalkind, who was still Terrell Walker's trial lawyer by virtue of his court appointment six years before, then made an extremely favorable plea deal with Newman Flanagan, who was now the elected district attorney, no longer the mere first assistant. Flanagan's unconstitutional error in his argument to the jury had been a major factor in our appellate win, and he may simply have wanted the case over and done with. Another consideration for Mr. Flanagan was that no one can ever predict the outcome of a retrial, especially in an old case, where witnesses sometimes die, disappear, or change their stories.

From Newman Flanagan's standpoint, at least the terms of his deal included a guaranteed outcome for the state: guilty pleas to everything and continued incarceration for Terrell Walker. This wasn't abject surrender, but to those in the know, it was close to it. Under the plea agreement, Walker pled guilty to the lesser charges of manslaughter and armed robbery, and on March 25, 1980, Superior Court Judge Andrew Linscott imposed the maximum sentences of eighteen to twenty years on the convictions—to run concurrently, however.

According to the *Boston Globe*, the district attorney explained his decision as follows: "Unfortunately, a circuit court of appeals made new law to the benefit of the defendant and to the detriment of the public, a law prosecutors must live with but with which I do not agree."

The Fifth Amendment to the Constitution was not, of course, "new law" in 1980. It was ratified in 1791, but it wouldn't have been collegial, or at all helpful to the client, had Norman pointed this out. The bottom line was this: Terrell Walker would be released from Walpole after serving twelve years. All considered, this was a tremendous victory, giving this young man a second chance at life.

At some point during the mid-1980s, Terrell telephoned me to let me know he was on the street. He hinted, without asking me directly, that he would like to travel to Vermont, where I was then living and practicing law, to visit and personally thank me.

I discouraged this as gently as possible. I had been one of Terrell's lawyers, and I cared about him and his future, but I was not his friend. Criminal defense lawyers lose their objectivity and they place themselves in harm's way when they befriend clients. One never knows what a client might do in the future; and were a lawyer out of friendship to become involved, even inadvertently or tangentially, in some criminal scheme, tsuris and disbarment await.

As I write this, the chill of an ill wind lingers in my soul, stemming from my failure to invite Terrell to visit me and my wife and stepdaughter in our home. I knew that he was essentially alone and that he needed a friend to help him make a life outside prison walls. But I couldn't be that guy—or so I believed.

I wished Terrell good luck and urged him to get some job training and find something positive to do with his life so that he would never again find himself behind bars. He seemed to want to change his life, but I know he was disappointed in me when we rang off, and that was the last time we spoke.

The odds are stacked like a snake-eyes dice-roll against a dark-skinned Black man, an ex-con, a convicted felon, a cop-killer, with no education and no one to turn to other than the wretched of the earth with whom he grew up in the Columbia Point housing project, erected on the city dump, the symbolism of which was lost on no one.

I continued to follow Terrell in the press and on Google, hoping that he would be able to turn things around. I learned that in 1994 Terrell was arrested for armed robbery, and he was convicted and did prison time for that. Then he was arrested on drug charges.

According to press accounts, Terrell had become an enforcer for a drug mob controlled by Rhode Island organized crime.

A Massachusetts State Police lieutenant colonel was quoted as claiming that Terrell "is revered in the criminal world and feared. Everyone in that crime organization knew what he did. His purpose was to intimidate people to pay their debts, and he made sure the hierarchical structure was compensated."

In 2018, at age 63, Terrell was busted on drug and firearm charges. In his last mugshot, Terrell looks nothing like the naïve, appealing kid I knew. He looks old and defeated. I wish I had done more to help Terrell Walker, though in my opinion the elimination of systemic racism is the only remedy for lives like his, twisted by the effects of third world–level poverty, school and housing segregation, police, political, and public hostility, and the lack of educational and job opportunities other than robbery or drug-dealing.

Court decisions have recognized that race discrimination in housing, education, employment, and criminal justice—as well as in voting, a fundamental right that many state legislatures have restricted and even sought to nullify in the wake of Trump's loss in the 2020 election—are "badges and incidents of slavery." That is, they are historical vestiges and mirrors of the treatment of Black people during slavery and its post-Reconstruction aftermath: segregation, the system of sharecropping, lynching and other Klan-style violence, the refusal to allow Black people to vote, the use of all-white juries, and the like.

Unfortunately, however, many white people are either incapable of making this historical link or they find it politically disadvantageous to do so. They angrily deny that white privilege is an historical fact, and instead they view efforts to eradicate "badges and incidents of slavery" as forms of undeserved and unlawful racial preference.

In part this is the fault of our educational system, which taught, and in some places continues to teach, that slavery wasn't all that bad and that most slavemasters were kind to their pathetic, inferior charges, without whose discipline and help they would have been incapable of survival.

The recent movement to ban the teaching of "critical race theory," which isn't a theory at all but rather the academic world's acknowledgement that institutional racism still exists, is another way in which white society blinds itself to the continuing impact of slavery in American social, cultural, and political life.

It is impossible to deny that oppressed kids of color like Terrell Walker shouldn't rob pawnshops and kill police officers, but it isn't totally off base from an historical perspective to analogize this bad behavior to the slave rebellions led by Nat Turner, Denmark Vesey, and Toussaint Louverture.

CHAPTER 5

⚖

The Chad Green Case

Medicine Versus Quackery

In September 1977, I decided to leave the Zalkind firm and go off on my own. I rented a room in a dingy suite with two other solo lawyers, Samuel Meline (a nursing home operator) and Victor Brogna (the brother of Vincent Brogna, a Superior Court judge), on the fifth floor of 148 State Street in Boston, around the corner from the Quincy Market and an Irish bar called The Black Rose. My only "support staff" was a telephone answering service. I bought a robin's-egg blue IBM Selectric, which in those precomputer word-processing days was the Ferrari of typewriters, with a tiny rotating ball in its well that made the inked impressions, without any need for keys linked to metal bars for each character.

Laboriously, as I'm a two-fingered typist, I sent letters to the local district courts letting them know I was available for appointment in criminal cases for the poor. The courts were happy to hear from me because these cases paid only $15 an hour for out-of-court time and $25 an hour for in-court time. It was the newly admitted lawyers, who needed the experience and exposure, who wanted these appointments. Only the most idealistic of the old-hand defense counsel would volunteer to represent indigent clients at this bottom level of the court system. During my district court travels, I met one of the best of these idealists, former Governor Foster Furcolo, a kind soul as well as a first-rate lawyer. I'd read his novel *Let George Do It!*

(1957), a satire on Boston politics, and let him know that I'd enjoyed it a lot.

My district court cases were routine misdemeanors that usually resolved with plea bargains at the first or second court appearance. I became reasonably adept at persuading prosecutors to agree to a disposition unique to Massachusetts known as "continued without a finding," where if a client gets into no further trouble for six months to a year, the case is dismissed, and the criminal charge and dismissal may sometimes be "sealed" and hidden from the public eye.

I traveled all over Massachusetts, as far away as New Bedford in the south and Great Barrington in the west. Each district court had a different culture. My favorite venue was East Boston, home of Logan Airport, where the late Judge Joe Ferrino presided in a friendly, kindly, ego-free manner. He seemed to enjoy dealing with the motions I filed instead of viewing them as a pain. I did not like practicing in West Roxbury, where Judge Paul Murphy always looked up at the ceiling when I spoke, never ever meeting my eyes, an odd demeanor that was challenging because it was impossible to tell what he was thinking. His tough, unsmiling chief probation officer, Sister Rose Paula Mace of the Sisters of Notre Dame, dressed in her full nun's habit in court. So much for the separation of church and state.

Ishmael, the narrator of *Moby-Dick*, Herman Melville's great novel, tells the reader: "A whale-ship was my Yale College and my Harvard." My formal education never prepared me for dealing with the overwhelmingly sad and troubled lives of the raggedy, clinically depressed people I represented in the district courts, an experience that earned me a bachelor's degree in other people's misery.

A few private clients hired me, but I was terrible at collecting fees. Silly me: I trusted folks who were charged with crimes to do the right thing and pay me. Getting money "up front" is a must in criminal cases. I hadn't yet been schooled in the apocryphal yet instructive tale of the defense lawyer who would beg the courts for continuances of his cases because he was "waiting for Mr. Green"—that is, to be paid.

A wealthy interior designer, antique dealer, and family friend who owned real estate on Boston's decidedly upscale Newbury Street got himself in big trouble and came to me for help. The housing court had sentenced him in absentia to jail (he hadn't shown up for his hearing) for failing to have the required fire escapes on one of his tenant buildings. I was able to get the jail sentence stricken after presenting the court with photographic proof that my client (finally, on my insistence!) had installed the proper outdoor metal landings and stairs to the street. I never got a dime from this man, and I learned after my mother's death that he had stolen some valuable items from her apartment.

Bill Waldron, the general counsel of Massachusetts General Hospital (MGH), came to my rescue. He had been looking for a young, relatively inexpensive lawyer ($50 an hour) to represent that venerable institution in child abuse and neglect cases, primarily in Boston Juvenile Court (BJC), because he wanted his staff attorney, Marvin Guthrie, to concentrate his efforts on hospital rate-setting litigation.

My late mother, Margaret Bonnell "Peg" Saltonstall, had been Bill's executive secretary when he was commissioner of administration under Governor Endicott "Chub" Peabody in the 1960s. She was working as a volunteer for Bridge Over Troubled Waters, a Boston social service agency dedicated to helping street children. I suspect that Bill and Peg connected; Bill offered me the work, consisting of civil cases, but they were righteous ones. And since I wouldn't be on the MGH staff, I could continue representing poor people as their public defender.

MGH filed what is known as "Care and Protection" petitions when a severely abused or neglected child was admitted as a patient. Kids showed up with broken bones, and their X-rays often revealed the existence of old fractures as well, to the extent that the social workers might diagnose these little helpless patients as victims of Battered Child Syndrome.

Burns from cigarettes, matches, lighters, and boiling water were common. Gross parental failure to supervise resulted in wandering children being hit by cars, taking disastrous falls, or suffering other harm. Child victims of sexual abuse, usually perpetrated by family members, also came to the attention of emergency room physicians.

Medical neglect—the failure of parents to provide children with necessary, lifesaving treatment—was a significant problem faced by MGH medical and social work staffs. This usually occurred when devout parents of certain faiths, such as Christian Scientists and Jehovah's Witnesses, refused on religious grounds to authorize medical intervention, even when their children were dying from untreated illnesses.

The main purpose of the Care and Protection petitions in cases of medical neglect was to obtain judicial orders for treatment. Sometimes, after a statutorily mandated investigation that was done in each case by a neutral person with appropriate training, the judge would place the child in the legal or even the physical custody of the state, but MGH generally took no position on custody except in the most extreme cases. The hospital staff always hoped to obtain the cooperation of abusive or neglectful parents, and they didn't want to alienate them by advocating for removal of children from their homes unless that was necessary to save their lives.

My first task was to go to the BJC with MGH staffer Marv Guthrie for a formal introduction to the court clerk, John "Jackie" Bulger. Clerk Bulger's older brothers were two of the most feared and most powerful men in Massachusetts, and as a result Jackie was far more formidable than his job description would suggest, requiring a kind of bowing and scraping in his presence.

Jackie's "good" brother, William "Billy" Bulger, the oldest of the three, was president of the Massachusetts Senate. One of his important accomplishments as a legislator was to revamp the state's laws on child abuse and neglect. For a time, he was a trustee of MGH. After retiring from politics, Republican Governor William Weld appointed Billy, a Democrat, as president of the University of Massachusetts. By all accounts, Billy did an outstanding job there, especially as a fundraiser. Billy was forced to resign his post under pressure from Governor Mitt Romney and others for refusing to testify against his brother Whitey before a congressional committee. Billy followed the precept that blood is thicker than water, even at the cost of his career. I think that this was an honorable decision. I would never testify against my brother, no matter what the circumstances, which in this case were admittedly egregious, given what a lowlife Billy's brother Whitey was.

Jackie's "bad" brother, James Joseph "Whitey" Bulger Jr., was a ruthless killer and head of Boston's Winter Hill Gang, whose evil deeds were later the subject of Martin Scorsese's Oscar-winning film *The Departed* (2006) as well as the biopic *Black Mass* (2015), starring Johnny Depp. Whitey's willingness to inform on rival mafia families earned him the protection of the FBI, whose "handler," Special Agent John Connolly, allowed Whitey to commit unspeakable crimes with impunity. After the FBI reversed course and decided to prosecute, Agent Connolly tipped off Whitey, who fled Boston and lived underground for sixteen years. Ultimately, Whitey was caught in an apartment in Santa Monica, California, extradited to Massachusetts, and convicted in Boston of eleven murders. After committing a murder, Whitey would remove the victim's teeth and fingers, so if the body were found, the authorities wouldn't be able to identify it. In 2018, while Whitey was incarcerated in a West Virginia federal prison, a group of inmates beat him to death as he sat in his wheelchair.

Given his extraordinary family ties, the BJC clerk, Jackie Bulger, wasn't someone to be trifled with. Au contraire, MGH lawyers and physicians were compelled to treat him with respect bordering on obeisance. We always addressed him as "Your Honor," even though he wasn't a judge. In fact, Jackie was an arrogant pretender whose demands made it unreasonably difficult for MGH to do its job. In 2003, Jackie was convicted of lying to a grand jury about stashing his brother Whitey's ill-gotten cash in various bank safe deposit boxes around town. But I knew Jackie in the late 1970s, when all three Bulgers were Boston royalty, and Jackie was in absolute control of MGH's access to the BJC.

Whenever MGH filed a Care and Protection petition at the BJC, we had to convince Clerk Bulger of its merits before he would deign to pass along the paperwork to Chief Judge Francis G. Poitrast (uncharitably referred to by some as "Pot Roast Poitrast" because of his great bulk and ruddy face) and schedule a court date. Bulger would hold hearings in his office at which I, often accompanied by a member of the medical or social work staff, would have to persuade him that court intervention was appropriate. We would have to make appointments in advance to meet with Clerk Bulger at his convenience, and this unnecessary, ego-driven hurdle was a source of delay.

In one case, Bulger's behavior may have had fatal consequences, although no one can be sure of that. The matter involved Jehovah's Witness parents who had refused to allow MGH doctors to perform blood transfusions that were needed to save their daughter's life. Based on my memory of visiting this child in her hospital room with an MGH social worker and her parents present, I believe she was ten or eleven years old.

After a delay of a day or so due to Clerk Bulger's unavailability for unstated reasons, I was finally able to get into court, and Chief Judge Poitrast issued an emergency order for the transfusions. The little girl received the blood her physician had ordered, but it came too late to be effective, and she died in her hospital bed. I learned from an MGH social worker that the girl's ultrareligious parents told her before she expired that, because she had received a transfusion, she was going to Hell.

MGH sometimes resorted to other courts for relief in matters involving children. Such was the case with Chad Green, age two, who in October 1977 began treatment for acute lymphocytic leukemia with John T. Truman, MD, the hospital's most experienced pediatric oncologist, reputed to be one of the best in the country. The Greens had arrived from Omaha, Nebraska, where Chad's leukemia had been diagnosed and chemotherapy begun.

Chad was one of the cutest little boys I had ever met, with blonde hair, big eyes, and a soulful expression that made my heart sink, knowing that he was gravely ill. He was a physically active child and deeply bonded to his mother, Diana, though less so, I thought, to his father, Jerry, who came off as a bit of a domineering tough guy. Chad's pasty white, unhealthy-looking complexion was the only indication that he had a health problem. Chad's cancer was in remission when Dr. Truman first saw him as a patient. At that time, his statistical chance for a cure was better than 50 percent; those odds have since improved to about 80 percent, as more historical patient outcome data have become available.

Chad's physicians in Omaha had wanted to use a medical protocol, developed by the Saint Jude Children's Research Hospital in Memphis, Tennessee, which included cranial radiation, a procedure that Chad's parents opposed, prompting their move to the Boston area.

In deference to Mr. and Mrs. Green's wishes, Dr. Truman agreed to utilize an additional chemotherapy drug instead of radiation. Dr. Truman also acceded to the parents' request that they put Chad on a diet of vegetarian foods, distilled water, and vitamin supplements. Dr. Truman stressed, however, that the diet would have no effect on their child's leukemia.

In November 1977, Chad's parents asked Dr. Truman what would happen if chemotherapy were terminated. Dr. Truman responded that there was a 100 percent chance that the cancer would return and that Chad would die. The parents assured Dr. Truman that they would continue chemotherapy, which included 6-mercaptopurine, a drug in pill form that had to be administered at home every day.

In February 1978, Dr. Truman found after conducting a bone marrow test that Chad's leukemia had returned. During a series of conversations with the doctor, Diana Green admitted that they had stopped giving their son the mercaptopurine pills three months earlier, without telling anyone at MGH.

During the next four days, Dr. Truman called the parents repeatedly, trying to persuade them to resume treatment. He told them that the chance for cure had diminished due to the recurrence of the disease but that there still existed a substantial possibility for healing if chemotherapy were resumed. Dr. Truman also made clear to the Greens that he had an ethical responsibility as a physician to do his utmost to save Chad's life and that he might have to seek a court order.

Nonetheless, Diana and Jerry refused any medical help for Chad. Accordingly, on February 24, 1978, MGH staff attorney Marv Guthrie and I raced to the Plymouth County Probate Court in Brockton, where we obtained from Judge James R. Lawton a temporary order of guardianship requiring the Greens to return Chad to MGH for treatment.

Jim Lawton was an old-school Massachusetts pol who had progressively climbed the greasy pole, all the way from state representative, to legislative secretary for Governor Endicott Peabody, to commissioner of motor vehicles, and finally to the not particularly demanding but prestigious and well-paid post of probate judge.

I represented MGH at a hearing that swiftly followed. The courtroom was filled, including with a multitude of newspaper and television reporters and even a sketch artist. (In those days, photography was not permitted in most state courts, and this ban continues nationwide in the federal court system.) Chad's parents, through counsel, moved the probate court to vacate the temporary guardianship.

At a bench conference, Judge Lawton made it clear that he wanted no part of the case. I thought that this politically connected and savvy guy, who enjoyed the perks of his cushy judgeship, was freaked out by the sudden and unanticipated explosion of media coverage and the potential threat to his position it could pose if he made the wrong move.

The media coverage, which Chad's parents had deliberately generated, and which was expanding exponentially, favored Mr. and Mrs. Green. They had relentlessly cultivated and schmoozed with reporters, and they had sown widely their distorted and sometimes blatantly untrue version of events. Dr. Truman had remained silent in deference to their privacy and doctor–patient confidentiality.

As a result, the Greens were winning in the court of public opinion. For the most part, the media accounts followed an underdog narrative stressing that the Greens were loving and thoughtful folks who wanted the best for their son while portraying Dr. Truman and MGH as officious and insensitive violators of their parental rights.

After calling the litigants and their lawyers to the bench, Judge Lawton whispered, so that the gallery couldn't hear what he was saying, that MGH should file a Care and Protection petition in the Hingham District Court, which he deemed a better place for the litigation, and he vacated the guardianship of Chad without hearing any evidence. Then out loud, he proclaimed that there was "no way" he could find Mr. and Mrs. Green to be unfit parents.

I was startled by Judge Lawton's refusal to let us present Dr. Truman's testimony. Given that a little boy's life hung in the balance, I did my best to change his mind, arguing that without the guardianship Chad would die for lack of proper medical care. I failed. Chad's mother, Diana, in her book about the case titled *Chad's Triumph: The Chad Green Story* (2015), says that I "didn't quit," "was in a frenzy to be heard," and that I had irritated the "nervous" Judge Lawton with my "repeated objections" to his refusal to hold an evidentiary hearing. Frenzy or no, I was able to persuade Judge Lawton to stay his ruling until we could litigate a Care and Protection petition in the Hingham District Court, which I filed on behalf of Dr. Truman and MGH the next day.

In response to our filing, District Court Judge Martha Ware appointed counsel for Chad as well as an investigator from the private nonprofit agency Children's Protective Services, who submitted a report within a few days recommending that the MGH petition be granted and that potentially lifesaving medical treatment should be continued. Chad's lawyer, John H. Wyman of Plymouth, supported the investigator's conclusion that Dr. Truman must be allowed to continue chemotherapy.

On March 29, 1978, Judge Ware, surely mindful of the unfavorable publicity that would be heaped on her if she found in the hospital's favor, returned full custody of Chad to his parents after an abbreviated hearing that was closed to the public and media. Dr. Truman had testified, telling the judge that his protocol of chemotherapy might well cure Chad of his leukemia and that the boy would die without it. His MGH nurse, Genevieve Foley, testified that she observed Chad carefully during and after his treatments and that—contrary to his parents' claims—the chemotherapy he received had not resulted in any substantial pain or other negative side effects. The Greens presented no medical evidence to the contrary. But we lost again.

Diana Green, in *Chad's Triumph* (published under her current name, Diana J. Meyer), accurately quotes Judge Ware explaining her decision to Dr. Truman at the conclusion of the hearing, telling him that while she held his medical opinions "in high regard, . . . these parents are intelligent and loving people, and I will not make them give this therapy to their son; although I might hope that they would choose to do so on their own."

Judge Ware's deference to parental authority has its origins in the seventeenth-century laws of the Massachusetts Bay Colony. Those laws placed on parents a legal responsibility to teach their children to read and write, give them religious instruction, and train them in "some honest, lawfull calling, labour or employment, either in husbandry or some other trade." Hence children were not exactly chattels.

However, the law was such that parents, subject to the above responsibilities, ruled their offspring with an iron fist. The *Charters and General Laws of the Colony and Province of Massachusetts Bay* provided that, if children "behave themselves disobediently and disorderly toward their parents," judges could order them to be whipped "not exceeding ten stripes for one offense." The law also mandated that if any child over age 16 "shall curse or smite their natural father or mother, he or they shall be put to death" except when "extreme and cruel correction" resulted in legitimate acts of self-defense.

The near-absolute rule over their children that Massachusetts Bay Colonist parents enjoyed is no longer the law. Now in appropriate cases, Massachusetts has the authority to step in and overrule parental dictates and wishes, even when they are based on sincere religious beliefs.

The United States Supreme Court began to recognize in the early part of the twentieth century that states, particularly in matters of public health, possess what is known as "police power" and may require compliance with enactments designed to protect the community. In the pioneering 1905 case *Jacobson v. Massachusetts*, the Supreme Court upheld a Massachusetts statute requiring that adults and children be vaccinated against smallpox. Given that precedent, those who complain today about loss of "freedom" due to state public health laws requiring masking against the coronavirus, or who rant about sinister underground government forces plotting to require vaccinations in order to change our DNA, have no legal leg on which to stand —that is, unless the Supreme Court decides to overrule more than a century of public health precedent.

Four decades after its decision on smallpox vaccination in *Jacobson*, the Supreme Court in *Prince v. Massachusetts* (1944) upheld a child labor law despite a parental objection based on religion. In that case, a Jehovah's Witness mother claimed that she had a "God-given right" to require her nine-year-old daughter to distribute religious tracts at all hours on the public streets of Brockton, Massachusetts—the same city where Judge Lawton had thrown us out of his probate court. The Supreme Court disagreed with the mother's claim of total power over her child, holding that "[a]cting to guard the general interest in youth's well being, the state may restrict . . . the parent's control" and parents may not "expose the community or the child to communicable disease or the latter to ill health or death."

The Supreme Court added, in memorable words directly applicable to the Chad Green case: "Parents may be free to become martyr themselves. But it does not follow that they are free, in identical circumstances, to make martyrs of their children."

It is more than a bit ironic that both *Jacobson* and *Prince* originated in Massachusetts, where two courts had thus far ignored their obvious applicability to the continued life of the critically ill child Chad Green. Neither Judge Lawton nor Judge Ware exhibited any fidelity to these Supreme Court cases, which properly limit the rights of individuals, including parents, in medical neglect cases where a child's life is at stake.

Judge Ware's decision received wide coverage in national publications, including in the *New York Times*, which quoted Jerry Green's presumptuous nonsense to the effect that "God prevailed" in the hearing. The *Times* reporter repeated the parents' contention that chemotherapy is harmful, both physically and emotionally, as well as their bizarre insistence that they "can better treat their son" with health foods. In a later interview with the *Sunday Times Magazine* reporter Marion Steinmann, Jerry said of his son: "We'd rather have had him go to God than to go through . . . chemotherapy."

That afternoon, I returned to a communal living situation on Garden Street in Cambridge and turned on *CBS Evening News*. To my dismay, the lead story featured a favorable video clip with the Greens, while hardly mentioning Dr. Truman's position and the urgent medical reasons for it. My roommates accused me of being a party to child abuse. The pressure I was under—doing my best to help save Chad's life under the surreal glare of national publicity, when I had been a lawyer for only a year and a half in a profession where experience matters and matters a lot—was such that I couldn't cope with hostility in what had been a place of refuge. I moved out of there.

Missing from the media coverage, including the *New York Times* piece, was the fact that the Greens had told their allies of their decision to substitute prayer sessions and the administration of the unapproved, illegal drug Laetrile in place of chemotherapy. Unbeknownst to us, the Greens had already started Chad on Laetrile. Mrs. Green had become a dedicated religious fundamentalist after being converted to Christianity and "saved" while watching the Reverend Billy Graham on his television program. This inspired her to adopt a belief in prayer as medical treatment.

A few words on the Greens' unwise decision to use Laetrile. This drug, also called Amygdalin, consisting of ground-up apricot pits and detritus from other fruits, was in 1978 fast becoming a trendy "natural" alternative treatment for cancer. Its use was backed by an oddball coalition of far-right conservative foundations and individuals and groups, including the John Birch Society, left-wing health-food proponents, and profiteer quack treatment providers who were based in Mexico to bypass FDA regulations banning the importation of Laetrile.

The best-known quack then touting the supposed curative powers of the drug, the late Ernesto Contreras, MD, ran a for-profit Laetrile clinic in Tijuana while simultaneously owning and operating a manufacturing facility there that produced the substance—a clear conflict of interest. Contreras was a pathologist whose training was in postmortem diagnoses, not on people still alive, a skill fit for a quack whose remedies for cancer meant certain death.

The National Cancer Institute had warned that Laetrile contains hydrogen cyanide, which is changed to cyanide when ingested into the body, a fact well known to the medical community and to Dr. Truman in 1978.

According to the NCI, potential side effects of Laetrile "treatment" include liver damage, trouble walking caused by damaged nerves, fever, confusion, coma, and death. In phase one and phase two clinical trials, performed after the Green case in response to intense pressure from Laetrile advocates, the drug was proven ineffective as a cancer cure.

Back to Chad Green's Care and Protection case. I challenged Judge Ware's decision of March 29 by scribbling on my legal pad and filing a notice of appeal with the district court. By statute, an appeal from the district court in Care and Protection cases meant that a completely new trial, also known as a trial de novo, would be held in the Superior Court. Given the emergency nature of Chad's case, all parties were ordered to appear the next day for a second trial, this time before Judge Guy Volterra in Plymouth.

I first met Judge Volterra as a student when he was a visiting teacher of a trial practice class at Northeastern University School of Law in Boston. (Direct as he always was, he told me that my advocacy skills were in dire need of improvement.) After I passed the bar exam, Judge Volterra generously invited me to do indigent criminal cases by appointment in the Taunton District Court, where he sat before being promoted to the Superior Court, so I was familiar with his judging style, which had taskmaster qualities. He was invariably polite and fair, but he did not suffer fools or unprepared lawyers.

With the help of staff lawyer Marv Guthrie, MGH had arranged for the presence of four excellent witnesses, whom we prepared for court beginning in the wee hours of the morning. These included three pediatric oncologists, including Dr. Truman, doctors from the Sidney Farber Institute and Boston Children's Hospital, and Chad's nurse Gen Foley. We also called the investigator from Children's Protective Services and the grateful mother of a child whose leukemia had been cured by Dr. Truman's chemotherapy protocol.

The Greens' only witness was Chad's mother, Diana, who testified that if the court were to allow her to control her son's medical care, she would stop chemotherapy and substitute an unspecified dietary program for her son in its place. On the advice of her lawyer (I later learned), her direct testimony deliberately omitted any reliance on the curative powers of prayer sessions. It took my cross-examination to bring out her belief in faith healing as a substitute for MGH leukemia protocols for Chad's cancer.

At bottom, the best case for upholding the parental "right" to dispense with a proven medical course was based on an understandable empathy for Chad's sincere and loving mom, Diana, and a reluctance to add to her emotional pain by removing her authority to make medical decisions for her little boy. Knowing Judge Volterra as I did, I was sure that he would have to decide the case on science rather than emotion or religion or run the risk of looking like an idiot to the medical establishment and his judicial peers.

The testimony went on until around 7:30 p.m. Judge Volterra retired into his chambers and returned a few minutes later, when he read aloud a brief interlocutory (temporary) order, which would be in force until the issuance of a detailed written decision. His order provided that the Greens must remain in Massachusetts and bring Chad to MGH for Dr. Truman's care. To enforce that, Judge Volterra placed Chad into the legal custody of the state Department of Public Welfare, while allowing the parents to retain physical custody so long as they obeyed the orders of the court.

On April 18, 1978, Judge Volterra issued his written decision. Volterra found as facts that "denial of the recommended medical treatment means certain death for the minor, whereas continuation of such treatment offers him a substantial hope for life." He added that the side effects of the chemotherapy were minimal, consisting of stomach cramps and constipation, which were treatable and transitory. The court held that "the minor's right to live" and "the state's duty to enforce that right" overcome the familial rights of the parents.

Judge Volterra brought further weight to his decision by ruling that we had proven our case "beyond a reasonable doubt," the law's highest standard of proof, usually reserved for application in criminal cases.

The parents appealed Judge Volterra's decision to the Massachusetts Supreme Judicial Court. Before the filing of briefs and scheduling of oral argument, the Greens attended a conference in Hartford, Connecticut, held by an organization called the National Health Federation (NHF).

The National Health Federation is a well-subsidized nonprofit lobbying group that promotes the freedom to use health foods, vitamins, supplements, and other "alternative" medical treatments without any government restriction whatsoever. The NHF opposes the fluoridation of public water supplies and compulsory childhood vaccinations, and it promoted Laetrile as a cancer cure. At this writing, the NHF website claimed falsely that the vaccines for the COVID-19 pandemic are only 1 percent effective, and it promoted "natural remedies" such as crushed garlic cloves, zinc, acidophilus, and vitamin D as more effective against COVID than vaccination. It warned darkly that the Moderna vaccine is designed to "alter your genetic makeup" as part of some sinister effort to make people "guinea pigs" in a "mass medical experiment."

The Greens made speeches at the NHF convention, which (according to Diana's book) triggered substantial donations for their living and legal expenses. There they met with the constitutional lawyer and professor John Remington Graham, who agreed to take over as their lead counsel. Graham, a Minnesotan and one of the founders of the Hamline University School of Law there, had made a national reputation for himself by doggedly pursuing litigation opposing the fluoridation of drinking water.

I found John to be a friendly but strange lawyer who took positions that were hobbled by adherence to his extreme political views, which sometimes caused him to overlook legal precedent and common sense.

To give you an idea of what I mean, the list of Mr. Graham's pseudo-scholarly legal writings includes the 800-page tome *Principles of Confederacy* (1990), which argues that the South had the constitutional right to secede from the union and also defends slavery as a benign institution. According to Graham, slavery "had been woven into a social fabric which had a gentle and quiet beauty, as well as a workable and pleasing balance. The personal relations between whites and blacks were actually in excellent order. And there was then an evolving civilization of very high and noble bearing in the South."

Graham's neo-Confederate view of the Old South is ahistorical bunk. His romantic view of slavery is central to trashy Hollywood films such as *Gone with the Wind* (1939), with its happy and caricatured "Mammy" played by Hattie McDaniel. It's only in this racist fantasy world that the relationship between slave and slaveholder is "excellent" and the South's culture of bondage, rape, whipping, legally required illiteracy, and separation and sale of family members is considered "very high" and "noble."

In retrospect, I believe that John Remington Graham's legal strategy, which was to continue an unwinnable legal fight to the end, was driven in part by political ideology and a desire to please the fringe element that was the source of much of his legal business. Graham's lawyering contributed to an atmosphere that made it impossible for the Greens and Dr. Truman to come to a reasonable accommodation on the issue of Chad's medical treatment.

Under attorney Graham's wing, the Greens embarked on a destructive quest for popular support and fame. They appeared three times on Phil Donahue's nationally broadcast daytime talk show, which also brought in substantial financial assistance from viewers. Diana and Jerry were television stars. Thousands of people viewed them as antiestablishment heroes. The adulation and cash with which they were showered clouded their judgment. An inner need to maintain fragile self-images as righteous rebels against an oppressive medical establishment was their Stockholm Syndrome; they became willing, easily manipulated captives of an "alternative" health care industry based on unscientific fantasies and lies.

The Greens' Massachusetts Supreme Judicial Court appeal could not possibly have prevailed. In order successfully to challenge on appeal factual findings made by a trial court, a litigant must prove that the judge's findings were "clearly erroneous" and without evidentiary support. The Greens hadn't presented any medical testimony to rebut our case, so they were stuck with Judge Volterra's findings: that Chad would die without chemotherapy, that the chemotherapy had produced no serious side effects, and that Dr. Truman's regimen gave Chad a better than 50 percent chance of cure.

At oral argument on the appeal before the SJC, attorney Graham told the Justices that, if given the opportunity, the Greens would "treat" Chad with Laetrile, which would cure his cancer. This became the front-page headline in the *Boston Globe* the following morning, but it was nothing the SJC could consider, because this contention had never been raised in the trial court.

Given the trial court record, Graham's legal position amounted to this: that the Greens have an absolute constitutional right to determine Chad's medical treatment, even though death is certain to result. Rejecting this absolutism, the SJC affirmed the binding nature of *Jacobson v. Massachusetts* and its progeny, which, as we have seen, establish the state's police power in matters involving the health or survival of children. The SJC held that the evidence in the record supported the trial judge's finding that "the parents' refusal to continue with chemotherapy amounted to an unwillingness to provide the type of medical care which was necessary and proper for their child's well-being. Where, as here, the child's very life was at stake, such a finding is sufficient to support an order removing legal custody from the parents, even though the parents are loving and devoted in all other respects."

Attorney Graham's next move on the Greens' behalf was to sue Dr. Truman and the Department of Public Welfare in federal court in Boston for violation of their civil rights under 42 United States Code § 1983.

Congress enacted this law soon after the Civil War under the authority of the Fourteenth Amendment. Originally it was designed to protect the newly freed slaves against the rampant trampling of their civil rights by racist white public officials and their many allies. The Supreme Court has limited the reach of section 1983 to matters where the alleged misconduct is committed "under color of state law." Complaints of police brutality are one obvious example of cases that are covered by the Civil Rights Act. Police actions are imbued with and made possible by the authority of the state, so they are deemed to be "under color of state law."

I filed a motion to dismiss the litigation for a judgment on the pleadings or failure to state a valid claim upon which relief could be granted. I pointed out that the complaint filed with the court by Graham failed even to allege, much less to outline, the existence of any "state action" or involvement with respect to Dr. Truman's treatment of Chad Green. Dr. Truman's role had always been as a private physician practicing in a private hospital.

I felt badly for Dr. Truman that the Greens were dragging him into federal court. I could tell that this was exacerbating his high stress level, which was already part and parcel of his responsibility to make decisions involving critically ill children, and this new litigation forced him unnecessarily to take time and energy away from his important job as a cancer doctor.

I was concerned by the rigidity of John Remington Graham, who held himself out as a constitutional law expert while filing a patently frivolous case that would accomplish nothing more than harassment of Dr. Truman. I tried to persuade him to drop the lawsuit voluntarily, but he had or pretended to have no awareness of the Civil Rights Act's "state action" requirement, and he told me that he was determined to press the case onward to a conclusion.

I appealed to the Greens' local counsel, George Donovan, a native of East Boston, who had been with the Green family nearly from the start, working pro bono (for free), now in the diminished role of local counsel under John Remington Graham, who had taken charge of the case.

George, who died in Ireland in 2011 at age 83, was a rare bird of the species known in Boston as a "Triple Eagle." This mascot-inspired title is bestowed on those who graduate from Boston College High School, Boston College, and Boston College Law School. George's father, Daniel J. Donovan, was first vice president of a rough-and-tumble union, the International Longshoremen's Association, led until 1977 by a former member of the Communist Party, Harry Bridges. Despite our different backgrounds, George and I liked and respected one another, and we had always been able to agree on procedural matters such as scheduling.

I told George that I believed their federal case was an off-the-wall loser and why. George responded with a sigh that he no longer had any influence on Jerry and Diana and that all case decisions were the sole prerogative of John Graham, who was taking his cues from unspecified sponsors of the Greens.

United States District Court Judge Andrew Caffrey, who presided over the case, dismissed the litigation in a decision dated October 27, 1978. As to Dr. Truman, the court stressed: "Plaintiffs do not assert the state involvement necessary to transform the private acts of Dr. Truman, the plaintiffs' child's privately retained pediatrician, into state action covered by § 1983. Dr. Truman's resort to the judicial process under state law does not, in the absence of a claim of conspiracy with state officials, transform him into a state agent."

Judge Caffrey also found the lack of a justiciable case against the Department of Public Welfare (represented by Assistant Attorney General Jonathan Brant), noting that the United States District Court isn't a "springboard for an unhappy state litigant" to retry adverse state court decisions, and he ruled that the Greens were legally bound by the existing findings of those courts.

Judge Caffrey pointed out in his opinion that the Massachusetts Care and Protection statute provides for the right to a judicial review of custodial orders every six months, allowing the Greens the option of going back to the Superior Court to present new evidence. According to Diana in *Chad's Triumph*, the Green litigation team then decided to come clean about their treatment of Chad, including the administration of Laetrile, and they held an impromptu press conference to let the public know about it.

The Greens also took Judge Caffrey's advice and returned to the Plymouth Superior Court, where they laid out their preferred "alternative" treatment, which they called "metabolic therapy." In addition to Laetrile, the Greens' treatment plan, which they were already following, included megadoses of vitamins A and C and folic acid, as well as daily enemas with protein-ingesting enzymes whose ingredients included a commercially available meat tenderizer.

The Greens' expert witnesses, including Laetrile "clinic" operator Dr. Ernesto Contreras, admitted that they had no expertise in treating blood diseases and that, from what little they did know, they believed that the proposed "metabolic" therapy likely would be ineffective as a treatment for acute lymphocytic leukemia.

MGH and the Department of Public Welfare brought forward the testimony of five physicians with extensive experience in pediatric hematology, including Dr. Truman, Dr. Emil Frei, who was the director of the Sidney Farber Cancer Institute in Boston and a cofounder of a collaborative research group on leukemia, and Dr. Robert Young, the chief medical officer for anticancer drugs at the Food and Drug Administration.

According to these medical experts, whose testimony Judge Volterra adopted as factual findings, Chad was suffering from a low-grade cyanide poisoning from Laetrile and hypervitaminosis A, which was damaging his liver. The meat tenderizer enemas carried a significant risk of digesting parts of Chad's colon, thereby eating holes in his intestinal walls and causing possibly fatal bacterial infections.

Judge Volterra refused to alter his earlier order, and on August 9, 1979, the Massachusetts Supreme Judicial Court affirmed his decision on appeal.

Bill Waldron made the decision that MGH lawyers need not participate in that appeal, reasoning that it would surely fail, that the hospital and Dr.

Truman had suffered enough stress and public criticism, and that Jonathan Brant, representing the Department of Public Welfare, would do an adequate job on Chad's behalf. As Bill predicted, the Massachusetts SJC made it abundantly clear that it had lost patience with Mr. and Mrs. Green and their legal antics and that it would hear no more of their unschooled adventures in "metabolic" cancer treatment:

> The judgment of the parents has been consistently poor, from the child's standpoint, and his well-being seriously threatened as a result. Their persistence in pursuing for their child a course against all credible medical advice cannot be explained in terms of despair of a cure, or by the suffering of serious side effects of chemotherapy. The chance for cure with chemotherapy is good; the side effects of chemotherapy in his case have been minor and readily controllable. The parents' actions must be viewed with compassion, but beyond doubt their poor judgment has added immeasurably and unnecessarily to their difficulties, and to those of the child.

Once again, John Remington Graham's legal strategy had failed Mr. and Mrs. Green, and this time it had subjected them to a judicial spanking that should have been a source of shame to the prominent law professor.

Diana and Jerry must have guessed in advance that they were going to lose the litigation. Before the Massachusetts SJC issued a denial of their second appeal, Mr. and Mrs. Green fled the state with Chad in violation of Judge Volterra's orders. After a cloak-and-dagger, shunpike drive on back-roads designed to evade law enforcement, they took Chad to the clinic operated in Tijuana by Dr. Ernesto Contreras.

There the Greens continued their public relations offensive. The February 12, 1979, issue of *Time* magazine featured them in an article titled "A Battle Over Cancer Care." It quoted Diana Green as stating that chemotherapy "doesn't cure" and that it had turned Chad "into a wild animal," both false claims that had been rejected by the courts. It added that the court proceedings are "not expected to have much impact on the Greens" because of financial support from the National Health Federation and private citizens. Jerry Green is quoted as touting the "loving atmosphere" at the Laetrile clinic, where its director, Dr. Contreras, "tells us, 'We'll be praying with you.' You just don't get that in the U.S."

Chad Green expired on October 12, 1979, in an apartment near the Laetrile clinic. Dr. Contreras did an autopsy on his dead body, the specialty in which he had been trained at Harvard Medical School, and he recorded Chad's cause of death as acute lymphocytic leukemia.

Diana Green eventually divorced Jerry after (she says in her book) she learned of his extramarital dalliance with a reporter covering Chad's case. She remarried, had three more children, and is known as Diana J. Meyer, published author.

Peter Chowka, who wrote the lead review on Amazon of Diana's memoir *Chad's Triumph: The Chad Green Story*, describes her work as "a loving mother's story for the ages" that "reveals how faith in God can help us find the courage to face life's most difficult challenges and how belief in our Creator goes hand in hand with man's deepest search for meaning and freedom."

But there is more to Diana's book than Mr. Chowka's religious interpretation. At the end of her sincere, well-meaning, and occasionally accurate account of the litigation, Diana Meyer admits that her son Chad's "survival would have been longer and more health sustaining if he had remained on chemotherapy."

Given that revelation, it is difficult for me to understand why Ms. Meyer titled her memoir *Chad's Triumph*. Diana and Jerry were vulnerable souls caught in a sinister web of free money and empty celebrity, a web cleverly spun by manipulative ideologues and profiteers. Under their influence, both parents rejected and disparaged the efforts of Dr. John Truman, whose medical skill and care had erased all traces of cancer from Chad's body. As a result, Chad died when he could have lived, as his mother now understands.

In a February 2022 telephone conversation, Dr. Truman told me that he is now in touch with Diana, who sent him her book, and that their relationship is much improved. But for me, at least, Chad Green's saga has never been a "triumph." Chad's death invariably brings tears to my eyes whenever someone asks me about his case. It's a source of pain that gnaws at the edges of my consciousness.

In the big picture, Chad Green was a pawn in an ongoing political fight, an unhinged battle against the "liberal" establishment and a chimeral "deep state," waged by fierce and sometimes overtly antisocial, authoritarian, violent adherents of "personal freedom." A relentlessly weird alliance of zealots and profiteers insists that the people have an absolute (though unwritten) "constitutional right" to reject safe and effective medical care in favor of either no treatment at all or the use of quack remedies that deal death on a massive scale.

These warriors against science and reason deprived Chad Green of personhood. Their pitiless campaign changed Chad from a sweet, helpless, lovable little boy into a pasteboard propaganda symbol. For this he paid the penalty of death.

CHAPTER 6

⚖

Fighting to End the Death Penalty in Massachusetts

In the spring of 1979, when my participation in the Chad Green litigation had ended, I learned of an opening for a lawyer at the Prisoners' Rights Project. The organization had just been renamed Massachusetts Correctional Legal Services, probably to make this state-funded agency seem less radical. Now it's known as Prisoners' Legal Services. At this organization, I was able to become involved in the fight to abolish the death penalty.

During my one year at Prisoners' Rights, I compulsively worked at least six days a week, without taking a single sick or vacation day. I didn't have a girlfriend or much of a social life. I had almost no contact with my family, due to my father's disapproval of my career path. "Jock" Saltonstall was a senior partner in the strait-laced law firm Hill & Barlow with a corner office in the high-rise State Street Bank Building looking out on the city. He viewed my public interest career path as an embarrassment that somehow sullied his own professional reputation among his peers in Boston's legal establishment.

To this day, I'm confused by my father's attitude. During the mid-1940s, he'd worked briefly for the national office of the American Civil Liberties Union under its cofounder, my mentor Roger Baldwin. In 1947, as a lawyer in private practice in Boston, he'd won a freedom of speech case in the Massachusetts Supreme Judicial Court that reversed the criminal convictions of two socialists—one for making a speech, the other for passing out political literature, on Boston Common. In 1956, he'd successfully represented the late communist Harvard professor Leon J. Kamin, who had been charged in federal court for the crime of contempt of Congress because he had refused to testify and "name names" before the so-called McCarthy Committee. He'd been an advocate for civil rights and personally given an award to Rev. Martin Luther King Jr. I was the only one of his three children who'd become a lawyer, and I thought he would be pleased that I'd followed in his footsteps. But instead of praising me, he was relentlessly critical of the fact that, in his view, I wasn't making enough money.

Added to the weight of paternal disapproval, my case of The Walpole Blues became more pronounced because I was spending so much time behind bars with incarcerated clients. Nevertheless, advocating for these despised people gave my life meaning. The work kept me going at full speed, and it enabled me to forgive myself for my personal unhappiness and put it aside. In a conscious effort to avoid drinking too much or succumbing to another bout with deep depression, I spent my evenings doing five-mile runs around Cambridge, wearing the same blue and yellow Onitsuka Tiger running shoes as the famed Boston Marathon champion Bill Rogers. You might say that I was running away from loneliness, but thankfully physical survival and a little bit of self-respect were waiting for me at the finish line.

Death penalty work was something I wanted to do because I'd been against capital punishment from when I was a kid in middle school, after reading books about the notorious case of the Italian-born anarchists Sacco and Vanzetti and their kangaroo court trial for murders committed during a 1920 shoe factory payroll robbery in Braintree, Massachusetts. The presiding judge, Webster Thayer, was a virulent anti-immigrant who privately referred to Sacco and Vanzetti as "wops" and "dagoes."

Nicola Sacco and Bartolomeo Vanzetti were electrocuted in August 1927 at the state prison in the Charlestown section of Boston. They protested their innocence to the end.

In his final statement to the court, Mr. Vanzetti bravely told Judge Thayer that:

> I would not wish to a dog or to a snake, to the most low and misfortunate creature of the earth, I would not wish to any of them what I have had to suffer for things that I am not guilty of. But my conviction is that I have suffered for things that I am guilty of. I am suffering because I am a radical and indeed I am a radical; I have suffered because I am an Italian and indeed I am an Italian . . . [so] if you could execute me two times, and if

I could be reborn two other times, I would live again to do what I have done already.

As a boy in middle school I'd met Aldino Felicani, a close friend of Sacco and Vanzetti, who chaired their legal defense fund. An anarchist himself, Mr. Felicani owned the Excelsior Press on Milk Street near my father's law office, into which I'd wandered one day. In his ill-lit shop, filled mostly with hand-operated presses, and whose walls were covered with political posters adorned with prominent printers' union "bugs," Mr. Felicani told me that he thought Sacco might have been guilty but that he was certain Vanzetti was innocent. His was the unenviable task of visiting with Sacco and Vanzetti in prison to let them know that all legal avenues had failed and they were going to be executed.

My involvement as a lawyer against the death penalty came about after the Massachusetts legislature in 1979 passed, and Governor Edward J. King signed into law, a new capital punishment statute, modeled on a Georgia law that the United States Supreme Court had deemed constitutional despite the heroic efforts of the abolitionist attorney Michael Meltsner and his colleagues at the NAACP Legal Defense Fund.

In January 1980, Suffolk County district attorney Newman Flanagan (the same guy who had prosecuted Terrell Walker) filed an original action in the Massachusetts Supreme Judicial Court seeking an advance advisory ruling on the constitutionality of the new law. The case was *District Attorney for the Suffolk District v. Watson.*

Under the Prisoners' Rights Project banner, I filed a written motion, granted by the SJC, to allow Prisoners' Rights to intervene in the litigation on behalf of our client, John Real. Mr. Real was an inmate in Walpole Prison, charged with murder while serving prison time, which made him subject to the new death penalty statute. Three other defendants with pending murder charges and the Attorney General's office also affirmatively sought and received party status. I was excited and daunted by the opportunity to work on this case.

I arranged for our office to draft a joint legal brief in *Watson* on behalf of all defendants and their counsel. Fellow staff lawyer Ann Lambert and I did that crucial, mind-bending work. I orally argued the case for our side before the SJC along with the veteran Boston criminal defense lawyer William P. Homans.

In the past, I'd visited Bill at his workplace to ask for advice on cases. His office floor was strewn with papers and books, and client files and correspondence were stacked high randomly on his desk. His office was so disorganized and unkempt that it resembled a room in the house of a hoarder. Bill was a chain-smoking, hard-drinking guy who years earlier had walked away from a serious one-car accident on Storrow Drive, a highway that skirts the Charles River between Cambridge and Boston. The *Boston Record American*, a tabloid newspaper in the Hearst chain, had featured on its front page a photo of Bill standing by his smashed vehicle, along with the banner headline "Attorney Cheats Death." Despite his foibles, Bill was a great lawyer—one of the very best in the state.

Bill had been chief counsel in two previous death penalty cases where the SJC had found in favor of the condemned and overturned statutes authorizing capital punishment. Naturally it devolved upon Bill to make those winning arguments again in *Watson*, which were succinctly and convincingly set forth in the portion of our brief written by my Prisoners' Rights officemate, and unsung legal genius, Ann Lambert. Our goal, and our solemn pact, was to end the death penalty in Massachusetts once and for all.

I'm simplifying the procedural history of the earlier Massachusetts death penalty cases here, but the essence of those decisions was that all people have a constitutional right to life. Before the state may legitimately deprive a person of that right, it must first demonstrate that extinguishing that life will serve a compelling purpose that cannot be achieved by some other means. As there is no proof that the death penalty deters people from committing murder or serves any state purpose greater than that already provided by the imposition of a life prison sentence, the death penalty violates the State Constitution's prohibition against "cruel or unusual" punishments. The doctrine of federalism enables state supreme courts to interpret their states' constitutions to provide more civil rights to their people than are contained in their federal cognate. Thus, even though the United States Supreme Court had deemed the death penalty lawful and constitutional, that ruling was no barrier to the SJC deciding otherwise under Massachusetts law and ordering its abolition.

I wrote three of the legal points in our *Watson* brief, and Ann, a Harvard Law School graduate who was more experienced and more effective than I, was responsible for putting the document together. She placed the arguments that I had written at the very end, almost as afterthoughts, an editorial decision that I must admit hurt my feelings a little, even though she was right to do that. Two of my arguments were inventions—or maybe divine interventions?—whose ghostly but vivid appearance out of the ozone shook me awake at night. To my knowledge, they had never been used previously in death penalty litigation.

My first argument was that the death penalty impermissibly discriminates against men in violation of the Equal Rights Amendment (ERA), which had been made a part of the State Constitution. The Massachusetts version of the ERA provides, in relevant part: "Equality under the law shall not be denied or abridged because of sex, race, color, creed or national origin." According to U.S. Justice Department records that I cited, women commit 15 percent of all homicides, but 99 percent of those executed in the United States between the years 1930–1978 were men, and no women had been executed since 1962. No woman had been executed in Massachusetts during the entire twentieth century.

Next, I argued that the death penalty is inherently unfair because, due to advances in the law over time, some of those who had been convicted and executed in the past would, under contemporary standards, have had their convictions reversed and granted new trials or released outright. After much reading and studying of old cases in the Massachusetts Reports, I was able to identify defendants who were put to death despite egregious legal errors that had passed muster with the SJC at the time but would never be countenanced today.

These cases included a defendant who was tried twice for the same offense in violation of the Double Jeopardy Clause, a constitutional provision that the United States Supreme Court hadn't yet made binding on the states; a trial where the judge refused to allow the defense to present evidence proving that the police had bribed witnesses to testify falsely against the accused; a capital case where the three mentally challenged defendants were shackled together in the courtroom in full view of the jury; and a death sentence that was imposed on a developmentally disabled man with an IQ of only 50.

I found that at least twelve Massachusetts citizens convicted of homicide during the twentieth century were electrocuted without benefit of an appeal of their convictions, a shocking denial of justice. Like the victims of police murders memorialized by the Black Lives Matter movement, these were real people.

Say their names:

John D. Cassels, age 35, executed May 6, 1902.
John Schidlofski, age 29, executed July 9, 1906.
Andrei Ipson, age 19, executed March 7, 1911.
Wassilii Ivanowski, age 22, executed March 7, 1911.
Biago Falzone, age 23, executed May 11, 1915.
Francis Ducharme, age 27, executed September 11, 1917.
Paul V. Hurley, age 20, executed September 15, 1931.
Sylvester N. Fernandes, age 24, executed August 12, 1932.

Henry Clay Bull, age 22, executed February 22, 1934.

Alexander Kaminski, age 25, executed February 19, 1935.

Joseph Rousseau, age 29, executed April 22, 1941.

Raphael Skopp, age 36, executed August 16, 1946.

Finally, I stressed a familiar argument in death penalty litigation: because of the rampant existence of racial prejudice, execution will invariably be imposed in a discriminatory fashion against people of color, a practice that mirrors the history of lynching.

I cited cases where Massachusetts courts had been forced to combat racial discrimination in schools, in housing pattens, in the building trades, and in the hiring of police, firefighters, and public transit workers.

Prior Massachusetts cases also told of Black citizens being subject to attacks by roaming bands of racists using rocks, bottles, and baseball bats; when police were called, the officers responded by clapping and chanting as the violence continued. Yes, this happened in Boston, the racist capital of the north, not in Alabama or Mississippi.

Black candidates for public office in Massachusetts had been the victims of threats and physical assaults, and their campaign workers had quit because it was too dangerous to support them.

White prosecutors had purposely challenged Black jurors to obtain all-white juries more likely to convict Black defendants. In some cases, prosecutors had also selectively prosecuted Blacks while allowing white criminals to go free.

I referred to national statistics showing that the death penalty is imposed primarily on those who kill white victims, while the killers of Black people get lesser sentences. Black defendants also suffer the death penalty in numbers grossly disproportionate to their percentage in the population.

On her own, without letting me know beforehand, Ann Lambert filed a brilliant friend-of-the-court brief on behalf of Henry Arsenault, who described his mental anguish as he waited in a prison hallway outside the death chamber while the guards prepared the electric chair, with fear so extreme that he peed in his pants. Fifteen minutes before his scheduled demise, the governor commuted his death sentence to life imprisonment.

BILL HOMANS WENT FIRST in our oral argument before the seven Justices of the SJC. Bill was great, and the court seemed extremely receptive and deferential to this lawyer with such a long and stellar track record, including in death penalty cases.

Because of a paucity of allotted time, I didn't argue orally the issue of unfairness resulting from changes in the law. The court appeared open to my argument on race discrimination, but not so much on gender. Justice Ruth Abrams, the first woman appointed to the SJC, jumped all over me when I raised the gender discrimination issue, and to my distress, the tone of her questions suggested that the argument might have offended her.

I had pointed out in our brief that the SJC, only a year earlier, had held that a statute that prohibited boys from joining a "girl officer regiment" at a public school violated the ERA. Also, in 1977, in *Attorney General v. Massachusetts Interscholastic Athletic Association*, the SJC had noted that "although women have been the usual victims of sex discrimination, there are significant exceptions to this generality, for example, legislation imposing harsher criminal penalties on men."

The SJC issued its decision in *Watson* on October 28, 1980. It struck down the death penalty on the basis that it constitutes "cruel or unusual" punishment under Article 26 of the Massachusetts Constitution. The court opinion in *Watson* is based only on Article 26; the decision makes no mention of the Equal Rights Amendment or any other constitutional provisions.

The court held that the death penalty is contrary to "the evolving standards of decency that mark the progress of a maturing society" in its "unique and inherent capacity to inflict [mental] pain"; that it will inevitably be applied arbitrarily; and that it discriminates against poor people, racial minorities, and members of unpopular groups.

On the issue of race, the court took what is called "judicial notice" of racial prejudice in Massachusetts, meaning that the existence of same is beyond any reasonable dispute. The court cited the statistics showing racial bias in the imposition of the death penalty. It expressed shock that in Texas, "of the 143 whites who killed blacks, *none* were sentenced to death."

The *Watson* decision made no mention of gender discrimination. But it adopted my argument that the death penalty is unfair because changes in the law inevitably will produce "anomalous results" in capital cases.

Chief Justice Edward F. Hennessey's opinion went so far as to plagiarize from what I had written on this issue, which I suppose is the highest compliment that an appellate lawyer can receive.

From my legal brief, at pages 72–73: "While this court has the power to correct constitutional errors retroactively by ordering new trials for capital defendants whose appeals are pending, or who have been fortunate enough to obtain stays of execution or commutations, it cannot, of course, raise the dead."

From *Watson,* in Volume 381 of the Massachusetts Reports at page 662: "While this court has the power to correct constitutional or other errors retroactively by ordering new trials for capital defendants whose appeals are pending or who have been fortunate enough to obtain stays of execution or commutations, it cannot, of course, raise the dead."

UNFORTUNATELY, *District Attorney for the Suffolk District v. Watson* was not the end of the death penalty fight.

The legislature reacted swiftly and specifically to the decision in *Watson* by passing an amendment to Article 26 of the State Constitution that the voters approved on November 2, 1982. That amendment provides as follows:

> No provision of the constitution, however, shall be construed as prohibiting the imposition of the punishment of death. The general court may, for the purpose of protecting the general welfare of its citizens, authorize the imposition of the punishment of death by the courts of law having jurisdiction of crimes subject to the punishment of death.

The legislature then passed another death penalty bill. The bill strangely reserved capital punishment for those murder cases in which the defendant had gone to trial and lost. Defendants who pled guilty and accepted a life without parole sentence could not be sentenced to death.

Once again Massachusetts prosecutors sought an advisory ruling on whether the new death penalty law was valid under the State Constitution. In *Commonwealth v. Colon-Cruz*, decided on October 18, 1984, the SJC ruled that it is not. By then I had moved to Vermont, and so I wasn't involved in this litigation. But here is what happened.

First, the SJC had to interpret the meaning and scope of the amendment to Article 26. It decided, in language that I find somewhat confusing, that the amendment does not prevent the court "from invalidating a particular death penalty statute under the Massachusetts Constitution on a ground other than the imposition of death is forbidden."

The court reasoned that the basis for its decision in *Watson* was limited; that case held that the death penalty may not be imposed because it is per se (as a matter of law) a "cruel or unusual" punishment under Article 26, without reliance on other clauses of that provision or the rest of the State Constitution. The legislature's purpose when it drafted the amendment to Article 26 was to overrule *Watson,* which was narrow in scope.

Given the legislature's limited intent, the court remains free to strike down other death penalty statutes if its reasons for doing so are based on different provisions of the State Constitution or on Article 26 grounds not relied upon in *Watson*. At least that is how I understand *Colon-Cruz*.

The court's assertion of its ability to invalidate death penalty statutes for reasons other than those covered in *Watson* makes much sense. Otherwise, the legislature would be free to enact, for example, an abhorrent statute that provides for the death penalty only for people of color and Jews, and there could be no judicial review of such a law. Similarly, as the SJC noted in *Colon-Cruz*, without the check of Supreme Judicial Court review, "a statute authorizing the imposition of the death penalty for shoplifting or prescribing the use of torture to carry out a death sentence would be valid under the Massachusetts Constitution."

The SJC in *Colon-Cruz* then examined the new death penalty law and found it to be invalid under Article 12, which guarantees the privilege against self-incrimination and the right to trial by jury. The court held that the new statute violated those principles because it imposed the death penalty only on those defendants who refuse to admit guilt (which they have a right to do under both the U.S. and State Constitutions) and who demand their right to a trial.

The court's decision in *Colon-Cruz* preserves the ability of the SJC to strike down death penalty statutes on a panoply of other grounds, and there is every reason to believe that it will do so if the legislature, in its less than infinite wisdom, were to try again.

The court could rely on the Equal Rights Amendment (the constitutional provision that was never mentioned in *Watson*) and hold that, based on statistical data, a death penalty statute violates its ban on race discrimination. It could reach the same result based on statistics demonstrating gender discrimination, as I argued in *Watson*, an issue that the SJC left undecided.

Hope in that regard is embodied in *Commonwealth v. Long*, decided on September 17, 2020, in which the SJC unanimously recognized and condemned the existence of systemic racism in police traffic stops and made it easier for defendants to show that such a stop was racially motivated. The court reached its decision under the ERA *and* under the Equal Protection Clause (Article 10) of the State Constitution. Such an analysis is directly applicable to systemic racism in the application of the death penalty.

Another potential attack on a capital punishment law is that it discriminates against the poor. The old saw to the effect that "only those without the Capital get the Punishment" is in fact the case, and such discrimination is mentioned in *Watson* (though only in passing) and in other case law. In a 2009 study of capital punishment in Harris County, Texas (which includes

Houston), for example, *no* defendants represented by privately hired counsel were sentenced to death. Capital defendants with private counsel were twenty times more likely to be acquitted than indigent defendants with appointed counsel. Based on their zip codes, an overwhelming majority of capital defendants lived in low-income neighborhoods.

The Common Benefits Clause of the Massachusetts Constitution, a provision that is also in the constitutions of other states, provides, in relevant par:

> Government is instituted for the common good; for the protection, safety, prosperity and happiness of the people; and not for the profit, honor, or private interest of any one man, family, or class of men.

The text of this article provides a good legal basis and foundation for an argument that the death penalty is in its application impermissibly class-based and that it unconstitutionally discriminates against the poor.

In the wake of *Watson* and *Colon-Cruz*, I'm reasonably confident that there will be no more executions in Massachusetts. Hopefully, other states and the federal government will follow this lead eventually.

CHAPTER 7

Vermont Law Practice

After my brief tenure at the Prisoners' Rights Project, I decided to move back to Vermont and practice law there. I missed rural life, especially landscapes dominated by mountains. I must admit that I also yearned to work in a place where my last name wasn't well known, where people would judge me on my own merits rather than on their opinions of family members like my cousin Leverett Saltonstall, a Republican of the old school who had served Massachusetts as governor and as a United States senator, retiring from the latter post in 1966. I was stripped of that hope when, at my swearing-in to the Vermont Bar, Chief Justice Albert Barney of the Vermont Supreme Court interrupted the ceremony to ask me from the bench, in front of everyone, whether I was one of "the" Saltonstalls from Massachusetts.

My main reason for leaving Boston, though, was a love of wild Nature and affection for a little-known place in Bennington County, the Town of Sandgate. Sandgate is a land that is surrounded by high, rugged mountains, and when I moved there the population was only 234. It's a place so cut off from the rest of Bennington County, and it's so remote, that it served as a refuge for Daniel Shays, who fled from western Massachusetts authorities after the failure of Shays' Rebellion.

Shays' Rebellion was a short-lived armed conflict, a kind of microscopic civil war, begun by Revolutionary War veterans in 1786 who returned home penniless after their military service on behalf of our country, only to find that their farms were being foreclosed upon. Shays and his followers responded by attacking courthouses and sacking and burning their records. When arrest warrants were issued and a large posse organized, Shays repaired with his followers to Sandgate. The remains of the foundations of houses where Shays and his allies lived are still visible there.

Shays's former hideout seemed to me to be the most agreeable sort of home for a lawyer whose practice is based primarily on opposing state power, and I had made friends in Sandgate during the time when I was living and working in Bennington as a night-shift gas station attendant.

I became part of a circle of artists, writers, and "back to the land" counterculturists led by Lothar and Bunny Wuerslin, who owned a large, rambling old farmhouse with a separate wood-fired sauna next to their pond. In the winter, in groups of ten to twenty people, all nude, we would get as hot as possible in the Wuerslins' sauna, then jump off their dock into the water through a hole they'd cut in the ice. After which we'd run barefoot in the snow back into the sauna for another round.

In the summer of 1980, along with three friends, using a "Sun-Loving Saltbox" plan ordered from the magazine *Country Journal*, I built a south-facing, twenty-by-twenty four-foot passive solar cabin on 54.32 acres of cheap mountain land (a bargain, I thought, at $475 per acre), nearly a mile from my nearest neighbor, with panoramic views, no artificial lights visible at night, and gravity-fed spring water that, in Buddy Guy's words, tasted sweet as cherry wine. When I found our spring, 550-feet up our mountain, there was a wooden pipe stuck in it, surely dating back to the mid-nineteenth century.

During construction, I fell in love with my bright and beautiful wife, Ellen Bosinoff, a middle school teacher and teachers' union activist, and at this writing we've been together for more than forty-two years, thirty-five of those in Sandgate. On a typical winter morning, looking south from our front deck, our mountain view was obscured by smoke from the wood stove that was our primary source of heat. In our early years, before my back went bad, I cut our firewood with a chainsaw and split it with an orange, triangular-headed maul.

Ellen's job as a middle school teacher, like my job, carried with it a very high level of stress, and getting away from civilization and living with the animals—from eastern coyotes (a species that is now part wolf) to bobcats, deer, flocks of wild turkeys, black bear, and seventy-five different species of birds—was an emotional boon.

After building my cabin, I worked for two years doing child abuse and neglect work for the Massachusetts Department of Social Services (DSS) as the agency's only lawyer for all of Berkshire County, Massachusetts. This required a three-hour daily commute in good weather. Given my Jimmy Carter–era mortgage with 12.5 percent interest, plus law school loans to pay, I had to rely on a tiny green Saab 96, with 46 horsepower and a bent frame, bought for peanuts from native Vermonter mechanic Laurie Reed of East Arlington; it would die periodically and strand me at inconvenient times on snowy roads.

The DSS job was emotionally challenging. The agency for the most part brought litigation under only the most serious circumstances, involving broken limbs or a failure to supervise resulting in terrible injuries. In one case, a young mother was using turpentine to remove tar from her two small children in a bathtub when the bathroom's gas hot water heater started up and flames incinerated the kids. They survived but were so severely burned that their overwhelmed single mom gave the state permanent custody without a fight.

I also learned at DSS how class-biased the foster care system could be. A rich and prominent businessman in Pittsfield had disciplined his high school–aged son so severely with a baseball bat that he had broken the boy's leg. The presiding judge, the late Clement Ferris, refused to remove the boy from the home or to allow social workers to visit him to make sure he wasn't abused further.

Another judge, known among local lawyers as "Mad Mike" Donahue, who sometimes presided in the Town of Lee, Massachusetts, would spend much court time loudly berating the DSS and its social workers for perceived failings, often singling me out for special criticism. On one occasion, he yelled at me for making a perfectly reasonable argument on the constitutional limitations placed on judicial power to give orders to the executive branch, which he said was akin to slapping him across the face with a wet fish. All that a lawyer can do in this situation is to apologize profusely to the judge for giving offense, which I did. I fared better with an older and wiser Berkshire County judge, the appropriately nicknamed "Gentle Ben" Apkin of North Adams, who was far more protective of abused kids than his brethren and addressed their problems with an even hand without regard to financial or family status.

In 1982, I managed to find work closer to home, at a Bennington law firm. The firm had two partners, Harvey Carter and Marshall Witten, both former Republican state legislators who had recently switched parties, though

Marshall retained his Republican voter registration. To get me going, and because they thought it was the right thing for the firm to do, they applied for a public defender contract. To obtain the contract, I had to drive to Montpelier to interview with Defender General Andrew Crane. This wasn't a problem; Andy and I were on the same wavelength on the duty and need to represent poor people with as much energy and thought and commitment as humanly possible. The public defense work kept me extremely busy, though its modest honorarium (a thousand bucks per month) didn't come close to covering our overhead, a tribute to Harvey's and Marshall's unselfish commitment to providing legal services to the indigent.

On my first day on the job, Harvey Carter escorted me to the Bennington County Superior Court to watch him cover a final, uncontested divorce case and to introduce me to the court staff and the presiding judge, John Morrissey. Judge Morrissey resigned his post a year later after a head-on collision while driving drunk on the wrong side of U.S. Route 89, a divided multilane highway, resulting in his third DUI conviction. But as far as I could tell, he was sober that day when I met him in chambers.

We waited for Harvey's divorce client, but he neither showed up nor responded to Harvey's telephone call. A half-hour after the scheduled hearing, Harvey got permission from the court clerk to leave the building to look for the client, and we drove to his house to try to find him.

The door was unlocked, so we went inside and wandered around, calling out for him, but to no avail. Tuned in to his sensitive side and his client's personality, Harvey went straight to the bedroom closet door, opened it, and there he was, standing behind his hanger-hung clothes. He hadn't wanted the divorce in the first place, and the thought of going to court was so depressing and emotionally overwhelming that he couldn't face it, even to the point of hiding from his own lawyer. Harvey put his arm around this man, and he was able to reassure and calm his troubled mind sufficiently that he came to court with us, and his divorce went through.

This incident typified for me the difference between cool, disembodied big city law practice and the relative patience and sensitivity that was engrained in the legal system in a rural town like Bennington, whose population has for the last forty years remained at a little over 15,000.

Harvey died in 2020 after a long bout with progressive dementia. He was a dear friend and mentor who taught me a lot about trial work. Harvey was always a gentleman with the juries and judges; even when he destroyed a witness on cross-examination, he was never unkind. During my second year with Witten & Carter, we had a jury trial together in Brattleboro, with Harvey as lead and yours truly drafting pretrial motions and physically carrying the files from Harvey's rusty but trusty Volvo station wagon into the court and back.

Our client, Joe Maillet, a forester, was charged with the crimes of leaving the scene of an accident (LSA) and negligent operation, death and serious bodily injury resulting. One evening in late November 1983, Joe had been in his pickup truck, driving under the speed limit on a dark, wooded, two-lane blacktop. The right-front bumper of his truck struck two boys, aged 14 and 11, dressed in dark clothing, who were walking on the right side of the road, in the same direction as the traffic, a violation of Vermont law, which requires pedestrians to walk on the left side of the highway, facing traffic. Joe never saw the young men before the collision. The older boy died, and the younger child was seriously injured.

Our defense on the LSA was that Joe had driven to his home, only eight houses away, to telephone for help, a necessity in this very rural place before cell phones, and that he and his wife both returned immediately to the accident site. On the more serious careless and negligent driving charge, a felony, our defense was that, given the prevailing conditions, it wasn't possible for Joe to see the boys, and so the accident wasn't Joe's fault.

I concluded, and Harvey agreed, that we needed to provide a scientific basis for our defense. I found and hired Paul L. Olson, PhD, an expert from the University of Michigan, who had written books in the field of human factors in traffic safety and driver vision and perception. Dr. Olson testified at Joe's trial that, given the lack of any light, the darkness of the teens' clothing, and the fact that they were walking in the same direction as Joe's truck, it would not have been humanly possible to see them until it was too late to react.

After a two-day trial, which closed with the testimony of our expert witness, Dr. Olson, the jury was out for five hours, deliberating after supper and into the night, and then came out of their room to report that they were deadlocked, 11–1 for acquittal.

Our Brattleboro District Court judge, Robert Grussing III, was a fair-minded guy and former secretary of the Vermont Senate with a good politician's human touch. He was the rare kind of jurist who wasn't afraid to rock the boat. In one of my cases, Judge Grussing issued a written decision finding that a Bennington police officer, Hank Haverkoch, had committed an illegal, warrantless search of a local head shop and that he had lied about what he had done while testifying at a hearing on my motion to suppress the marijuana he had seized. For this radical departure from the judicial norm, Bob Grussing became anathema to the entire Bennington police force and to the local State's Attorney Office for the rest of his career on the bench. Haverkoch, a genial and likeable liar and corner-cutter, was later disciplined for "cooping," police jargon for sleeping in one's patrol car while on duty. Hank had parked his car behind a local restaurant to avoid detection, but he was nabbed nonetheless.

Faced with a possible mistrial in the Maillet case, Judge Grussing instructed the jury to keep trying. After an hour or so of further deliberation, the jury found Joe not guilty.

The holdout had been a sour-looking woman on the far left of the front row of the jury box. We had been getting bad vibrations from her all along. Some jurors have such meanness in their hearts that they just want to hurt the person on trial. Eventually the other eleven jurors persuaded this holdout to change her vote. The fact that it was a snowy Friday night probably helped them do that. Harvey drove us back to Bennington over the spine of the Green Mountains in a blizzard, our forward progress slowed by a lot of scary sideways skidding. It was well after midnight when we made it back into town.

Harvey Carter was the lead lawyer, and I the second banana, motion writer, and briefcase carrier when we appeared in court together, but in our firm's public defender cases, I was always on my own.

That is, until Charles "Chopper" Lake Jr., age 18, was arrested on September 29, 1984, at his family home in Beech Court, a low-income housing project in Bennington, for the shotgun murder of his father. A few days later, Defender General Crane called from Montpelier and asked me to take the lead on Lake's defense team with help from one of his full-time staff lawyers, David Howard. Andy told me that the state would pay our firm $5,000 if I accepted the assignment, with the possibility of another $5,000 if the case were tried by jury to a conclusion.

Harvey and Marshall had made me a partner in the firm a few months before, but I asked their permission to represent Lake because I knew that the firm, even with a $10,000 fee, would lose a substantial amount of money, with or without an actual trial. A case like this, with the client facing the possibility of a life sentence, would from start to finish probably require the expenditure of close to an average year of attorney time. I told Harvey and Marshall that I would do my best to lessen the financial blow by working more hours, and they agreed.

If the fate of a defendant in a murder case depends in large part on who is killed—and I am convinced that it does—we had a built-in advantage. The elder Mr. Lake had a significant record of drug offenses and physical assaults, and the local cops despised him as a scofflaw and lowlife. After interviewing the potential witnesses, David Howard and I agreed that we had a potentially winning case based on self-defense and defense of others.

We were able to get Chopper's bail reduced from $50,000 to $20,000, and a relative came forward to post bail, so he was released pending trial.

We learned that the "victim" had been constantly beating and threatening with death his wife, Patty, and his children, including Chopper, the accused, and two younger kids, Henry and Stephanie. When the family gathered outdoors for occasions such as picnics, he would fire one of his guns over the heads of his children and laugh as they cried. He would tell his wife and kids that they had better not sleep deeply, because he was going to kill them. Late at night he enjoyed dressing in military camouflage clothing, and he would crawl through the yard, pretending to be a Special Forces commando, and wriggle into the house through a bedroom window to wake and intentionally terrify his kids. He had once riddled a girlfriend's car with bullets when she said something that offended him. In the last week of his life, he punched Chopper repeatedly, and for the first time Chopper defended himself by punching his father back. After this occurrence, Lake told his wife that he was for sure going to kill Chopper—and that he would do it soon.

The elder Lake's menacing behavior escalated to the point where, on the night of his demise, he repeatedly stabbed the kitchen walls with a hunting knife while yelling death threats at the family. When the family sat down at the kitchen table, he slammed the knife into the middle of it, telling them that this was the night he was going to do them in. In response, Chopper left the kitchen, picked up his father's shotgun from the living room, and returned and shot his father once in the chest, killing him.

As required by court rule, David Howard and I formally notified the prosecutor's office of our intent to rely at trial on the doctrines of self-defense and defense of others. Ray Bolton, the elected State's Attorney, who was helped in the case by Assistant Attorney General Robert Gagnon, opposed our ability to do that. Ray and Bob argued that, even assuming Mr. Lake was potentially dangerous, Chopper was not entitled to shoot his father because the threat he posed was not "imminent," as the law requires; when he died, the elder Lake was sitting at the kitchen table, rather than actively advancing toward his son with his knife raised in attack mode.

Ray Bolton took the pretrial depositions of the Lake family members other than Chopper, who recited litanies of terrifying incidents where Mr. Lake had assaulted and threatened them over the years. Their testimony didn't seem to affect Ray Bolton's legal position, and it appeared from Ray's demeanor, at least, that he was not a huge fan of this family of "woodchucks," a term that affluent Vermonters sometimes use to refer to people on the economic bottom like the Lakes, who survived on welfare and food stamps and lived in government-subsidized "section 8" public housing.

During one of these formal Q&A sessions, Chopper's younger brother, Henry, mentioned an afternoon when he'd gone on a successful squirrel hunt, brought home several of the critters that he'd shot, and used them to cook a stew for the family. Ray Bolton screwed up his face, looking as though he would vomit, and asked Henry, "You *eat* squirrel?" as if that were the equivalent of dumpster-diving and serving up fried garbage for dinner.

I had taken the compulsive step of reading and photocopying every reported Vermont Supreme Court case on homicide, and I made a thick notebook of the decisions, going back to the early nineteenth century. When the time came for motions, I used that law when I filed a memorandum describing every violent or threatening incident perpetrated by the deceased Mr. Lake that we intended to introduce at trial to establish Chopper's right to defend himself and his mother and siblings. I made clear in the paperwork and in oral argument that our theme would be to portray at trial the reign of terror that the elder Lake used to control his family, which justified the homicide. In essence, we would put the "victim" on trial.

Our assigned Judge, Theodore S. Mandeville, decided that we would be limited at trial to delving into violent incidents that Chopper knew about when he killed his father. I had argued, without success, but with a possible appeal in mind, that other such incidents were admissible because they were relevant to the objective reasonableness of Chopper's action in shooting his dad, even if he didn't specifically know about each one.

Andy Crane was kind enough to permit us to hire (from his limited budget) a professional consultant from the National Jury Project to advise us during jury selection. We were able to persuade Judge Mandeville to allow the questioning of prospective jurors privately, one at a time, in the judge's chambers. the Judge gave us the latitude to ask the jurors indirect questions bearing on their suitability to serve from the defense perspective, as recommended by our consultant. The question that I thought the most effective was "What are the most important values that you believe a parent should teach a child?" If a juror were to cite the "golden rule," or compassion for others, or the need to help people in trouble, or kindness to animals, that was a plus. But if they answered things like obedience to parental commands, or strict adherence to the law, or never driving over the speed limit, we would try to get them bounced from the panel, either "for cause" because they were obviously biased or by using one of our six "peremptory challenges," for which we didn't have to give a reason for removal.

We spent an entire week on jury selection, and when it was over, David Howard and I were optimistic and ready for trial. During the ten months between Chopper's arraignment and the trial date, Ray Bolton had never offered any deal or even mentioned the possibility of a negotiated plea.

It turned out that Ray was bluffing. I believe he thought that we would cave and beg him for leniency, but we did nothing of the sort. On August 5, 1985, just moments before the jury were to be called in to hear the opening statements of counsel, Ray called David and me over to the prosecutor's table and offered us a plea to manslaughter, a crime for which the penalty in Vermont is a minimum of one year and a maximum of fifteen years to serve. The state would recommend five to fifteen years, with at least three years in prison. We would be free to ask for any sentence we wished. There would be a month's delay to allow the probation department to conduct a presentence investigation and make its own sentencing recommendation for the court's consideration.

Although our case was strong, it's impossible to forecast what a jury will do. Chopper wisely accepted this offer, and instead of going to trial that morning, he entered a plea of no-contest to manslaughter.

The probation folks prepared and issued a detailed report on Chopper, with the recommendation that his entire sentence be suspended with *zero* jail time. I had never heard of a presentence report recommendation as lenient as this in a homicide case.

The sentencing hearing began on September 17, 1985, and lasted for two days. We brought to the fore much evidence about the brutality of the deceased, Mr. Lake. One witness, a former lover named Geraldine Ross of Sunderland, testified that the elder Lake had once loaded a .357 magnum pistol with a single bullet, spun the gun's chamber, pointed the gun at her, and pulled the trigger, Russian roulette–style. The gun did not fire. She said that Lake "didn't have any feelings for anybody." Bolton's witnesses stressed that our client had smoked marijuana and drank alcohol on the night of the shooting. We presented testimony from Chopper's employer and two former teachers, who told the court that our client was hardworking and respectful.

In the end, Judge Mandeville imposed a sentence of two to eight years, with two years to serve and the remainder of the sentence suspended on probation. I was disappointed that the judge gave Chopper any jail time, but a totally suspended sentence would have been unprecedented for a Vermont judge to issue in a homicide case.

David Howard and I were pleased with the result. After his release from jail, the Town of Bennington hired Chopper as a member of its road crew, a job at which he excelled. As a hobby, Chopper took up competitive weight-lifting, and one year he won the title of "Vermont's Strongest Man."

But murder cases and serious felonies did not occupy all of my time at Witten & Carter. I signed up to be a cooperating attorney with the Vermont chapter of the American Civil Liberties Union. Heavily influenced by my elderly mentor and father figure Roger Baldwin, a founder of the national ACLU, I found that I liked doing freedom of speech cases, and I tried always to carry at least one of these on my case list.

CHAPTER 8

⚖

The Cowboy Snodgrass Case

I filed my first ACLU-sponsored lawsuit in November 1985 for Cowboy Snodgrass—his real name—a carpenter who worked just down the road from the Killington ski resort. That huge facility had unveiled a plan to use treated sewage (including feces from toilets) to make snow with the "spray irrigation" method of disposal. At the bottom of Killington Mountain is the Ottauquechee River, a beautiful, 41-mile tributary of the Connecticut River, which eventually flows into Long Island Sound. The treated sewage would make its way downhill into the Ottauquechee when the snow melted. Two Vermont state legislators, Donald Chioffi and William Mares, distributed a humorous pro-environment bumper sticker opposing the sewage disposal plan; Cowboy Snodgrass bought one from a carpenter friend of his and stuck it on the back window of his truck. It read: "Killington, Where the Affluent Meet the Effluent."

In April 1985, Cowboy was working for $9 an hour on a crew constructing the Glazebrook Townhouses, a development located in a cul-de-sac off the Killington ski area's access road. Cowboy's boss, developer Horace "Red" Glaze, was infuriated by the bumper sticker's environmentalist political message. Glaze believed he had the right to censor the political views of his employees. He ordered Cowboy to remove the sticker from his truck and fired him when he refused.

Glaze was a former selectman for the Town of Sherburne, where the Killington ski area is located, and he had served on the committee responsible for regulating the town's water and waste disposal. Glaze was lauded at a meeting of the Rotary Club for firing Cowboy. Other Vermont developers and a pro-development lobbying group sent Glaze letters of commendation for his action. Preston Smith, the president of Ski, Ltd., the company that owned Killington, personally visited Glaze and offered to support him in the anticipated litigation, which the ACLU-Vermont had indicated it would file unless Glaze were to reinstate Cowboy, bumper sticker and all.

That's when I heard from Scott Skinner, the executive director of the Vermont chapter. Vermont. Scott, one of the youngest Eagle Scouts on record at age 13, had dedicated his life to public interest work. He'd been a Peace Corps volunteer in Nepal, and he'd served as the first director of the Vermont Public Interest Research Group (VPIRG), when he was responsible for persuading the legislature to pass the "Tooth Fairy" program, which provides funding for low-income children to go to the dentist. Scott called and asked me to take on Cowboy Snodgrass as a client, and of course I said I would.

I filed suit on Cowboy's behalf against "Red" Glaze in the Rutland Superior Court, the only place with appropriate jurisdiction.

There is an old saying that the best way to see Rutland is in the rearview mirror. It's Vermont's ugliest burg, scarred with commercial strip development along the main drag, U.S. Route 7, and politically it's solidly conservative. In Vermont the trial Judges rotate, riding circuit from place to place, so that James Morse, a liberal from Montpelier who would be appointed to the Vermont Supreme Court several years later by Governor Madeleine Kunin, was the presiding judge in Rutland. I felt we'd get a fair shake from him.

The First Amendment protects freedom of speech only when government is involved, which wasn't true in Cowboy's case; "Red" Glaze was a private employer. Hence the only available legal basis for bringing our case was the doctrine of wrongful termination.

Vermont, like many states, follows something called "Wood's Rule," first articulated in 1877 by Horace G. Wood in his legal treatise, *Master and Servant*. Under this doctrine (also called "termination at will"), in the absence of a written contract an employer may fire an employee for any reason or no reason at all without incurring liability. There are instances where Wood's Rule doesn't apply, and one of them is when the termination of the employee violates "a clear and compelling public policy."

The issue of whether the public policy exception protects employees from being fired for expressing their political views was one of first impression in

Vermont. There was no Vermont case law directly on point, although the Vermont Supreme Court issued a decision six weeks before trial holding that firing someone because of old age violates public policy.

As with the issue of the prisoner's dock in the Terrell Walker appeal, my challenge was to research Vermont law for an analogous line of cases that I could use to persuade Judge Morse to make new law by applying the public policy exception to political speech. The only case law that I was able to find dealt with *contracts* involving political speech and activity that the Vermont Supreme Court had deemed void as against public policy. That wasn't the same as Cowboy's employment situation, where there was no contract, but it was the best I could do.

In the 1902 case *Livingston v. Page*, the Vermont Supreme Court refused to enforce a contract between a political candidate and a newspaper, where the candidate had agreed to pay the editor for his support. The court reasoned that the contract was void because "as long as the editorial column is relied upon as a public teacher and adviser, there can be no more dangerous deception than that resulting from the secret purchase of its favor."

The 1860 Vermont Supreme Court case *Nichols v. Mudgett* involved a contract providing that a political candidate would pay for the vote and the active political support of a constituent. Though the candidate won as a result, the court refused to enforce the deal, holding that it would violate public policy to do so. The Court stated: "Every voter is bound to use his influence to promote the public good according to his own honest opinions and convictions of duty. If for money or other personal profit, he agrees to exert his influence against what he believes to be for the public good, he is corrupt, and the agreement void."

I argued in my trial brief that these decisions stand for the proposition that public policy is implicated whenever freedom of political speech is banned or hindered by private action. With respect to the public policy exception to the termination at will doctrine, I emphasized that it should be construed to protect the exercise of the political speech of employees because "any other rule would mean that Vermont workers would be little more than robotlike serfs, condemned to parrot the employer's 'party line' or join the unemployment line. Such a result . . . has no place in a society which favors free and open political debate."

This might have been a bit of an overstatement, but it was mildly so compared to the written submission by Paul Kulig, the lawyer for Red Glaze, a partner at a Rutland firm that represents many developers.

In his trial memorandum, Kulig cited as authority a case from another jurisdiction that held it lawful for a boss to fire an employee who was a member of the Ku Klux Klan—as if expressing environmentalist political views were somehow equivalent to participation in an organization known to engage in lynching and beating Black people and burning their homes and churches and denying them the right to vote. Kulig also wrote that Cowboy's pro-environment bumper sticker "is comparable to an employee building a hotel on the road to Disneyworld displaying a bumper sticker that says, 'Disneyworld, where the children meet the molesters.'"

The trial took only a few hours. Glaze admitted that he'd fired Cowboy because of the bumper sticker. He testified that it was embarrassing for him as a developer, and against his business interests, to have employees who publicly oppose the spray irrigation sewage disposal system needed for the ski area's expansion, which would boost the number of skiers and thereby enhance the market for his townhomes. He admitted that Cowboy was an excellent carpenter but complained that he didn't like his "attitude."

Cowboy told Judge Morse that he put the bumper sticker on his truck because he is in favor of clean water and that the effluent flowing into the Ottauquechee River would degrade its quality to the point where it would harm the trout population and make the river a place where people would no longer want to use it for recreation. After all, who wants to swim in shit, even if it's "treated" shit?

Judge Morse found for us, agreeing that Cowboy's termination for expressing his political views via the bumper sticker violated public policy. He awarded Cowboy damages in the amount of $2,720 for his lost wages, but no punitive damages, which I'd asked for.

Cowboy was pleased. The January 9, 1987, edition of the *Rutland Herald*, Vermont's newspaper of record, quoted Cowboy as follows: "It made me feel really good inside that the court system upheld the law like it should have. It kinda hurt my career really bad, what he [Red Glaze] done to me. We were doing it for the principle of the thing, for the effluent, to let people know what was going on at ski resorts. Basically, we got our message across. It was like a political view thing."

Glaze chose to refrain from appealing Judge Morse's decision to the Vermont Supreme Court. I was disappointed, because I thought that we would win there as well and make some good law that could be cited as a binding precedent in the Vermont Reports, unlike trial court decisions. It's likely that Paul Kulig didn't appeal the case for the same reason—he'd lose, and he knew it.

The case was over. Scott Skinner was happy about our win, but he discovered, after the appeal period had lapsed and Judge Morse's decision had become final, that he had forgotten to send me the usual ACLU retainer agreement, binding the client to pay a legal fee of one-third of any recovery, split evenly between the organization and the lawyer.

I didn't know about this policy; I'd assumed that all ACLU cases were pro bono and that any recovery went to the client alone. But I told Scott that I would ask Cowboy if he would please make a donation to the ACLU, even a small one. I was unsuccessful.

One of the things that I experienced when representing clients for free is that sometimes they will tell you that they wish that they had a "real lawyer," as if doing a case out of a commitment to social justice, or a desire to help out a fellow human being in distress, means that you are a lesser species of professional. Sometimes such clients feel that their case was so strong anyone could have won it; they could have done it themselves, without a lawyer. So, "Thanks for nothing."

I don't know what Cowboy thought. The case was done. I simply wished him luck, and I never heard from him again.

CHAPTER 9

⚖

My Most Troubling Walk-In Cases

The Cleaning Lady and the Doctor and
the Gun on My Desk

One of my duties as the most junior lawyer at Witten & Carter was to speak with "walk-ins," prospective clients with no appointment, but with a legal problem they viewed as pressing or of an emergency nature. Most of the time these weren't real cases worth pursuing beyond the initial consult, but often I was able to calm people down and give them some constructive free advice; they often left in a better emotional state. Sometimes, however, the walk-in cases were serious, requiring my attention after the first meeting.

During the year 1985, a woman in her twenties from Bennington whom I'll call Nancy (not her real name) worked cleaning the houses of the affluent. She and her husband had a special-needs toddler who was afflicted with serious neurological problems. This low-income family was on food stamps and Medicaid.

Nancy found work cleaning the home of Dr. Z (not his real name, either), a successful physician who lived on a dirt road in North Bennington, in that village's most desirable and expensive neighborhood. The physician's home stood across from the Park–McCullough House, a 35-room mansion built during the Civil War on the grounds of a 700-acre farm owned by Vermont Governor Hiland Hall, of which Dr. Z's land was once a part.

The job paid reasonably well because the house was large, and Nancy was grateful that Dr. Z had taken an interest in her son's medical condition.

Although Z wasn't a neurologist, he had been kind enough to arrange for her boy to be seen by a specialist in Boston who had agreed to accept Medicaid payments. Dr. Z even befriended Nancy and her spouse, and he would have the family over for dinner and as overnight guests.

On December 14, 1985, a Saturday night, Nancy's family went to Dr. Z's house for dinner. While her husband was out of the room, Dr. Z allegedly fondled and propositioned Nancy, telling her that she would look beautiful without clothes.

Dr. Z cooked sloppy Joe sandwiches, and the group sat down to eat. Nancy's husband noticed that his sandwich tasted bitter, and he opened it up; he and Nancy saw that it was laced with numerous broken-up capsules of a drug later identified as a prescription tranquilizer.

They spat out their food, told Dr. Z that they were going home, and headed for the door. Dr. Z stood in front of the door to block them, and when they tried to get around him, he hit Nancy's husband with his fists and the butt of a pellet gun, breaking his jaw in two places and causing dental damage.

After a trip to the hospital emergency room, the couple went to the Bennington police headquarters and reported what had happened. Nancy turned over to the police two pills that Dr. Z had given her that night and she had refused to ingest, found by authorities to be a Valium derivative. The following Monday morning, Nancy and her spouse appeared in our office and asked for the help of a lawyer.

The first thing I did was to call State's Attorney Raymond Bolton, and I demanded that he do something about Dr. Z. Two days later, On December 19, Sergeant Tom Otero of the Bennington Police Department sought and obtained a warrant to search Dr. Z's home. He found and seized a Valium container, seventeen yellow pills, and a pellet gun. Prosecutor Bolton then convened an inquest, which is a closed court proceeding where he could call witnesses to determine whether a criminal charge was warranted.

Bolton had full authority to prosecute on his own without an inquest, simply by drafting a States Attorney's "information," a formal charging document, attaching to it a sworn police report, and filing it with the district court. I am not sure why Ray resorted to the secret inquest procedure. Maybe he wanted to have the opportunity to assess the credibility of my clients in live courtroom testimony prior to charging a local physician with the felony of aggravated assault, which carries a prison sentence of up to fifteen years. Maybe he wanted to give Dr. Z every procedural break by holding a hearing at which Z would have the opportunity to have his say. I've telephoned Ray Bolton several times recently to ask him about this, but he never returned my calls.

When the inquest ended, Bolton decided to charge Dr. Z with two counts of felony aggravated assault: one count for intentionally causing serious bodily injury to Nancy's husband, and one count for using a deadly weapon to inflict that injury.

After my initial contact with Ray Bolton, I reported the matter to the Vermont Board of Medical Practice, which held an emergency meeting in Montpelier in January 1986. I was not present, but the board held a hearing at which testimony was taken, and Dr. Z agreed to a temporary suspension of his license pending a full investigation and the outcome of his criminal charges.

That month I filed a civil complaint against Dr. Z in the Bennington Superior Court, seeking money damages for his assault. I added a count for medical malpractice, based on what I had learned about their young son. A couple of weeks before the assault, the baby was having a seizure, and Nancy called Dr. Z for advice. Rather than sending him to the hospital, Dr. Z suggested that she bring the boy to his home, where he would minister to him. The youngster fell on the floor of Z's house, sustaining a closed-head injury that was upsetting but deemed not serious.

The malpractice count was viable but not very strong. The baby wasn't Dr. Z's patient of record, the injury wasn't permanent, and Dr. Z was probably entitled to raise the defense of the Good Samaritan, which by Vermont statute might have immunized him from any liability.

The main reason I added the malpractice claim was to involve Dr. Z's professional liability insurance company. Intentional wrongs such as Z's assault are not insurable, and Z's homeowner's carrier would have denied coverage and refused to defend him in court. With no insurance available, prevailing in such a case likely would have meant a paper victory only. Sophisticated defendants hire lawyers who are schooled in the art of sheltering assets in such a way that it might have taken years to recover any money, and perhaps my clients would never see a dime. One way to do that is for a malefactor like Dr. Z to mortgage his house and land and automobiles to the hilt, so that there is little or no equity available to satisfy a judgment. But the medical malpractice insurer would have to defend Dr. Z, and I thought that I might be able to persuade the carrier to come up with some money to settle the case, even though the claim, while colorable, was relatively thin.

In May 1986, Dr. Z was found guilty of two counts of simple assault on Nancy's husband. Pursuant to a plea agreement, the charges were reduced from felonies to misdemeanors despite the serious injuries he had inflicted. Dr. Z received suspended sentences of one year, and he was ordered to pay my clients' uninsured medical bills, which amounted to $1,800. After that I was able to resolve the civil case with the malpractice carrier; to the best of my memory, the amount of the settlement was small, but the modest sum was of some help to a family living at or below the poverty line.

Had Dr. Z cooperated with the Board of Medical Practice, admitted wrongdoing, and agreed to get therapy and alcohol treatment, he would have been able to resume his medical practice in short order. In December 1986, the board found him guilty of misconduct and entered an order to that effect, allowing him to practice while receiving appropriate professional help and monitoring.

Instead of grabbing this arguably undeserved lifeline, Dr. Z called the allegations against him "trash," even though he had already been convicted of them by plea agreement in criminal court. He refused to admit any professional wrongdoing and instead unwisely chose to litigate the licensing matter. Represented by a sincere but mindlessly aggressive lawyer who was later disbarred for misappropriating client funds, Dr. Z appealed the board's decision and sued the board and the state for $750,000 in damages for wrongfully suspending his license. Predictably, that litigation went nowhere, and Dr. Z's licensure status was further complicated by his 1988 arrest for driving under the influence, where his blood alcohol level was alleged to be 0.30 percent, three and a half times the current legal limit and not far from causing unconsciousness.

According to the website of the Board of Medical Practice, the license of Dr. Z is still under suspension.

From a 2016 Vermont Supreme Court bail appeal decision, it appears that Nancy's special-needs son has not fared well as an adult and that his acting-out has been a big problem for her. In 2014, the state of Vermont charged Nancy's son with various serious offenses involving her. The Vermont Supreme Court opinion states: "Defendant's mother was the representative payee for defendant's social security disability benefits. Defendant, who suffers from severe cognitive disabilities, went to his mother's residence in a motel called the Iron Kettle to pick up money from his social security disability check. When she refused to give him money, he threatened to harm and kill her."

The court's decision contains no information on how Nancy's son's cases were ultimately resolved. I do not know whether Nancy was able to remain as her son's financial caretaker given his abusive treatment of her or whether Nancy has ever experienced anything other than poverty and pain in her life after she refused to let Dr. Z have his way with her.

I do know that, during the legal fiasco with Dr. Z, false rumors spread around town that Nancy was a gold digger and that she had probably set the whole thing up for money. I learned this from our office receptionist.

In truth, Nancy was the victim of a prominent local physician who assumed that he could do whatever he wanted with a cleaning lady. He was unable to succeed in his mischief, which is a tribute to Nancy's courage and moral values. But the criminal justice system treated Dr. Z with great lenience, even after breaking a man's jaw in furtherance of a selfish seduction scheme. As usual, money and power prevailed, and the offender was able to skate with no felony conviction or jail time, leaving Nancy to deal with an ugly whisper campaign and her son's neurological disability.

STRANGE THINGS WILL HAPPEN to criminal defense lawyers. Shocking and unpredictable things. A particularly egregious example involved another of my walk-in clients, around the same time as Nancy's case. One afternoon, a man from nearby Williamstown, Massachusetts, appeared at our office without notice and hired me to represent his son, who had committed an armed robbery the night before. The Williamstown cops had no suspects. After retaining me on his son's behalf, and without warning, dad dropped on my desk the handgun used in the robbery and hurriedly left the building.

What to do with it? The gun was evidence in a serious crime, and I couldn't keep it; that would be obstruction of justice, which is a felony. Under the law as I understood it, I had to turn over the gun to law enforcement. But if I did that, I might be viewed unjustly as an accessory after the fact, and cops might arrange to charge me to learn more about the significance of the gun and my client's connection to it, something I could never ethically reveal. Moreover, possession of a handgun without a license is illegal in Massachusetts, and conviction carries a mandatory minimum sentence of one year, so I couldn't take the gun across the state line and surrender it to the Williamstown authorities without the risk of being charged with that offense.

The "gun on the lawyer's desk" is a legal ethics problem so classic that versions of it have appeared on bar exams, and there is an ongoing debate in legal circles and law reviews on how to handle it without violating the criminal law or the Rules of Professional Responsibility. I chose an option that worked on a practical level, though I'll never be entirely sure whether I did the right thing.

I hired my own lawyer to represent me, a former Assistant DA from Pittsfield, Massachusetts, a city in the same county as Williamstown, though it's a half-hour drive away, over the Berkshire Mountains. My lawyer had a license that allowed him to carry a handgun. At my request, he took the gun to the office of the criminal division of the Massachusetts Attorney General's office in downtown Boston. He turned over the gun to an Assistant AG, telling him only that it was evidence in a crime. Then he returned to Pittsfield.

I had done what I had to do—surrender to police a gun used in an armed robbery—but in a way that would make it difficult for law enforcement to tie the gun to my client or to me. My lawyer was barred by law from disclosing the identity of his client, yours truly. The robbery witnesses never identified my client as the perpetrator, so he was never charged. Walk-in case closed, though it has remained open in my own mind because my effort to deal with competing and contradictory ethical and legal requirements included an element of deception that I regret.

CHAPTER 10

⚖

Continuing with Public Defense

After the Chopper Lake murder case was over, I was able to focus with re-newed zeal on the other, less serious charges on my public defense caseload.

Unfortunately, Theresa St. Helaire, the prosecutor with whom I often dealt at the office of the Bennington State's Attorney, didn't always exhibit the collegiality and restraint that characterized the Bennington County court system generally. Theresa was an unhappy zealot in our cases, particularly in those involving small amounts of marijuana, citing the "War on Drugs" as her main agenda and the reason that she'd decided to become a prosecutor.

In one case I defended, Terry charged a local married couple with felony cultivation for possessing three spindly little marijuana plants growing in a flowerpot in their home. (At the time, cultivation of marijuana in small amounts was a felony.) Deputy St. Helaire subpoenaed the couple's teenage son as a witness against his parents to a pretrial deposition, in an effort to use him to establish their guilt.

On the advice of a pro bono lawyer I found, David J. Williams of Mont-pelier, the son took the Fifth Amendment, and he refused to testify against his parents. Terry retaliated by charging the boy with the same felony culti-vation offense, a move that, to me, at least, smacked of prosecutorial over-reach; it was a morally questionable way of dividing the family.

Terry's plea offers were off the mark in terms of their proportion to the seriousness of the offense in many a case in which I opposed her. As I remember, she posted a homemade sign in her office that read "No deal!" I felt sorry for her, angry with her, and at the same time upset with myself for my inability to connect with her better on a human level. She didn't like me, and after a while I gave up trying to persuade her that her philosophy was too punitive and her plea offers too draconian.

In frustration, I sometimes adopted a strategy of trying cases for sentencing purposes, knowing that I would almost certainly lose them before a jury, thereby following the trial lawyer's old saw "settle your winners and try your losers." I made it clear to our usual judge, Theodore S. Mandeville, who presided in the Chopper Lake murder case, that Terry's harsh plea offers were the reason I was trying those cases. As a result, Judge Mandeville sometimes gave lenient sentences to my clients after trials where all the facts came out, not just the skewed version of events set forth in prosecution paperwork, even though the jury had returned the expected guilty verdict. So at least in that respect my strategy worked.

One of my public defense cases involved a bar fight at the local Ramada Inn. My client was charged with breaking a beer bottle over the head of another patron during a drunken melee that involved ten or twelve others. The only independent eyewitness who appeared for the state, the hotel's bouncer, Robert "Bubba" Davis, now dead, testified on direct examination by Terry St. Helaire that while standing by the "ladies' room door" he had seen my client commit the assault.

I brought out on cross-examination of Bubba, using an architectural drawing of the Ramada, that the ladies' room was located far from the open, doorless entrance to the bar, on the other side of a wide hallway. I suggested that it would have been impossible for him to have seen the fight well enough to identify my client while stationed in front of the door to the ladies' room.

Bubba agreed in principle but claimed that "ladies' room door" was the term that he and the rest of the staff used for the barroom entrance doorway, because it was the barroom entrance *nearest to the actual* ladies' room door. I asked Bubba, with stagey faux astonishment that elicited giggles from the jury: "OK, so let me get this straight. You all call the open barroom entrance, which has no door, 'the ladies' room door,' even though it *isn't* the ladies' room door, and the *real* ladies' room door is across a hallway?" Bubba had to answer "yes."

I thought I had made a telling point that went straight to reasonable doubt and an acquittal, but I was wrong. John Shanahan, the manager of the Ramada Inn, the prosecution's next witness, came off as a sweetheart of a guy, so genuinely sincere in all his dealings that no one could possibly doubt his word, and he backed up Bubba: the staff called the doorless, wide-open barroom entrance the "ladies' room door." The jury returned a verdict of guilty, late in the afternoon after a three-day trial.

Judge Mandeville was no shrinking violet. He had been a CIA agent and a judge in the United States Navy before becoming a judge in Bennington. He was generally so strict with defendants and their lawyers that his nickname among some defense counsel was the deliberately counterintuitive "Mandy." A lawyer wag said that the problem with this militaristically inclined guy was that he'd never understood the difference between the naval marching music played in the service and civilian rock 'n' roll. Judge Mandeville's strictness applied across the board. One morning, when the prosecutor was late to court, he dismissed all the cases on the docket. The State's Attorney's office then had to do the time-consuming scut work of redrafting and refiling the charges. When one of the prosecutors arrived to find the courtroom empty and learned what had happened, he slammed the door so hard that one of the hinges came off.

In my bar-fight case, the prosecutor demanded before trial that my client plead guilty and agree to serve a jail term. He was a contrite college student from Long Island who had no previous criminal record. "No, Terry," I said, "that's a deal I cannot and will not swallow." And from the judge's perspective, Theresa's refusal to settle the case reasonably before trial was going to clog the docket by consuming three valuable court days, during which she called a total of nineteen witnesses.

After the jury had spoken, and Terry and I made sentencing arguments, Judge Mandeville imposed a fine and brief jail time on my client, which he suspended. This was appropriate lenience that Deputy State's Attorney St. Helaire failed to appreciate. Even though her office prosecuted an almost identical beer-bottle assault by a local college student whom I'd represented. In that case, a different prosecutor had agreed to a deal for a deferred sentence; after the young man completed a year of probation successfully, his conviction was expunged and he had a clean record. This result enabled him to become a police officer and later a police chief, with whom I dealt occasionally in cases involving his department. .

In 1991, Vermont's Democratic Lieutenant Governor, Howard Dean, ascended to the top job when our Republican governor, the highly competent Richard Snelling, had a heart attack while swimming in his backyard pool and died. Governor Dean's first judicial appointee was Terry St. Helaire, and she became the first in a series of "lock 'em up and throw away the key" jurists that Dean picked for the bench. Dave Williams and I testified against

Terry at her Vermont Senate confirmation hearing, citing the marijuana case where she had subpoenaed a child to testify against his parents and later charged him with the same crime after he took the Fifth Amendment. But the Senate confirmed her anyway, and Theresa was now a judge, one that I did everything I could to avoid, and she probably felt similarly.

As a presidential candidate in 2008, Howard Dean appeared to be a liberal. But as governor, he was a conservative figure. For example, he used teacher-bashing rhetoric in opposing their quest for decent salaries and health benefits. Dean did this with such virulence that the relatively mild-mannered Vermont chapter of the teachers' union, the National Education Association, distributed bumper stickers to their members with the polite slogan "I've Soured on Howard."

Dean's budget proposals cut public defense appropriations to amounts below the bone. He justified doing so by telling reporters, with apparent conviction: "They're all guilty anyway." His judicial appointees imposed so many long jail terms that Vermont had to send prisoners to out-of-state institutions, many of which are so far away (including Virginia and, most recently, Mississippi) that low-income family members couldn't afford to visit their kin. The Department of Corrections (DOC) budget exploded with the need for more probation officers, more court officers and clerks, more prison guards, and food, shelter, health care, and other required services for the ballooning prison population.

Soon the DOC budget exceeded the amount that Vermont allocates to support the University of Vermont and the Vermont State Colleges System. Ironically, a DOC study in 2000 found that 95 percent of Vermont prisoners under the age of twenty-two lacked a high-school diploma, and roughly half were formerly students with special needs. The same study calculated that 7 percent of Vermonters between the ages of eighteen and twenty-one were under DOC supervision.

When a state spends more on prisons than higher education, that is a serious problem, in my opinion. To fund his budget increases, Dean persuaded the legislature to "borrow" from the teacher retirement fund, a debt that was never repaid, resulting in a current pension deficit of more than $1.5 billion in a state with a population of only 625,000, with many politicians proposing deep cuts in retiree compensation. Debt and too many people in prison are Howard Dean's main legacies. But it was the famous televised scream, not errors in policy, that ruined his presidential prospects.

DEAN'S LAST TRIAL JUDGE APPOINTMENT, made in the year 2000, was an excellent one. He named to the bench Karen Carroll, a prosecutor who could be tough but who was honorable and fair in her dealings with me and other defense lawyers I knew. After starting off as a Deputy State's Attorney, she was promoted to the job of Assistant Attorney General, and she served simultaneously as a Special Assistant United States Attorney. Karen Carroll was admired in the legal community on both sides of the street for her ability and integrity.

In my most memorable case against Karen, I represented a client named Steven Shearer of Bryant Pond, Maine, charged with barging into the office of Brattleboro lawyer Bob Fisher, who worked part-time as a local prosecutor but also maintained a busy private law practice. Fisher had represented Shearer's spouse in a contested divorce case the day before. Steven had no lawyer at the final hearing, and Bob Fisher cleaned his clock on the money issues. Outraged by this, Shearer punched Fisher, shoved him onto the carpet, smashed his laptop computer, and threw a chair at him.

In addition to a couple of misdemeanors for assault and trespassing, Shearer was facing charges of felony unlawful mischief for destroying the laptop, plus an additional count for hitting Bob Fisher—not only for misdemeanor simple assault, the usual charge brought in this instance, but also for violating a Vermont statute that makes it a felony (obstruction of justice) to hinder public officials, including prosecutors.

I made a motion to dismiss the latter charge. Judge David Suntag, a Howard Dean appointee, denied the motion, even though the language of the operative statute required proof that the defendant hinder the victim "while acting under the authority of this State." Bob Fisher was acting in his role as a private divorce lawyer in the case with Mr. Shearer, not in his official capacity, and there was no evidence that Shearer was even aware that Fisher was also a part-time prosecutor. So how could his conduct reasonably be deemed obstruction of justice?

Judge Suntag's unfair ruling was now what is called "the law of the case," and the only way to get it reversed would be with a Vermont Supreme Court appeal, an unlikely prospect, as my client wanted his case over and done with as soon as possible. Moreover, in my opinion, if Shearer had gone to trial and been found guilty, Judge Suntag would have given him substantial jail time. (In another of my cases involving Judge Suntag, my client spent a year and a half in prison until the Vermont Supreme Court granted his appeal, holding that the behavior for which he was convicted did not constitute a crime. The Supreme Court ordered the entry of a judgment of acquittal, at which point my client was set free.)

I took a pretrial deposition of Bob Fisher's secretary, a witness to the assault, who had been frightened by my client's behavior, and she testified shaking and in tears. After she left the room, I told Karen that I thought my client's impact on the secretary, even though she was physically unharmed, was far worse than anything he had done to attorney Fisher.

My frank comment broke the ice between us, and Karen and I were able to come to a deal that involved Mr. Shearer "doing time" on the street. Technically he would be in the custody of the Commissioner of Corrections for sixty days but not physically in jail during that period, as long as he showed up faithfully and on time for work on a road crew supervised by probation officers, cleaning up Vermont highways.

In the event of compliance, Mr. Shearer would remain on the street and be allowed to return home to Maine after two months of work. Steven was delighted, and according to the probation folks, he didn't merely show up; he was the best worker they'd ever had. I was happy. Karen was happy. Justice was done.

I had two trials before Judge Carroll. In one of them, a misdemeanor assault case, a prosecution witness, whose father was the alleged victim, testified that I had been his father's lawyer in a similar recent case. Were that true, which it was not, it might have established that my representation of a client charged with assaulting a former client was improper and a conflict of interest. This false testimony threatened to blow up the trial or at the very least utterly confuse the jury, probably to my client's detriment. I went up to the bench with the prosecutor and told Judge Carroll that the witness was lying about my having represented his father, but because I was a lawyer in the case, I was barred from testifying, so would she please do something about the lie.

Taking me at my word, Judge Carroll immediately instructed the jury that the testimony about me was false and that they should disregard it. It takes guts to do that. Judges aren't supposed to tell juries that a piece of testimony they've just heard is a lie. But in this situation, it was the right thing to do to avoid a mistrial or a miscarriage of justice, and in the end the jury found my client not guilty of the assault.

In 2017, after I'd retired and left the state, Vermont Governor Phil Scott, a Republican, promoted Judge Carroll to become a Justice of the Vermont Supreme Court.

I LOVED CRIMINAL DEFENSE WORK during my public defender days. I spent long hours researching, drafting, and filing every conceivable motion, raising odd defenses, and asking for unusual jury instructions, which made me unpopular with some of the Deputy State's Attorneys in Bennington.

For example, in a prosecution charging my client, a logger, with grand larceny because he'd failed to pay a client in full for trees he'd cut, I successfully asserted the defense that, under American common law, which is derived from English law, trees are considered part of the land rather than personal property, so that the prosecutor should have charged him with theft of realty, not larceny. Unfortunately for the prosecution, however, the statute of limitations for theft of realty had expired. Case dismissed.

Some other unusual motions I made never failed to annoy prosecutors. When a defendant runs from police, judges invariably instruct the jury that they may deem flight as "evidence of guilt," even though fear of the cops is often the motive. In every case where my client *had not* fled the scene, I filed a motion asking the judge to instruct the jury that they should consider *lack* of flight as "evidence of innocence." No judge ever agreed to give that eminently even-handed instruction. Judges also always denied my motion that the defendant and I be allowed to sit at the table closest to the jury box, which by custom was reserved for the prosecution, despite the lack of any rule or court decision to that effect, and this Vermont custom is not followed in other jurisdictions, including Massachusetts. I wanted the jury members to get a good look at my client. The accused is a human being, after all, not merely an impersonal "defendant" who is sitting so far away from the jury as to appear more like an object or a television image than a real person.

My client list included the most impoverished people I had ever met. They lived in uninsulated hovels with no indoor plumbing and dirt floors, packed together in areas near railroad tracks and abandoned freight cars. I had never been in a home with a dirt floor before visiting one of these clients. I hadn't realized that such places existed in Vermont.

One of my regular public defense clients would walk into our office barefoot—because, he said, he couldn't afford shoes! And he and many others smelled awful, as if rancid cooking oil were coming out of their pores. Carol Cameron, our receptionist and bookkeeper, complained about this, and I had to buy Ozium to spray my office and the waiting room after they left. She would rate the clients by the number of sprays necessary to kill the smell. This was her joking way of telling me that she had empathy for these folks. I returned the favor. Knowing that Carol entered every possible sweepstakes contest, I would kid her by placing on her desk the calling card of Robert H. Treller, the mythical chief of prize awards from Publishers Clearing House, or by leaving phony "sorry I missed you" phone messages for her, with callback requests from Bob Treller, the always elusive PCH money man.

In my thirty-two years as a lawyer in Bennington County, I represented three generations of Vermonters from the same families, with last names like Grover, Wilkinson, Morse, Secoy, Skidmore, and Jenks. Their offenses ranged from drunken assaults to break-ins to violation of relief from abuse orders by making forbidden phone calls to their spouses. These were people the cops loved to target and would arrest whenever possible, even for the most trivial wrongs.

In one public defense case I handled, my indigent client drank part of a bottle of Coke in a Bennington supermarket, screwed the cap back on, then placed the half-empty container back on the shelf, which is technically a form of retail theft despite the negligible loss to the store. The fact that the Bennington cops bothered to arrest this man, and that the State's Attorney decided to prosecute the case, was a typical example of the class-biased, unequal justice that permeates the system.

The criminal conduct in a lot of my cases, involving people with the same surnames, seemed almost as if it were handed down from grandparent to parent to child as a kind of weird family custom and tradition. Is there a sociobiological component to this? Or is it simply the result of lack of education, terrible health and dental care, a food stamp diet of starches and sugary drinks, having to wear raggedy hand-me-down clothing, and being bullied and scapegoated and shunned from early childhood by those more fortunate, who thoughtlessly dismiss them as "dirtbags"?

America's class system, even in a relatively tolerant place like Vermont, is stratified and reminiscent of societies that scorn Untouchables and other low-caste beings. I'm not sure what to do about this problem. The efforts of people like Tenzin Gyatso, the 14th Dalai Lama, whose aim in life has been to teach others to feel compassion toward all sentient beings, is one way to start. This living Buddha has said that, "to end war, we must first end the war within ourselves," and to that end, he teaches that every person should strive to eliminate the emotion of anger toward others.

These are inspiring insights, though they are far from easy to effectuate, either on an individual or macro level. One of the jobs of a criminal defense lawyer is to try to minimize the anger of others toward the client, including from cops, prosecutors, victims, and the public, thereby to make it possible to lay the groundwork for a favorable plea agreement. This is especially important in cases where death has resulted from the client's wrongdoing, even when the misconduct is unintentional.

⚖

CHAPTER 11

Homicides by Auto

In Vermont, most homicides aren't intentional or malicious or premeditated; they're caused by drunk or grossly negligent drivers. I've been able to forget some of the cases in which I represented the driver, though not all. Flashbacks of old tragedies during otherwise happy times are part of a criminal defense lawyer's unwelcome baggage. I'm sure that's true of other helping professions, pediatrics being a likely candidate. I'm not complaining here, just reporting my experience. Prospective law students, please take note before taking the plunge.

Raymond Mohr's Case

In June 1986, a teenage boy named Jimmy, age 15, was riding his bicycle down an extremely steep and long incline on Center Hill, a street in Manchester Center. It was dusk. At the bottom of the hill, likely going faster than was safe, Jimmy tried to make a left turn onto Vermont Route 11, cutting the corner, when an antique Triumph sports car, turning right from Route 11 onto Center Hill, hit him head-on and killed him. A middle-aged man named Ray Mohr, now dead, was the driver of the Triumph. When police arrived at the scene, they smelled alcohol on his breath. Mohr called another lawyer,

Jeremy Dworkin, after which he refused to take a breath test for alcohol level. Dworkin then referred the case to me.

State's Attorney Raymond Bolton charged Mr. Mohr with DUI death resulting, a serious felony carrying a penalty of a minimum of one and a maximum of fifteen years in prison.

Raymond Mohr was a former New York City actor and voice-over ad man, a profession that prepared him well to serve as the coproprietor and front man of an extremely successful, high-end jewelry store in town, Nina's of the Village.

There is a certain level of con needed to be successful in that business, where markups on diamond engagement rings average 300 percent nationally. Ray was a charming fellow, and he was popular in Manchester, but his huckster overlay wasn't terribly helpful in my dealings with the State's Attorney.

Our defense was that Ray Mohr was not under the influence of alcohol, even though his refusal to be tested was highly suspicious. I had in my possession a handwritten receipt from a local bar, from which Ray had departed two or three minutes before the accident occurred, and it showed the number of drinks Ray had imbibed, what they were, and the amount of the tab. If the receipt were genuine, the amount of alcohol involved could not possibly have put him over the legal limit of .08 percent.

At first blush, this receipt business seemed to me a bit too convenient and cute, and there is no way that I would ever knowingly use false evidence to help a client. I took the receipt back to the bartender, and he acknowledged its authenticity and accuracy, told me that in his opinion Ray was okay to drive, and gave me a written statement to that effect. I sent copies of the receipt and the statement to State's Attorney Bolton, and I suggested that he send his own investigator to speak with the bartender.

After a month or so, Bolton called and told me that he had verified the bartender's story. We met and reached a plea agreement, providing that Mohr would plead guilty to a traffic ticket for a defective headlight, a cracked windshield, and bald tires, pay a $100 fine, and accept an eighteen-month license suspension for refusing to take a breath test after the accident. No criminal conviction and no jail time when a teenage boy had died? There is no way that a client of mine would turn down this "deal of the century."

At the time of the accident, my wife, Ellen, was an English and Holocaust history teacher at the Dorset School. (The Town of Dorset's claim to fame is that it's the hometown of Bill W., a founder of Alcoholics Anonymous. He is buried there, and his family home became an inn for AA members.)

The father of Jimmy, the boy who was killed, whose first name is Greg, was the superintendent of schools for Ellen's district. Greg was Ellen's boss. It's a tribute to Greg that he never retaliated against Ellen, even in a small way, due to my role in Ray Mohr's case, though many people in his position would have been furious with me. He told her that he knew I was only doing my job. He was always fair and professional in his dealings with Ellen. They had a great working relationship for years, and Greg retired.

Ray Mohr's attitude toward me was different. He wouldn't pay his legal fee. Not a farthing. Our firm had to sue him. He didn't bother to respond to the suit, and so we got what is known as a "default judgment" against him. He still would not pay. The firm then filed a foreclosure action on his home, based on the default judgment. No response to that either. The court gave us a judgment of foreclosure.

Ray Mohr's home was in the most expensive and swanky section of Manchester Village, on Route 7A near the Equinox Hotel. It was worth a lot of money. Why would Ray risk loss of his home when his jewelry business was doing so well? His wife was reputed to be independently wealthy. Separately or together, I believed they could pay our firm's reasonable fee with no problem. I couldn't figure it out. My efforts had helped save Ray from prison.

In Vermont, there is a "redemption period" of six months, allowing people who are foreclosed upon to avoid losing their home if they pay the amount due, including interest, attorney's fees, and costs, within that appropriately generous time frame. Ray Mohr waited until the last day of the redemption period, and then he paid up in full.

My less-than-compassionate side had fantasized sending the sheriff to evict Ray and then moving into his house myself, a violation of the Dalai Lama's teaching on the uselessness and futility of anger. Ray had done likewise by succumbing to his anger toward me, holding off until the last possible minute to pay his legal fee.

I never learned why Ray Mohr was so upset with me.

Matthew Wolff's Case

The picturesque, agricultural village of West Rupert is directly north of Sandgate, located on the border of Salem, New York, on Vermont Route 153, a narrow, winding two-lane blacktop. A house there was the site and set of Chris Kimball's PBS series *Cook's Country*, and Chris still owns a home there, next to Sherman's, the only store in the tiny village.

My client Matthew Wolff, an Air Force veteran, artist, and antiques restorer, lived in a house on the other side of Sherman's from the Kimball manse. On September 19, 1998, Matthew was driving his van while his son, age 14, rode in the front passenger seat. There is an ultra-hazardous, double-hairpin S-curve on Route 153, and Matthew's van crossed the center line there and crashed head-on into a 1988 Plymouth driven by Ruth Kirchner, Rupert's town clerk and a local Sunday school teacher.

Mrs. Kirchner was killed, and her husband and two children were seriously injured. A rescue helicopter flew them to Albany, New York, for treatment. Matthew's collarbone was broken, and he suffered compound fractures to his left leg. After months of almost unbearable pain, his doctors decided that the leg could not be saved, and they amputated it.

Bennington County State's Attorney Bill Wright charged Matthew Wolff, then age 55, with two counts of grossly negligent operation, death and serious bodily injury resulting, both felonies and each carrying a maximum fifteen-year sentence. At the scene, Matthew had taken full responsibility for the accident, telling police that he was "fooling around" with his son and that he crossed the center line due to his own inattention.

Matthew was heartbroken by what had occurred. Every one of my private conversations with him was tear-filled. Despite his genuine remorse, the prosecutor's office was seeking significant jail time in the case.

While the litigation was in progress, I drove Matthew's son alone to the accident site, and I questioned him about his memory of what had happened. He said that he had been playing with a squirt gun, and he shot his father in the eyes, temporarily blinding him with water and causing him to lose control of the van on the curve.

Matthew had lied to the police to protect his son. I arranged with Bill Wright to accept a written statement from the son, with the verbal understanding (I always trusted Bill's integrity) that it wouldn't be used against him. He was too young to be charged as an adult in any event, so the stakes for him were low. Luckily for Matthew, the cops had found a squirt gun in the van after the accident, and that discovery corroborated the son's truthful though belated account.

It was a tough row to hoe despite the squirt-gun revelation, especially given the understandable feelings of anger shown by the surviving accident victims as well as by the prosecutor and the public, but eventually I was able to negotiate a plea agreement that didn't involve jail time for Matthew.

Frankly, the amputation of Matthew's leg was the event that dissipated the widespread anger that had been hindering a rational resolution of the case. Having only one leg is a lifelong punishment, and that became clear in a dramatic way that a cold medical report can't possibly demonstrate when Matthew appeared in the Bennington District Court after his surgery for all to see.

Despite the harm that had been done, it was difficult to avoid feeling compassion for Matthew as we watched him struggle, sweat pouring down his face with exertion and with obvious residual physical pain, just to get around the courtroom. Bill Wright and I were able to make a deal providing that Matthew would plead guilty to a felony charge with a suspended sentence of one to six years, probation, and 100 hours of community service, in addition to the unwritten understanding that the State's Attorney's office would not prosecute his son.

Matthew's antique restoration business went bust. The car crash was reported so extensively in the media that he lost all his clients. Because of Matthew's guilty plea to a serious felony, and the popularity of the deceased Ruth Kirchner in West Rupert, a tightly knit community of only a few hundred people, the locals shunned him, and he had to sell his home and leave Vermont. He moved to Florida and died there in April 2010. His son grew up, got married, and works as an artist in a large city. I hope for his sake that he doesn't think about the accident as much as I do, but I suspect that it will continue to haunt both of us.

CHAPTER 12

⚖

Representing the Worst Person
in Vermont

In 1988, Steve Blodgett, a former college classmate and friend who was practicing law in Burlington, asked me for help on a case. Steve was an excellent lawyer, but his first love has always been performing as a rock musician. In 1967, our senior year, the Compass record label released a 45rpm single, with a song Steve wrote called "Grey Eyes Watching." Steve sounds a lot like the Everly Brothers on that record. He called his group "Steve Sargent and the Pride." I liked the single (it's still available on YouTube), but it never made the Cashbox Top 40. Now Steve has retired from law, and he's a full-time musician. He tells me that he's popular in Finland.

Steve asked me to take over a federal criminal case he'd lost, which was on appeal to the United States Court of Appeals for the Second Circuit, located in New York City. That court has jurisdiction of federal cases originating in Vermont and Connecticut as well as New York. Steve's client was Edwin A. Towne Jr., who had been convicted under the "ex-con with a gun" statute. Because the trial court had designated Towne as a "dangerous special offender," he'd received consecutive sentences adding up to seventy years. On two of the counts, which carried sentences of fifteen years each, the judge had ruled Towne ineligible for parole under a sentencing enhancement applying to those with three violent felony convictions.

Steve was understandably burned out on the case, and he was having trouble finding anyone willing to represent Towne. I wanted to help an old friend, but even more important for me was that no one else would agree to take on this client. I believe that the many other qualified lawyers in the Burlington area were concerned (realistically) that their reputations and legal business would be affected negatively by representing Mr. Towne.

There is a heightened professional responsibility to represent the unpopular defendant, no matter how horrible a person the client may be or how sick the crimes are. One of the American Bar Association Standards governing the practice of criminal defense states that "qualified lawyers should stand ready to undertake the defense of an accused regardless of public hostility toward the accused or personal distaste for the offense charged or the person of the defendant." Sure, the behavior of a loathsome client invariably rubs off onto the lawyer, but that's part of what I'd signed up for when I decided to practice criminal defense. I agreed to replace Steve Blodgett, though if a poll had been done, Ed Towne easily would have won the title of the worst, most hated person in Vermont.

Here's why. Towne's firearms charges arose out of the murder of Paulette Crickmore, a 15-year-old who disappeared on the morning of September 10, 1986, as she waited for the bus to take her to school in Richmond. On November 19, a deer hunter discovered her decomposed body in the woods in Duxbury. She had been raped and shot three times in the head with a .32-caliber handgun, probably a revolver, as no shell casings were found at the scene. Unlike revolvers, semiautomatic weapons expel a shell casing after each firing. Police often find them at crime scenes because the shooter is too careless or in too much of a hurry to pick them up or they fly unseen into the underbrush.

Creative police work by Vermont State Police Sergeant Leo Blais culminated in Towne's arrest for the murder of Paulette. During a search of the home that Towne had built himself, and armed with a valid search warrant, Sergeant Blais, on a hunch, X-rayed its foundation. There was a gun inside it. Police ripped up the foundation, seized the gun, and determined from a ballistics examination that it was the murder weapon.

The state of Vermont filed a first-degree murder charge in a local district court, but the United States Attorney General decided to prosecute Towne first under the Federal Firearms Act, which generally requires proof that the defendant has a prior felony conviction or is a proven domestic abuser or is awaiting trial on such charges. Ed Towne's rap sheet showed four prior convictions arising from two separate rape–kidnapping incidents.

The first such crime occurred in July 1976. While living in New Hampshire and driving to work, Towne abducted and raped a woman twice in separate wooded locations. He told her he was going to kill her, but she escaped when he stopped for gas. A jury convicted Towne, and he received the extremely lenient sentence of five to ten years.

These were the bad-old days of sexual assault cases, when, due to ignorance and sexism, rapes weren't always treated with sufficient seriousness or good sense. Towne won a transfer to a minimum-security joint in New Hampshire after serving "max" time for only three years, and he was released shortly thereafter. Incredibly, even for the era, the prison mental health professional in charge of Towne's case boneheadedly characterized him as a person "who responds to basic human needs. The described sexual episode appears to be more the response to common basic human needs rather than the act of any criminal." This evaluation was contrary to the generally accepted view that rape is a crime of violence and domination, bearing little or no relationship to normal sexual desire.

In 1980, Towne did it again, this time in Vermont, kidnapping and raping a woman repeatedly and taking her to an abandoned hunting camp, from which she escaped when he left to buy groceries. This time, Towne received a six-to-eight-year sentence, and he was placed in the prison sex offender program. He was released in 1987 on parole, and he was still participating in state-mandated outpatient treatment for sex offenders when he sexually assaulted and murdered Paulette Crickmore.

The main basis for the federal appeal wasn't one that would get Mr. Towne released or a new trial. It was a systemic sentencing issue of statutory interpretation: whether the no-parole enhancement law, which is triggered when a defendant has three prior violent felony convictions, applied to his type of case. I argued that the two rape–kidnapping convictions should not be counted as four convictions (as the trial judge had ruled), because they were the product of only two criminal incidents, each a part of the same ongoing and temporally related criminal scheme.

The solicitor general of the United States, who is the lawyer in charge of representing the government in all cases before the Supreme Court, had issued a formal opinion that agreed with my interpretation of the statute.

This split of authority diminished the weight of the opposite readings of the statute given by the trial judge in Towne's case, as well as that of the Attorney General, represented in the Second Circuit by Vermont's United States Attorney, George J. Terwilliger III.

Unlike the First Circuit's old Boston culture of good manners, appearing before the Second Circuit is akin to being thrust into a heated argument with three highly articulate New York City cab drivers after a multitaxi crash. The judges are uniformly brilliant, but politeness isn't their strongest point.

The morning of the Towne case was "take your daughter to work day," and a young female lawyer had a case before mine. The judges (all male) so aggressively attacked her legal argument from the bench that they reduced her to tears, and one can only imagine how badly this impacted her young daughter, watching her mom getting raked over the coals in a rude and insensitive fashion. I felt like walking over and giving this lawyer a hug, but such a gesture likely would have been misinterpreted.

My panel was composed of three conservatives. Judge Lawrence W. Pierce was a Nixon appointee, as was United States District Court Judge Charles E. Stewart Jr., sitting on the court of appeals that day by designation, something that happens when there is a shortage of judges due to illness or vacations. I'd never heard of these guys.

Ralph K. Winter Jr. was the third member of the panel and was well-known to all. A Ronald Reagan appointee, Winter was a former Yale Law School professor and resident scholar at the American Enterprise Institute, a Republican think tank. Winter was in the process of lobbying relentlessly for a spot on the United States Supreme Court. His imperious and domineering behavior in the courtroom was such that it seemed as though his elevation had already occurred and that, by his very presence, he was doing us peons a favor.

All one can do with judges like this is to show them the utmost respect, without any overlay of fear or slavish pretense of intellectual inferiority. And as an advocate you must always be prepared, to the point of memorizing relevant page numbers in the court record that contain material helpful to your cause, so that if a judge asks a question about the facts, you can immediately cite chapter and verse in the client's favor.

My opening to the Judges went something like this: "Good morning, Your Honors, and may it please the Court. This is a case where the government is at war with itself." I don't remember much else, but that set the tone for the arguments on both sides and the questions from the bench. Judge Winter seemed especially upset that the government was split on the interpretation of an important federal criminal statute. I liked that.

AFTER THE ORAL ARGUMENT, in the elevator on the way back to the street, U.S. Attorney George Terwilliger, who did a fine job for his side, was there when someone asked me why I thought that a no-parole life sentence for a monster like Ed Towne was such a bad thing.

My response was that stripping an inmate of all hope, even a remote or vain hope, makes incarcerated sociopaths even more dangerous, to other prisoners and staff alike, because they have absolutely nothing to gain by good behavior and nothing to lose by doing more bad things. I could tell from his body language that George didn't agree with me, but he seemed to understand where I was coming from.

The Second Circuit decision on the no-parole issue was in Mr. Towne's favor. I lost every other legal point that I had argued in my brief, including an illegal search issue that might have resulted in dismissal of the charges. Did this "win" make any practical difference for Towne? No, because he still had seventy years to do, and practically speaking, the possibility of his being paroled wasn't realistic. Release became impossible after Towne was convicted in Bennington District Court for the sexual assault and first-degree murder of Paulette Crickmore, for which he received a life sentence, to be served "on and after" his federal time.

Ed Towne's murder trial was held in 1990 in Bennington, after a motion for a change of venue was granted based on adverse pretrial publicity up north, so I was able to watch some of the proceedings. The specially assigned trial judge, Frank "Skip" Mahady, unfairly called "Freedom Frank" by his detractors, was known by defense lawyers as someone who would "due process you to death." That is, he would grant every defense motion he possibly could, went overboard to be fair in his evidentiary rulings during trial, and when the jury found the defendant guilty anyway, there was almost nothing in the record to form the basis for a winning appeal. It isn't widely understood, either by the public or by the judiciary, for that matter, that if you want to be a "hanging judge," fairness to the defense is the most effective route.

A Republican who had run George Romney's presidential campaign in Vermont, Skip Mahady grew his greasy black hair down to his shoulders, and he looked like a warmed-over hippie badly in need of a shampoo. But his calm and friendly demeanor and his modestly displayed intellect made him the most popular Vermont judge with trial lawyers. By the time of the Towne murder trial, Skip was being treated for intestinal cancer, and he didn't look well. But he did a superb job, and he was fair to the despised Ed Towne.

The case against Towne was overwhelming. Ed made a terrible impression as a defendant. For reasons known only to him, badness was something he seemed to want to project, with an untrimmed, scruffy backwoods beard, dirty clothes (his choice; prisons do have laundries), and a perpetual mean sneer that was scary and intimidating. The outcome of the trial was never in doubt. After all, the murder weapon, a .32-caliber pistol with three spent shell casings still inside it, didn't somehow magically appear within the foundation of the home that he had built for himself. Ed had raped Paulette

Crickmore, and after he was done with her, he shot her in the head three times so that she couldn't live to tell the tale. He had earned his reputation as the worst person in Vermont.

Towne died in prison in Butner, North Carolina, a destination warehousing the craziest federal mental cases, on March 15, 2020. Before his death, Towne filed on his own, without a lawyer, at least eleven appeals of his murder conviction with the Vermont Supreme Court, all of which were denied. Ed was the rare client in my career whose inner light was so obscured—maybe switched off permanently—that he was too dangerous ever to be allowed on the street.

Sometime in late 1991, after the conclusion of my representation of Mr. Towne, I received an unannounced visit from two FBI agents, who asked my opinion on the character and qualifications of George Terwilliger III, whom President George H. W. Bush was considering for the job of chief of the Criminal Division in the Justice Department in Washington, D.C. I told the agents that, while I disagreed with Mr. Terwilliger's politics and what I perceived to be his overly harsh approach in criminal matters, I thought he was trustworthy, talented, and qualified and that his character was beyond reproach.

George got the job. He became acting Attorney General when his friend and boss (William Barr, of all people) left the Justice Department. I think I must have been the only liberal lawyer in Vermont to give George high marks, because for several years he sent me Christmas cards, with handwritten notes like, "I'm gone, but you are not forgotten."

As I write this, Mr. Terwilliger is a partner in a D.C. law firm specializing in white-collar criminal cases. During the Trump years he wrote a series of op-ed pieces in the *New York Times*, defending his former Justice Department colleague, the now twice-retired Attorney General Bill Barr. One of George's specialties is representing Republican politicians in trouble, including former Trump Chief of Staff Mark Meadows in connection with the congressional investigation of the January 6, 2021, attack on the U.S. Capitol. It's likely that George will be on the short list for Attorney General in a future Republican administration.

In my last email to George, I asked him to please use his influence to urge his friend Attorney General Barr to bring federal civil rights prosecutions against those police officers responsible for the death of George Floyd. To my disappointment, Terwilliger didn't respond, and Bill Barr's administration never brought any federal charges in the case, although Attorney General Merrick Garland has since done so.

It's easy to contrast William Barr's nonresponse to the Floyd case, where a white police officer cruelly tortured and murdered a Black man on video for no reason, with how he dealt with the murder of Paulette Crickmore, the white victim of a civilian offender. Barr's Justice Department did nothing on Floyd, the kind of murder once readily ignored by law enforcement as just another "shine killing." But it raced to the courthouse to be the first to prosecute Ed Towne, beating the state of Vermont to the punch in a transparent effort to enhance its white-bread crime-fighting image. There is a hoary Latin phrase sometimes used in the legal profession that applies to that obvious double standard: *quod erat demonstrandum*—it's proof that institutional racism persists.

CHAPTER 13

⚖

Getting Rid of a Bad Judge

In 1983, a year after I started practicing law in Bennington, Republican Governor Richard Snelling appointed fellow party member Arthur J. O'Dea Jr. of Arlington, Vermont, as a Bennington County judge. Art had been effective as a trial lawyer. But some lawyers are temperamentally unsuited to the bench. As soon as they have judicial power over others, their personalities become rude and authoritarian, and their judgment and legal rulings unpredictable, even tyrannical.

Sadly, such was the case with Arthur O'Dea. No lawyer I knew wanted to appear before him. He was moody, and without warning he would lash out with abusive and threatening dressings-down of lawyers and litigants, especially women and low-income people.

All the trial lawyers I knew had war stories about their appearances before Judge O'Dea. I had a civil jury trial, a commercial dispute involving several defendants and their various lawyers, with a single plaintiff, who was represented by Jeremy Dworkin of South Londonderry. Judge O'Dea's demeanor toward Jeremy was disdainful and sarcastic. He insisted on calling Jeremy "Mr. Dorkin" during the proceedings, apparently his way of telegraphing to the assembled, including the jury, that he considered him a "dork."

Jeremy was the only Jew in the room. My Jewish wife has conferred on me the title of Honorary Member of the Tribe, based on my marriage to her and my acceptance into a welcoming Bosinoff family fold, including her parents and her aunts, uncles, cousins, and especially her immigrant grandparents, who found refuge in America after escaping an antisemitic pogrom in what is now Belarus. Perhaps I was being overly sensitive or even a mite paranoid, but this repeated "Dorkin" business set off a tocsin in my head.

In a Rutland divorce case where the issue of custody was contested, Judge O'Dea appointed me as guardian ad litem for the child, to advocate for her best interests. Jane Adams Esq. of Pownal, a farmer as well as a lawyer (not unusual in Vermont), represented one of the parents. I liked Jane a lot. She was an outspoken, brassy overweight feminist whose mere presence in the courtroom seemed to offend Judge O'Dea, probably because of her politics and her appearance; her gestalt, which I found equally brave and charming, brought out Judge O'Dea's worst proclivities.

At a pretrial conference I attended, one of the agenda items was to discuss the ramifications of a psychological evaluation of the child that had just been filed. The psychologist's report recommended that the court place custody with the parent whom Jane Adams did not represent.

Judge O'Dea made it clear that a trial would be a waste of his valuable time given the content of the evaluation, and he indicated that he had already decided to follow the custodial arrangement recommended therein. Jane Adams stood up and objected, telling the judge that there was another side to the story and that her client was prepared to present compelling evidence that would prove that the psychologist was wrong. Judge O'Dea angrily ordered Jane to stop talking and sit down, and then he bellowed, "Ms. Adams, the Fat Lady has sung!" The judge had decided the outcome of the case before the trial, and he didn't mind saying so in open court in language that was not only insulting but also cruel.

Judge O'Dea's worst treatment of me was in a criminal case, and it came on the heels of a Vermont Supreme Court appeal that I had argued, ordering a new trial in litigation over the terms of a will.

The appeal was from a jury verdict overturning the will of Lena Raedel, late of Stamford, Vermont, who left her 100-acre farm to two of her nieces while omitting half a dozen other kin. The two nieces named in the will came to our firm to represent them after their trial lawyer lost the case. The basis for my successful appeal consisted of legal errors made by the trial judge, Arthur J. O'Dea.

In a decision titled *In Re Estate of Raedel* (1989), the Vermont Supreme Court held that Judge O'Dea had mistakenly allowed the jury to find the existence of "suspicious circumstances" surrounding the drafting and signing of the will. Judge O'Dea's erroneous ruling had the effect of shifting the burden of proof to our clients, the will proponents, rather than placing it on the will contestants, which is the usual rule.

As a general matter, courts bend over backward to uphold wills, based on the ancient legal doctrine of "the sanctity of wills." Outright fraud such as a counterfeit will is a rare event, because of the universal requirement that the signing of wills be witnessed by people who have nothing to gain. Thus, in nearly all cases, there are only two legal grounds available to invalidate a will.

The first basis for overturning a will is "lack of testamentary capacity," which applies only when the author of the will is so mentally disabled or debilitated that she isn't able to understand the nature and amount of her property or identify the "objects of her bounty," antiquated legalese for those who stand to inherit. The second, which was the issue in the *Raedel* case, is that of "undue influence." To prevail on that theory, those contesting a will must prove that the beneficiaries exerted such extreme, improper, and overwhelming influence over the will's author that they were in fact able to substitute their own self-serving wishes for those of the decedent.

I found a Vermont Supreme Court case from 1898 titled *In Re Barney's Will*, which suggested that the burden-shifting doctrine of "suspicious circumstances" in the creation of a will should be limited to instances where there is what the law calls a "fiduciary" relationship between the will's draftsperson and the beneficiaries—though the court didn't explicitly use that term in its opinion. According to *Barney*, this means that, in relationships such as "guardian and ward, attorney and client, spiritual advisers and persons looking to them for advice—in fact, all relations of trust and confidence in which the temptation and opportunity for abuse are so great," justice requires that the beneficiary should have to prove that "he did not betray the confidence placed in him." In *Barney*, the Supreme Court overturned a will providing that its draftsman, a lawyer, would inherit all the decedent's estate, even though they were not related by blood or marriage.

Justice James Morse, who had presided over the Cowboy Snodgrass trial before his elevation to the Supreme Court, wrote that the matter of Lena Raedel's will was not such a case, because it involved two nieces who were not acting as her fiduciaries. Justice Morse reasoned in the court's unanimous opinion that courts should not "presume undue influence when the relationship between testator and beneficiaries is one between aunt and nieces and nephews, at least where the beneficiaries do not assist in preparing the will. Here, the evidence showed only that the beneficiaries wanted to inherit the farm, helped care for Lena Raedel during her illness, urged her to seek legal advice regarding her estate, and discouraged the other heirs from contact with their aunt."

The Supreme Court also found that Judge O'Dea had made a second mistake of law, stressing that the existence of "suspicious circumstances" is a preliminary issue for the trial court to decide. The judge had committed reversible error by submitting it to the jury instead of making the decision himself.

This was a double embarrassment. The Supreme Court's opinion made it appear that Judge Arthur J. O'Dea was the Superior Court's reigning Dunce on the Law of Wills. I was the guy responsible for pointing out that O'Dea had screwed up royally, and I was worried that there would be a price to pay down the road.

My first appearance before Judge O'Dea after the *Raedel* decision was a sentencing in an arson case in Bennington in 1990. My client was the late Carl Jones of Dorset. Carl was a developmentally disabled man in his fifties. He was the brother of a self-taught Dorset landscape artist, Arthur Jones, now dead; his sister, Gloria Jordan, makes custom flies and fly rods for trout fishing. I accepted one of Arthur's paintings as part of the fee in Carl's case and paid the firm its fair market value.

Poor Carl was a mess. Motivated by a childlike desire for attention and praise, he set fire to a barn in Dorset, and then he immediately called the volunteer fire department, hoping to get credit for his act of good citizenship. As the firefighters finished their work, the Vermont State Police officer who specialized in arson cases came to the scene. When the officer tried to question Carl, who was watching the blaze (as arsonists often do), he panicked and ran away. The cop tackled him roughly to the ground, warning him he'd better confess "or else," and the terrified Carl complied.

The State's Attorney's office charged Carl with second-degree arson, a serious felony offense that carries a minimum sentence of one year and a maximum of five years in prison. But the only damning evidence against Carl was his confession, and I filed a motion to suppress it from evidence because it was unlawfully coerced by the arson cop's unenlightened interrogation method of tackling and threatening him. The case was somewhat problematic from the defense standpoint, though, because Carl had an old rape conviction from when he was a young man thirty-plus years earlier.

I discussed the case with Bill Wright, the prosecutor, who already knew from community sources that Carl had the mentality of a young child. I had learned that, after the rape conviction and his release from prison, Carl's parents had him castrated. I shared that information with Bill, who was appropriately shocked. Bill also must have realized that my motion to suppress the confession had significant merit. That surely influenced his negotiating position, because if my motion were granted, the court would be compelled to dismiss the case for lack of sufficient proof. Bill and I agreed to a two-year deferred sentence, which would keep Carl on probation for that period. Assuming good behavior, he would remain on the street and his arson conviction would be expunged from his record after two years. But if he were to commit another offense, or violate the terms of his probation, he would have to do prison time.

I sent Carl to Bennington's sole licensed psychiatrist, James M. Toolan, MD, a veteran of New York City's Bellevue Hospital, who evaluated him and drafted a report on his mental disability that I shared with Bill Wright and with the probation officer who was preparing a presentence investigation. Dr. Toolan agreed to testify on Carl's behalf at his sentencing.

When we arrived in court for the hearing, I learned that Art O'Dea would be filling in for the regular judge, who was off for some reason. O'Dea was in high dudgeon. He thought the plea agreement was far too lenient given the old rape conviction, and he insisted that Carl would have to do jail time. When I responded that I wanted to call Dr. Toolan and Arthur (Carl's brother) as witnesses to support the no-jail plea agreement, Judge O'Dea refused to hear them. He ordered me to leave the courtroom, discuss the matter with Bill Wright, and return with a new plea agreement that included prison time. Then he bounded off the bench and into chambers. His behavior confused and frightened Carl, and his brother and I had to comfort him as best we could.

I was thoroughly intimidated, but I wasn't about to go along with this grossly unfair treatment of my client. Instead of meeting with Bill Wright as ordered, I drafted and filed a handwritten motion to recuse Judge O'Dea from sitting on Carl's case any further because he had prejudged the sentencing without hearing the defense evidence. After a fifteen-minute wait, a court clerk told me that Judge O'Dea had granted my motion and that another judge would be assigned to conclude the matter. Carl got his deferred sentence after all.

LATER I SPOKE WITH a local Vermont Legal Aid lawyer about Judge O'Dea. She told me that he was under investigation by the state's Judicial Conduct Board (JCB). She and other Vermont Legal Aid attorneys had filed complaints about the rude and biased way that he treated their indigent clients. She told me that in her experience Judge O'Dea hated women, both clients and lawyers, but especially low-income women. Whenever she drove to a Vermont Family Court hearing and saw Judge O'Dea's white Saab in the parking lot, with his last name emblazoned on his vanity license plate, she was certain she was going to lose.

This lawyer told me that she had represented the wife in a divorce case in which the children had told their therapists that their father was sexually abusing them. Even after hearing extensive testimony corroborating the sexual misconduct at the final divorce hearing, Judge O'Dea refused to believe the children or the professionals, and he awarded custody to the father. The Department of Children and Families then immediately removed the children from the father's custody and placed them in foster care, a terrible result that was understandably traumatic for the children and their mother.

My lawyer friend asked me to discuss my experiences with the JCB investigator, who then called me. I told him what I knew.

The Vermont Supreme Court had already come down hard on Judge O'Dea for his conduct in a 1990 divorce case, *Blair v. Blair*. During the trial, the wife told Judge O'Dea that her husband had severely abused her, threatened her life, and strangled her.

In verbal findings of fact issued from the bench, O'Dea determined that the wife had lied, based on his belief that she would have left the marriage if her allegations of abuse were true.

The Supreme Court rebuked Judge O'Dea, citing cases from other jurisdictions to the effect that many women, particularly those suffering from battered wife syndrome, are unable to leave abusive husbands out of fear that the husband will track them down and commit further violence or are motivated by an unrealistic hope that their husbands will reform.

The court added that Judge O'Dea's "reasons for discrediting the defendant's testimony about domestic violence are ones rendered suspect in the literature on the subject." The Court granted the wife's request for a new trial.

Then in February 1993, the Vermont Supreme Court issued an opinion upholding a finding by the Judicial Conduct Board that Judge O'Dea repeatedly had been guilty of misconduct in other divorce matters.

Judge O'Dea appealed the JCB's decision. The Vermont Supreme Court found that during his JCB hearing he expressed little or no remorse for his sexist and insensitive courtroom antics. Judge O'Dea stubbornly denied that his intemperate behavior had ever risen to a level sufficient to permit the JCB or the Vermont Supreme Court to impose discipline.

The court disagreed. It publicly reprimanded Judge O'Dea and stripped him of the authority to sit on Vermont Family Court matters for a two-year period. The court's opinion detailed some of the reasons for its decision.

The court's opinion highlighted a case in which Judge O'Dea had "refused to grant a continuance so that the litigant mother could obtain counsel, although she had appeared at the court expecting the matter to be mediated or continued. He cut off the mother's attempt to briefly cross-examine the father, gave her no opportunity to present testimony or evidence of her own, and questioned in a harsh and intimidating fashion the parties' daughter, who was not a party or sworn as a witness." The court continued: "When the mother began to comfort her daughter, who had begun to cry, he directed the mother to 'just leave her alone and let her listen.' He also threatened to transfer custody of the daughter to the father if the parties did not adhere to a visitation schedule, although the father neither requested nor wanted such a transfer."

In some states judges are elected, and in others they are appointed. In Vermont, judges are appointed by the governor subject to Senate approval; if confirmed, they serve for six-year terms. At the end of each term, the Senate and House of Representatives, sitting in joint session, vote on whether to retain or fire each judge. The vote in Judge O'Dea's case was scheduled for March 25, 1993, only a month or so after the release of the Vermont Supreme Court's opinion imposing discipline on him.

Despite his disciplinary problems, Judge O'Dea had many Republican friends in high places, and he mounted a surprisingly effective public relations campaign on his own behalf. One of his arguments, which gained traction with some legislators, was that he was only weeks away from the vesting of his full judicial pension, which he would lose in the event of nonretention.

Lawyers from Vermont Legal Aid and others lobbied against Judge O'Dea. The vote was expected to be close, though no other jurist during the twentieth century had been denied retention.

On March 25, minutes before the final vote, my lawyer friend and college classmate Steve Blodgett telephoned me. His wife, Jan Backus, was a state senator from Burlington. She was undecided, and she wanted advice from a lawyer whom Steve knew and trusted and who practiced in Bennington County, Judge O'Dea's bailiwick. I gave Steve my recommendation for a vote against retention and the reasons for it. Steve passed this info along to Jan. Hers was the deciding vote, which was 87–86 for termination. In Vermont's backwoods vernacular, O'Dea was "all done."

Though Art (as lawyers were able to address him now) deserved the boot, no one I knew wanted to see him without prospects or some decent means to support himself and his family. Locals, including my wife and I (Ellen had taught three of the O'Dea kids), were genuinely sorry that Art was experiencing such a public and humiliating fall from grace. We felt special compassion for Art's diminutive wife, Roberta, a kindly, humble, and sensitive person (the polar opposite of Art's public persona), who must have been going through hell.

Art was able to bounce back. After a course of study at Ohio State University, he became a hugely successful mediator, primarily in personal injury cases. He earned the respect of lawyers on both sides and that of those shadowy, impersonal, and ubiquitous deciders—the insurance company claims adjusters.

When Art had no power over others, other than his newfound ability to bring litigants together, he was a superbly effective professional. One of the techniques that he used to settle cases was to stress in private conversations with litigants on each side that, for a case to resolve successfully in mediation, both plaintiff and defendant must walk away unhappy with the result. That is so true, and it's something that Art was able to get people to understand.

I agreed to have mediations (which are required by court rule in civil cases) with Art at his peaceful Arlington farmstead many times, and I was always grateful for his efforts, even when they didn't result in a settlement, which was unusual.

After Art's sacking, I learned that his father, the senior Arthur J. O'Dea, had been a judge in Bergen County, New Jersey, for a total of twenty-five years. The elder O'Dea had broken new ground, being the first judge in the state to allow jurors to take notes during trials. The rest of the state's judiciary followed his example.

Perhaps Art Jr. was compelled by unconscious forces to follow in his dad's alluring and compelling paternal footsteps, even though he wasn't suited temperamentally for a judicial role. The fact that his father had been a successful and innovating jurist must have made Art's fall even more devastating. Ultimately, Art was able to overcome his problems and find a profession at which he excelled, and I admired him for that.

If Art ever learned that my recommendation to Senator Backus was a factor in his firing from the judiciary, he never mentioned it.

⚖

CHAPTER 14

Operation Rescue Accuses Me of Attempted Murder

During the late 1980s and early 1990s, a self-styled pastor with no divinity degree named Michael McHugh was the leader of the militant anti-abortion group Operation Rescue in Vermont, as well as the founder of his own organization, Operation Save a Baby. Between September 1988 and October 1989, his organizations conducted five protests that shut down the Vermont Women's Health Center in Burlington, employing tactics such as blocking the entrances to the clinic, yelling and screaming at patients, and chaining themselves to doors. They did the same on one occasion at the Planned Parenthood office in Barre.

Police made hundreds of arrests (mostly of people from other states), and courts issued various orders designed to stop McHugh and the two groups with interfering with clinic operations. The protestors ignored those orders. Finally, after an October 1989 anti-abortion action, the Women's Health Center in Burlington sought and received a contempt citation against McHugh and Operation Rescue, which the Vermont Supreme Court upheld on appeal in the 1992 decision *Vermont Women's Health Center v. Operation Rescue*.

Affirming the Superior Court's imposition of attorney's fees and prospective fines, the Supreme Court found that "a group led by defendant McHugh of more than fifty persons . . . physically invaded the grounds and building of the health center. They blocked doorways and exits of the building and positioned a ten-wheel truck to block the driveway. Many of them locked themselves to one another in the hallways of the building; they made a great deal of noise singing and chanting." The court continued: "As a result, health services for women scheduled for that day, including cancer-related examinations and other tests, as well as abortions, were cancelled. Two police officers were injured as they attempted to enter the building through doors pulled shut by protesters. The use of mace and tear gas was ultimately required to gain entry and control."

In 1993, the year after this Vermont Supreme Court decision, Judge Doris Buchanan of Bennington County Probate Court asked me to represent pro bono Joseph Schaaf, whom she had appointed to be the guardian of a man named Ronald Comeau. In Vermont, probate judges are elected, and they do not have to be lawyers. Judge Buchanan had been clerk of the Bennington District Court, but she was not a lawyer, a handicap when one is required to make complex or controversial legal decisions.

The Bennington Police Department had arrested Mr. Comeau, who was homeless and a drifter who had done prison time in Utah and Texas, for physically attacking other homeless people. While awaiting arraignment on an assault charge, he tried to commit suicide by hanging himself in his jail cell. He was taken to Southwestern Vermont Medical Center in Bennington, where physicians found him unresponsive and in critical condition. Hospital neurologists diagnosed Mr. Comeau as being in a persistent vegetative state, and after twenty weeks in the hospital with little or no improvement in his condition, the institution's ethics committee voted 11–3 to authorize removal of Mr. Comeau's feeding tube.

During this time, Joe Schaaf, a retired teacher who was serving as Mr. Comeau's guardian as an unpaid volunteer, made repeated, unsuccessful efforts to enlist a member of the Comeau family to replace him in that post and take responsibility for Ronald's care. On one occasion he was able to speak by telephone with Mr. Comeau's father, who told Schaaf that he wanted nothing to do with his son. During the twenty weeks, Schaaf visited Mr. Comeau in the hospital nearly every day. No one in Mr. Comeau's biological family ever did so.

Schaaf's observations of Mr. Comeau led him to believe that he was suffering horribly and was chronically in great physical pain. After the hospital ethics committee's vote, Schaaf decided that, were Mr. Comeau competent to make the decision, he would support the removal of his own feeding tube, even though that would lead swiftly to his death. Schaaf filed a motion with the probate court to authorize and direct the hospital to take that course of action. Judge Buchanan appointed me to assist Mr. Schaaf for the purpose of arguing in favor of his motion to cease feeding and hydration.

Enter Michael McHugh, stage far-right. After learning of the litigation on a radio program, McHugh filed a motion with the Bennington probate court to replace Schaaf as Mr. Comeau's guardian. McHugh, as the leader of the "right to life" movement in Vermont, made clear that, if appointed as guardian, he would oppose removal of the feeding tube and keep the patient alive no matter what.

Judge Buchanan held a hearing that evening. I argued on behalf of Mr. Schaaf that McHugh had no legal standing to petition the probate court to do anything. He was what the law calls an "officious intermeddler." He had had never heard of Mr. Comeau before finding out about him on the radio, and his interest in the ward was purely political.

McHugh claimed that he had automatic standing to litigate the case because of his role as a Christian minister, asserting that pastors are imbued by the Lord with a legally cognizable "interest in people they don't know who are being killed." The chairperson of the Vermont Right to Life Committee supported McHugh's position, adding that Vermont should "draw a line in the sand" and adopt the rule that, as a matter of law, food and water should never be withheld from an incompetent patient.

I wrote in opposition to McHugh's effort to intervene that, if adopted by the judiciary, "[t]he McHugh Rule would turn the Probate Court into an ideological battlefield of warring theologies" and that "in the fog of this war . . . the best interests of the ward would be totally lost."

Judge Buchanan decided, in the words of a Massachusetts Supreme Judicial Court decision, that, after "donning the mental mantle" of the incompetent, she believed that Mr. Comeau would want to die. She further held that Michael McHugh lacked standing to become a party to the case. When McHugh asked her to reconsider that ruling, Judge Buchanan determined that she had no power to do so given McHugh's legal inability to be heard.

He appealed to Superior Court, which reheard the case a day later, with a raft of newspaper and television reporters in McHugh's pastoral tow. While we waited for the trial, in a public room where the media was allowed, McHugh raised the level of rhetoric, announcing to all that he considered Joe Schaaf and me murderers, on the same immoral—indeed criminal— plane as physicians who kill babies by performing abortions.

As a veteran criminal defense lawyer, I was used to becoming the butt of scurrilous and defamatory charges by others, but Joe Schaaf was understandably upset by McHugh's mean-spirited spouting. Schaaf emphasized to the media, and to Superior Court Judge Ellen Maloney, that his decision to ask for removal of the feeding tube was a difficult one, made only after it appeared to him that Mr. Comeau was undergoing immense suffering, and that he had no reasonable chance of recovery. Schaaf repeated his position that, were a family member to come forward to assume the responsibility of making medical decisions, he would gladly withdraw as guardian.

After a hearing, Judge Maloney affirmed Judge Buchanan's decision on the merits as well as on the issue of Michael McHugh's lack of legal standing, and she ordered the feeding tube removed.

That evening, which was a Friday, a lawyer hired by McHugh sought and received by telephone from Chief Justice Frederic W. Allen of the Vermont Supreme Court a temporary stay of the lower court's feeding tube removal order. This was done ex parte, meaning without notice to me or the hospital's lawyer, Lon McClintock of Bennington, thereby denying us the opportunity to be heard, an ethically borderline tactic, in my mind.

McClintock told the local *Bennington Banner*: "This thing has been handled unethically and improperly . . . right from the beginning." The reporter quoted Joe Schaff as calling McHugh's latest gambit "[a]bsolutely outrageous. These churchmen that worry about heaven—I think they're keeping him [Mr. Comeau] in hell right now."

McHugh asserted that Mr. Schaaf and I "wouldn't kill a dog the way they want to kill him." Dog-lover Saltonstall responded that McHugh's litigation conduct was "inhumane and something that would only be done by a religious fanatic. We will do our best to persuade the Supreme Court to permit Mr. Comeau to die with dignity." I spent the weekend writing a brief, which I submitted to the court on Monday for a hearing it had scheduled for Tuesday. The brief made clear that Mr. Schaaf would gladly defer to the wishes of Mr. Comeau's family if one of them would simply agree to take over his guardianship.

Joe Schaaf and I arrived at the Vermont Supreme Court in Montpelier on Tuesday, with plenty of time to spare before our oral argument. Miracle of miracles, members of Ronald Comeau's family were there in person, ready to tell the court that they were in McHugh's corner, that they were now ready to assume the responsibility for Mr. Comeau's care, and that his brother Renald had agreed to become guardian.

I informed the Supreme Court Justices that in our view the case was moot, as Mr. Schaaf was enthusiastically in favor of the appointment of Renald as guardian and that he'd believed all along that Mr. Comeau's family should be the ones making life-and-death medical decisions for him.

As I walked down the stairs to the street to make the long drive back to my office in Bennington, Duncan Kilmartin, a conservative lawyer (retired recently from his post as a Republican member of the Vermont legislature) who was sympathetic to McHugh's political views, screamed down the stairs at me: "How does it feel to be a death penalty prosecutor?" That verbal assault from a colleague was hurtful, particularly given my lifelong opposition to the death penalty, but I did not respond.

Shortly thereafter, the parties filed a legal stipulation transferring the guardianship of Mr. Comeau to his brother, which Probate Judge Buchanan swiftly approved. Michael McHugh was not a party to this.

McHugh then filed a formal complaint against me with the agency empowered to impose discipline on lawyers, which at the time was the Vermont Professional Conduct Board (PCB). The *Bennington Banner* ran an article on McHugh's filing, with the headline "Right-to-Life Minister Says Local Attorneys Tried to Kill Comeau." It quoted me as saying that "McHugh is destructive and misguided, and I feel sorry for him. Nobody, as far as I know, did anything professionally wrong. He just disagrees with what happened, which is different from a professional error."

McHugh told the reporter that he would like to see the attorneys provide financial compensation to the Comeau family and a public apology. "Or maybe someone ought to chain them to a bed for three days, without food or water." The PCB dismissed his complaint.

After assuming the role as guardian and extracting a commitment from the state of Vermont to continue paying for his brother's care, Renald Comeau sent Ronald by ambulance to a Massachusetts rehabilitation facility. Mr. Comeau died on June 19, 1997, having never left rehab, after contracting pneumonia and choking on his own vomit.

"We didn't see a whole lot of progress, unfortunately," his sister, Patty Comeau of Worcester, Massachusetts, told an Associated Press reporter. "He eventually gave up."

CHAPTER 15

⚖️

Combatting the War on Drugs

I suspect that the widespread animus against physicians who perform abortions extends with equal or greater force to those who sell illegal drugs to children. Now that recreational and medical marijuana are legal in many states, it's easy to forget that, during the War on Drugs in the 1970s and the 1980s and into the 1990s, mere possession of that drug often meant jail, and distribution of it to others—even simply passing a lit joint to a friend—virtually guaranteed a prison sentence. In one such case, my public defense client, who was in his early twenties, was tagged with a felony conviction and a year in prison simply for *offering* a joint to a couple of teenage buddies; no marijuana ever changed hands.

I decided to make dope cases a priority. To develop some skill in defending drug prosecutions, and because I supported the legalization of weed, I joined the National Organization for the Reform of Marijuana Laws (NORML). For a few years I was the only Vermont lawyer who dared become a member of that organization; it was considered somehow seditious and dangerous, something that might attract police attention and get you busted. Many people I knew smoked marijuana, and some grew it in their backyards, so a certain amount of wariness was realistic, especially when one's professional license was at stake.

I smoked dope only on rare occasions and in the wilds of Sandgate, which has no police force and is a half-hour from the closest Vermont State Police barracks. Cops often get lost in Sandgate. Late one night, Ellen and I were awakened by a car coming up our long, uphill driveway. I grabbed my home-defense shotgun and Ellen went downstairs to answer the door. It was a pair of State Police Troopers on a domestic violence call, far away from the correct house. Ellen gave them directions, and fortunately the officers never saw me, armed and lurking in the shadows on our second-floor landing.

I became a regular at NORML's continuing legal education events, and I made friends with Keith Stroup, the organization's courageous and outspoken founder. I joined the NORML Legal Committee and went with my wife Ellen to its meetings in Key West, Florida and Aspen Colorado, towns where smoking marijuana was accepted. Freed from the specter of arrest and possible disbarment, many of the NORML lawyers walked around stoned to the eyeballs. Others disapproved, viewing such behavior as reckless and unprofessional.

After one of these meetings, Ellen and I were invited to dinner at the Aspen home of a famous and wealthy Texas drug lawyer (he'd represented the Panamanian dictator and drug lord Manuel Noriega, among others), where we were served a salad made with fresh marijuana leaves instead of lettuce, along with high-end, $500-a-bottle tequila with worms in it. The late Aspen writer Hunter Thompson was there, and he took a shine to Ellen—too much of one, I thought—and he drove her around town in his DeLorean sports car. Stoned, naturally.

The usual defense to drug arrests is that the police have committed an illegal search under the Fourth Amendment of the United States Constitution and (in Vermont) Article 11 of the State Constitution, which has stricter rules about these things than its federal cognate. When you win a motion to suppress the evidence (the dope) based on a constitutional violation, the case is dismissed. But when there is good police work, which does happen, that defense isn't available.

There is another angle that I learned, which drove the prosecutors crazy—not the main goal in criminal defense, but something I liked doing in drug cases during the bad old days, when jail sentences were the system's reflexive response to substance abuse. The prosecutors were so sure of their own righteousness and purity that I will admit, like bad boy Eddie Haskell in the TV series *Leave It to Beaver*, I derived pleasure from monkey-wrenching their efforts.

A part of the state's burden in drug cases is to prove beyond a reasonable doubt that the alleged illegal substance (which was almost always marijuana in my law practice before heroin replaced it as the favorite of street dealers) is in fact what the prosecution claims it to be. That's not as easy as one might think—that is, if the defense lawyer chooses to contest that element of the criminal charge. I realized that to be effective I had to do that. Dig we must, and dig I did, deep into the foreign, rarified earth of chemistry lab science.

This wasn't easy for me; I'd gotten a D-minus in third-year math in high school, and I had never taken a lab science course, just elementary physics and chemistry. In college, I stayed up all night standing in an outdoor line of freshmen seeking to avoid taking a lab science by signing up for a course on human evolution that had only 150 slots. The course's creator, the anthropology professor William Howells, publicly predicted that it would attract "all the least energetic minds in the university."

My roommate Ted Hammett and I were seventy-fifth and seventy-sixth in the line. A freshman who appointed himself to count and record our places, thereby to prevent anyone from getting into the course by cutting into line surreptitiously, became known during his student career by the name of "List Man" or, if he passed you by on the street, as "Hey, List!"

Ignoramus that I was and still am in science and math, I learned that prosecutors and their helpers, to prove that a substance is in fact marijuana, must rely on certain field and lab tests, all of which have flaws that make them vulnerable to attack, flaws that I studied assiduously.

The first method, still used by police, is the Duquenois-Levine (D-L) "presumptive" test. This is a field test used by officers, who place the sample of supposed marijuana into a pipette containing a chemical solution, which will turn purple when mixed with the drug.

This test is often used to establish "probable cause," the required legal predicate for a judge to issue an arrest or search warrant. The problem with this test, which was developed during the 1930s, is that it isn't specific for marijuana. Over-the-counter cough medications such as Sucrets, and many innocuous plants including ordinary tea, will sometimes produce positive test results. A 1972 study of D-L's accuracy found that twelve *legal* plants out of forty randomly chosen by researchers tested positive for marijuana.

The manufacturers of D-L test kits take pains to inform the law enforcement user of their limitations when it comes to accuracy. The instructions for the popular "Nark II" test kits warn in all-capital letters: "ALL TEST RESULTS MUST BE CONFIRMED BY AN APPROVED ANALYTICAL LABORATORY!" The reason being that a positive test result "may occur" with "both legal and illegal products."

The company warns that the D-L test "*SHOULD NOT BE USED*" in states where hemp (used to make clothing) or CBD oil are legal, as "everything tested will be positive." Nonetheless, police continue to rely on the D-L test, and unless defense lawyers object to it on scientific grounds, courts will admit the results into evidence for the purpose of validating the grounds for arrests or search warrants. I always objected to the use of this test, with some but not universal success. Habit sometimes overcomes scientific validity.

Most jurisdictions, including Vermont, send suspected illegal drugs to the state crime laboratory for further analysis after a formal charge is brought. These purportedly more "scientific" lab tests are fraught with problems that I discovered on my own by reading and by taking the pretrial depositions, under oath, of the state lab technicians involved, who were surprised that I cared about the details of their work.

Vermont's testing protocols provided that the lab technician must first examine a sample of a substance alleged to be marijuana under a microscope, to look for the presence of cystolithic, or "bear claw," hairs. Like the Duquenois-Levine "presumptive" test, however, the bear-claw test isn't specific for marijuana. Such hairs are found on many other plants, including hops, oregano, thyme, and rosemary. There may be as many as 200,000 plants with cystolithic hairs. One study could not differentiate such hairs on marijuana from those on eighty-two other plants microscopically examined. Thus, there is no scientific support for the proposition that this test can determine with accuracy that a plant is marijuana.

Assuming that the lab technician detects the presence of bear-claw hairs in the sample, the next test generally performed is thin-layer chromatography (TLC). This test uses a glass plate that has been coated with dried silica or a similar absorbent substance. Solutions are made with a "known" sample of marijuana and one or more of the "unknown" samples suspected to be marijuana. Drops of the solutions are placed side-by-side on the plate, and they travel up the silica-treated glass by capillary action. The technician then observes whether the unknown sample rises on the plate up to the same level as the known sample and whether their colors appear to be the same. If, in the opinion of the tester, both distance of travel and hue are identical, the unknown sample is deemed to be marijuana.

This test isn't scientific because it isn't truly objective. It relies on the lab technician's "eyeballing" of the glass plate and a subjective judgment as to the height and color of the tested samples. Moreover, substances other than marijuana, such as coffee, basil, and tobacco products, have in the past produced false positives using thin-layer chromatography. Even the proponents of TLC admit that it is reliable only as a presumptive test; it cannot distinguish accurately marijuana from legal products such as CBD.

During one of the depositions that I took of the state lab technicians under oath, I experienced a flash of insight, a weird kind of Beat Generation Zen *satori*, that blew my mind and his. I asked the technician how he knew that the so-called known sample used in testing is itself marijuana. The tech responded that the known sample is obtained from a commercial source, and to confirm its identity it is tested against a known sample previously obtained from that source and used by the lab.

The problem here is that, going backward in time, eventually there will be a known sample that can't be tested against a previous known sample, because it is the first of the known samples, and so there exists nothing to test it against. It follows that the validity of the known sample is based on speculation and blind faith, not science. The technician agreed with great reluctance that there is some logic to this line of reasoning—an admission that drove the prosecutors bonkers and caused them to use the far more expensive gas chromatography testing method in my felony marijuana cases.

With gas chromatography/mass spectrometry, the sample to be tested is heated into a gaseous form, its various components are analyzed, and a graph is produced, all by the same expensive machine. The instrument contains a "library" of graphs for various chemical components, and the test sample graph is compared to the machine's library graph to determine its chemical identity.

In my experience, while the graphs produced when marijuana is tested are very similar to those in the machine's library, they are never exactly the same, an argument the lawyer can use to suggest the existence of a reasonable doubt as to whether the sample that's been tested is marijuana. In addition, the machine's library is a form of hearsay, as it is an implicit out-of-court statement (in this case, that the graph in the library accurately depicts marijuana) used to prove the truth of the matter asserted (that the tested sample is in fact marijuana). The library's admissibility into evidence, required for admission of the test result, may be attacked as inadmissible hearsay. I would argue to prosecutors in plea negotiations that the state, in order to successfully admit the results into evidence, would probably have to call the machine's designer and manufacturer to the witness stand to give expert opinions on its reliability and the accuracy of its library, a costly hurdle that would make convictions substantially more difficult.

The result was that prosecutors, in many of my marijuana cases, would offer me no-jail plea agreements rather than risk a loss on the testing issue, which could have had systemic consequences. They would reduce felony charges to misdemeanors or agree to deferred sentences, which resulted in the expungement of the conviction from the criminal record after a period of successful probation.

But the pro-police, antidrug atmosphere in Vermont was overwhelmingly bad. So much so that the district court in Brattleboro, which is considered the most liberal town in an extremely liberal state, was imposing a condition of pretrial release for all those arrested for drug offenses "to submit to give a sample of your urine when requested by a law enforcement officer and pay for the analysis of same." At the request of the Vermont chapter of the American Civil Liberties Union, I appealed this release condition to the Vermont Supreme Court, which held, in a one-page decision, that forcing people who haven't been convicted of a crime to undergo random drug tests violates the search-and-seizure provisions of the U.S. and State Constitutions.

In *State v. Kenneth Sargent* and *State v. Corina Reagan* (issued on November 17, 1989), the court ruled in an unsigned "rescript" opinion: "Because of the unusually personal and sensitive nature of the condition, we hold that, as written, the condition is too broad and not based on sufficiently specific standards and guidelines."

Leslie Williams, who was director of the Vermont ACLU chapter, hailed the decision as "another victory for the right to privacy."

The fact that a Vermont Court would even consider imposing such a sweeping release condition forcing people to undergo drug testing on the whim of any cop at any time, and then requiring them to pay for it, demonstrates the extent to which the War on Drugs skewed the justice system and made it difficult for drug defendants, especially people of color and those without funds, to receive the fairer treatment accorded to others with money and white privilege.

A PRIME EXAMPLE OF THIS FLAW in our system is a case that I stumbled into in 1999, which exemplified the continuing hysteria and prosecutorial blindness and overreaching that the War on Drugs had wrought.

This was a prosecution where my client was innocent of the charges, which were for distributing marijuana and engaging in a conspiracy to do so. In the trial of such a case, it wouldn't have helped strategically to attack the lab analysis, because that defense is inconsistent (in my opinion, anyway) with saying "I didn't do it." In other words, I was prepared to concede that the marijuana was real, because no illegal drugs were ever found in my client's possession or in his apartment, and our whole case rested on the truthful proposition that my client was a "fall guy" wrongfully accused by others to protect their guilty friends, the real drug suppliers.

I happened to be the only defense lawyer present one afternoon in the Bennington Criminal Division when a 22-year-old man named Hugo Nieto, a Spanish-speaking native of Ecuador, was brought into court in shackles.

David Howard, the presiding judge, asked me to represent Mr. Nieto for the purpose of arraignment (although I was no longer a contract public defender), and of course I said yes; refusing such a request is considered extremely bad form.

The charges were serious. The state claimed that Hugo had sold marijuana to two students on the campus of Bennington Junior High School, where he had been working for a couple of years as a janitor. Vermont law provided for a heavy sentencing enhancement for selling or distributing even small amounts of marijuana to a minor, plus another, separate enhancement for doing that on school property.

The result was that Hugo was facing a possible sentence of forty-four years in the event of a conviction involving only a quarter of an ounce of marijuana, with certain deportation after that, even though he was a legal resident with a "Green Card" that allowed him to work. The state argued for bail of $100,000 given the length of sentence and the incentive for Mr. Nieto to flee. Hearing this, Hugo burst into tears. How could anyone calling himself a defense lawyer refuse to help this poor guy?

Hugo and I went into one of the rooms reserved for lawyer–client conversations. Hugo knew almost no English (he called me "Mr. Steve" throughout the case), which left me at a disadvantage, because my training in languages other than English was limited to Latin and Ancient Greek. To make matters worse, the only interpreter available for the arraignment was the Latina wife of the arresting officer in the case, Sergeant Ronald Elwell of the Bennington Police Department. Given that relationship, my conversation with Mr. Nieto was abbreviated. I was concerned that, despite Mrs. Elwell's sincere promise of confidentiality, the temptation would be too great for her to refrain from sharing with her husband my communications with Hugo.

Judge Howard reduced the bail from an initial $100,000 set by a different judge, Paul Hudson, to $20,000, a sum that the family was never able to raise,; the judge refused to reduce the amount further despite my entreaties. After Hugo entered a not-guilty plea, the judge remanded him to the regional jail in Rutland pending trial. This facility was far safer for Hugo than a maximum-security joint, but it is a stupefyingly boring and depressing place to live.

My relationship with David Howard wasn't all that great. We had worked together on Chopper Lake's murder case, but after that we'd drifted apart professionally. As time went by in his role of Bennington County's head public defender, particularly after Ray Bolton retired and Bill Wright took over as State's Attorney, David dealt with the prosecutors in what seemed to me to be an increasingly obsequious and deferential fashion that I found distasteful, a feeling that I found difficult to hide. In my experience, clients often view defense lawyer chumminess with prosecutors as a sign that "the fix is in" against them.

My approach to dealing with prosecutors was to be polite, but always to maintain a certain distance. They were opponents, not friends. They wanted to put my clients in jail. When Bill Wright took over as State's Attorney, the plea offers from his office became far tougher and, from my standpoint, fair. I organized a response from the private bar to combat this new policy. At my urging, we decided that at the weekly criminal court "calendar call" (during which all lawyers and their clients are present to discuss the status of pending cases with the judge and prosecutors), defense counsel would tell the court that we were "ready for trial" in every case. No plea bargains. Soon this tactic had the effect of clogging the system so dramatically that the plea offers became more reasonable. But the public defender's office wouldn't participate in this effective cabal.

In fairness, I'm sure that David Howard sincerely believed that his approach was the best way to get good results for his many clients, and he did well at that. Moreover, to have any chance of the judgeship he craved from Governor Howard Dean, David needed the imprimatur of State's Attorney Bill Wright.

Consistent with the servile persona that David Howard had adopted as his technique to deal with prosecutors, he unwittingly projected among his other colleagues at the bar a kind of sorry, shamefaced demeanor, as if to apologize for being such a wimp.

One morning I was assigned to represent a defendant charged with the unarmed robbery of a woman whose purse and money were ripped from her grasp in downtown Bennington. My client insisted that he was the victim of mistaken identity, and so with his assent I took a huge chance and arranged for an on-the-spot lineup at the courthouse.

The robbery victim stood inside a conference room with prosecutor Bill Wright and me, looking out of a panoramic window toward a group of shuffling "suspects," including my client, that we had assembled outdoors in the court parking lot. Without hesitation, the victim picked the guilty-looking David Howard as the robber. My client walked, right then and there, out of the courthouse to freedom. Poor David couldn't see the humor in all of this when I kidded him about it.

Now, equipped with a newly acquired "don't mess with me" judicial demeanor, replete with a multitude of different frown faces when displeased, David Howard was the boss of the Bennington Criminal Division and of my case with Hugo Nieto, which for sure would be a jury trial. Hugo had to win this case or be sent back to Ecuador after serving a long prison term. Even if the prosecutors had offered Hugo a lenient plea bargain, which they never did, he wouldn't have accepted it, because he was steadfast in his claim of innocence. Except in unusual circumstances, it's unethical for a criminal defense lawyer to allow a client who claims innocence to plead guilty.

I believed Hugo, and I still do. He did not commit this crime. But I had to cope somehow with the reality that, as the old saying goes, the state wanted to put this brown-skinned man not simply *in* jail but *under* the jail.

The police reports revealed a big problem with our case from the defense standpoint. After Hugo's arrest, the cops searched his apartment, finding nothing incriminating. But their drug-sniffing German Shepherd had "alerted" on his dresser and his jacket by sitting down in front of them.

By the way, I have often wondered why the Vermont State Police and many other police forces use German Shepherds, a breed used in Nazi concentration camps and death camps, to detect contraband, when Labrador Retrievers, who are sweet and nonthreatening, are used in airports and customs offices for the same work. I suppose it's because German Shepherds are so amenable to being trained to attack, that we "subjects," as cops like to call civilians in their official reports, are afraid of them.

In my opinion, this intimidation factor is unnecessary and lends less credibility to the dog's performance. Aren't ordinary people more likely to relate to and trust America's most popular breed, the Labrador, than a potentially vicious guard animal who will bite you on command?

There weren't any drugs in Hugo's apartment, either in the dresser drawers or in his jacket or anywhere else, for that matter. There were no marijuana paraphernalia, such as rolling papers or roach clips or pipes or bongs. However, the police were prepared to testify that, in their opinion, based solely on the dog's alerts, illegal drugs had been there at some point.

At our first status conference, I asked Judge Howard to allocate state funds so that I could hire an expert witness to contest this highly prejudicial opinion. I argued that I could locate an expert witness to testify that drug dogs are far from infallible in their sniffing ability. Independent research on the ability of dogs to detect the presence of trace amounts of drugs has shown that "canines," as police refer to them, are sometimes prone to alert due to cues unconsciously given by their handlers. Many dogs will alert when they sense that this is what their handlers want them to do, even in instances when there have never been any illegal drugs there.

I added that that the defendant and his family were unable to afford an expert witness. Hugo was indigent, of course, and I told Judge Howard that, after a small initial retainer, the family was unable to pay me anything further. I said that I fully intended to continue representing Mr. Nieto to the end of the case pro bono, thereby saving the state substantial funds, but that we needed the money to hire an expert.

Judge Howard denied this request.

After the status conference, a local newspaper reporter asked me why I had decided to continue to represent Mr. Nieto when a lengthy trial was certain, without being paid.

I almost never commented in response to a question like that. But I thought I should tell the reporter something truthful that might help Hugo, who had been the subject of a torrent of unfavorable publicity and community disgust as a result. The next day, the *Bennington Banner* quoted me as saying: "I took the case because I felt there was a real possibility for a miscarriage of justice. It's easy to blame someone like Mr. Nieto. He doesn't speak English and his skin color is different. . . . I felt there might be a rush to judgment."

To have any chance of winning the case, I knew I had to do something to get rid of the dog-sniff baloney. I filed a motion to suppress that evidence based on fundamental fairness and lack of relevance. I didn't have an expert witness, but I found some federal court decisions to the effect that 99 percent of all U.S. paper currency was then contaminated with cocaine, to a degree that drug dogs will always alert on it. I argued that this shows the irrelevance of a dog-sniff alert in cases where no drugs are found on the premises or the defendant's person.

At the motion hearing, I called as a witness Hugo's uncle, Jose Viera, who lived in the same apartment with Hugo and who had worked for many years as a janitor in the Bennington School system. He had been Hugo's immigration sponsor, felt that he had a responsibility to look after him, and believed that he was under a legal requirement to do so under the immigration laws—and to report him to authorities if he strayed.

Mr. Viera testified that he had never seen any marijuana or other illegal drugs in the apartment and that he had never seen Hugo use controlled substances. On the issue of the dog alerts, Jose said that he knew firsthand that Hugo had bought his chest of drawers used at a tag sale, and he was present when Hugo found and retrieved his jacket from a school garbage can, where a student had discarded it.

From this I argued that, even assuming the dresser and jacket had contained marijuana at one time, the German Shepherd's alerts didn't implicate Hugo, so that their evidentiary value was minimal to nonexistent and their use at trial would be unfairly prejudicial. Judge Howard granted my motion, and I felt that we had a chance. Nonetheless, in an effort to avoid a trial, I hired a retired cop to polygraph Hugo at the jail. His family was able to come up with the couple of hundred dollars needed for that. Unfortunately, the test was deemed "inconclusive."

In retrospect, I think that this was because of the language barrier. I wasn't allowed in the room. Had I been there, I would have slowly and carefully repeated and explained the polygrapher's questions to Hugo. Neither was a professional translator permitted to attend. If Hugo had passed, I would have shown the results to the prosecutors, whose usual practice was then to arrange for another test with a Vermont State Police polygrapher and to consider dismissal if both tests were exculpatory.

Judge Howard allowed my motion for a jury questionnaire that I had prepared, primarily out of concern for racial prejudice. Many on the jury panel were honest and up-front with their racist views. A question I asked was: "Do you think it's more likely that a recent immigrant from South America would sell drugs than a person who was born here?" One of the frank answers was: "Yes, because that's what they do."

There were other, similarly racist responses. To the credit of one of the prosecutors, David Fenster, who is now a judge in Middlebury, he agreed that the erstwhile jurors with obvious racial bias based on their questionnaires could be excluded from the panel for cause. But people often won't admit to racism or are unaware of it or go out of their way to conceal it, and I'm reasonably sure, especially given the outcome of the trial, that several of these closet racists were selected to be on our jury.

I made a motion to dismiss the entire jury pool of a hundred or so because every single one of them was white and my client had brown skin. I pointed out that we had a lily-white panel even though two or three percent of Bennington County residents were people of color. The problem, I argued, was that the jury pool was selected primarily from Department of Motor Vehicle records, a technique that excluded many low-income minority folks who didn't own a car. The county should have included lists of people on welfare and food stamps and Medicaid.

Judge Howard's reaction was, "How do you expect me to find minority jurors?" My answer was that the court should send law enforcement officers out on the "highways and byways" to look for people of color and bring them to court. That is exactly what is done when it turns out that the jury pool is too small for a particular trial and more people are needed. Motion denied. I expected that. This was something I could use for ammunition on appeal, should an appeal become necessary.

I awoke sick on the day of trial, with the flu or a very bad cold, I'm not sure which. The stress of preparing and worrying about my client's fate, especially for an innocent client, had rendered me susceptible. I wasn't about to ask for a continuance of the trial, though. With the jurors summoned, the witnesses subpoenaed, and my client incarcerated for eleven months awaiting trial, the judge would have denied a postponement unless I had been so ill as to require hospitalization. Armed with aspirin, nasal spray, and a lot of Kleenex, I arrived in court ready to go forward, and the high stakes for Hugo gave me the energy I needed to do my job.

The trial took three days, with the testimony of seventeen witnesses. Here is a reprise of the State's case.

Based on a telephone call from an anonymous source to the principal of Bennington Junior High School, Bennington police officers conducted a stakeout at the school. One afternoon, they saw two male students, Michael Radcliffe and Nathan Spencer, both age 15, leave the school and engage in a brief conversation with Hugo, who was working outdoors. Officer Paul J. Doucette (who at this writing is Bennington's police chief) stopped and searched the students when they walked downtown. Doucette seized approximately a quarter of an ounce of marijuana from them, parceled out in ten tiny Baggies, sometimes referred to as "nickel bags," seemingly for sale. Doucette radioed Sergeant Ronald Elwell, who was stationed at the school and immediately detained Mr. Nieto.

The two students fingered Hugo as the source of the marijuana. However, when I cross-examined the police officers, they admitted that they had conversed by radio about the bust and that the two boys could overhear what was being said. Sergeant Elwell had asked Doucette *before the boys had been questioned*: "Did they get the marijuana from the janitor?"

When the cops interrogated the boys at the police station, the questioning was similarly leading in nature. The police asked "Did you get the marijuana from Hugo?" instead of "Who gave you the marijuana?" The suggestiveness of this questioning telegraphed to the students not only whom they easily could implicate but also whom the police apparently *wanted* them to accuse as their source of supply. That is, a brown-skinned, Spanish-speaking, low-caste kid from Ecuador, a mere janitor who was out of place and an easy target in a place like Bennington.

The boys testified, but their answers as to their history of dealings with Mr. Nieto on times, quantities, and prices were inconsistent with one another and substantially different from the testimony that I had elicited at their pretrial depositions. One of the students testified that he had been buying marijuana from as many as ten different people in town, whereas in their depositions they had stated under oath that Mr. Nieto had been their only source. No witness other than these bad boys had ever seen Hugo possess or use marijuana. Jose Viera again testified that he had been living with Hugo, and he was not a marijuana or drug user. Darlene Jones, Hugo's supervisor at the school, testified that on one occasion she thought that she had seen Hugo and one of the boys engage in some kind of hand-to-hand transaction. But on my cross-examination, she admitted that she was too far away to be sure of that, and it could have just been a handshake.

Thus, the state's case depended almost entirely upon whether the jury believed the two boys, Radcliffe and Spencer, who were caught red-handed with marijuana that had been packaged for sale and who had been given lenient juvenile court treatment for their offense.

Reporter Todd Spivak, in his summary of the trial published in the daily *Bennington Banner* on April 14, 2000, suggested that the testimony of Radcliffe and Spencer was not credible. "Contradictions were rampant in Radcliffe and Spencer's testimony. Their statements under oath in the depositions about how much marijuana they allegedly bought from Nieto and how many transactions they made were drastically different from their court testimony."

But it was the jury that would have to make this determination. In final argument, I told the panel that Hugo Nieto was "the perfect fall guy" because of his brown skin, broken English, and different culture, that no one had ever seen him use or possess drugs, and that Spencer and Radcliffe had lied to protect their real source and to ensure that they would get lenient treatment.

John Lavoie, the lead prosecutor, whose job was to travel around Vermont trying major drug cases, argued with respect to the boy accusers that "they get the big stuff right and disagree on the details."

The jury was out for six hours, and they returned to tell Judge Howard that they were hopelessly deadlocked. Howard declared a mistrial and sent the jury home and Hugo Nieto back to jail. The judge told us that the vote was 8–4 for acquittal on the substantive drug distribution counts and 8–4 for conviction on the conspiracy counts. This contradiction made little sense to me, but the jury had spoken—sort of.

A year later, on the eve of the scheduled retrial, two previously unknown witnesses came forward and told the defense and the prosecution that they would testify that they knew that Spencer and Radcliffe had lied about who had sold them the marijuana. It wasn't Hugo.

Rather than retry a case that was problematic from the outset, prosecutor John Lavoie called me and David Silver, a talented lawyer and friend I'd asked to be my co-counsel on retrial, and told us that the state would dismiss all charges on the express condition that we promise to refrain from making any comment to the press. I figured that the prosecutors were concerned that we would criticize them for holding Hugo in prison for nearly two years for a crime he didn't commit.

Done. The case was over. State's Attorney Bill Wright told the *Bennington Banner* that his case had started "unraveling" when he spoke with the new witnesses. He then reinterviewed Spencer and Radcliffe, whose stories changed again. Bill Wright added, with apparent self-congratulation that I considered undeserved: "We have an obligation to uncover all evidence related to a case," and "that's why we dismissed" it.

Would the prosecution team have persisted as long as it did with such a weak case while the defendant languished behind bars for lack of bail if he had white skin?

No, I don't think so. Hugo Nieto was released after serving one month shy of two years in jail because his family didn't have the money to post bail set by Judge David Howard at $20,000. Ironically, this was the same bail amount that the court had set in Chopper Lake's murder case, on which David Howard and I had worked when he was a public defender.

Hugo's case was, after all, only a marijuana charge, where no one had been physically injured. I believe that this man was punished summarily for race and poverty. Based on my experience, if Hugo Nieto had been white, his bail would have been far lower, or he would have been released on conditions, including periodic reporting in person to the police station and/or the wearing of a radio transmitter ankle bracelet and the surrender of his passport.

The bail system in this country should be abolished. Only demonstrably dangerous people should be incarcerated before trial, when defendants are presumed by law to be innocent and sometimes are—people like Hugo, people of color with no money.

In his native Spanish, Nieto told the *Bennington Banner* that he chose the Town of Bennington "because it looked like a nice quiet place to live. But look what happened to me. I wish I had stayed in New York. Maybe it's safer for me down there."

I hear you, Hugo. A 2021 statistical study by the Council for State Governments concluded that, while white and Black people use and sell drugs at the same rate, Black people in Vermont are *fourteen times more likely* to be prosecuted for drug offenses than whites, and they are significantly more likely to get prison sentences than whites when convicted.

The CSG report noted that this isn't just a Vermont problem: racial disparities in sentencing are a "persistent and pervasive feature of the U.S. criminal justice system." The November 28, 2021, edition of *VT Digger*, a daily electronic newspaper based in Vermont, in an article reporting the results of the CSG study, noted that "national research has found that Black people are more likely to be arrested, more likely to be charged, more likely to be convicted and more likely to receive longer sentences than white people—even when comparing across the same severity of crime."

This systemic racism is well-known to defense lawyers and their clients of color but is rejected by 90 percent of Republicans, who, according to an October 2018 Pew Research Study, deny that "the way racial and ethnic minorities are treated by the criminal justice system is a very big problem for the country."

CHAPTER 16

⚖

Defending Nature

Living with the animals on a remote Vermont mountainside changed the way I felt about Nature. Our south-facing home on 54.32 acres of land adjoined a state-designated "deer yard," a south-facing slope where whitetails bunch up together during the winter to get whatever warmth they can from the sunlight and one another. We dug a hole for a pond, lined it with clay, and filled it using the same spring that supplied our house with water.

Our pond attracted a (mostly) Peaceable Kingdom, reminiscent of the painting of that name by Edward Hicks, from tree frogs to turtles, to ducks, turkeys, and great blue herons, to deer family groups (as many as a dozen individuals at a time), coyotes, foxes, weasels, porcupines, raccoons, and black bears. Bears liked to knock the bird feeder off our deck, feast on black-oil sunflower seeds, and peer at us through windows and sliding glass doors.

My wife, Ellen, and I developed over time a kinship with the animals and the land, a mysterious closeness that's hard to understand fully except in ways biological. In 1984, the late Edward O. Wilson, a Harvard professor, field biologist, and the world's greatest expert on leafcutter ants, published a theory that he called "Biophilia." Wilson believed, and defended eloquently the view, that there is a genetically based, inherent human need to experience and identify with Nature.

Henry David Thoreau tells us in his essay *Walking*: "In Wildness is the preservation of the world." Edward O. Wilson took this thought a step further. Wildness, he said, is programmed into our brain cells and bodies, and a relationship with Nature is an essential, biologically driven imperative. So that "in Wildness" lies the preservation of our species as well as that of the world at large. As the conservation movement founder and writer John Muir telegraphically put it in his journal entry of September 4, 1908: "I only went out for a walk, and finally concluded to stay out till sundown, for going out, I found, was really going in."

Related to Biophilia is Deep Ecology, which posits that it should be "intuitively clear and obvious" that all life-forms, not just our own, are equally entitled to live and thrive and that it is wrong—both scientifically and as an ethical matter—to think of and place humans in an exalted position. The Norwegian philosopher Arne Naess contends in *Ecology, Community, and Lifestyle* (1989) that the prevailing anthropocentric view of the world is superficial and false and deprives us of "the deep pleasure and satisfaction we receive from close partnership with other forms of life. The attempt to ignore our dependence and to establish a master-slave role has contributed to the alienation of man from himself."

The Nature Conservancy's Bat Cave Preserve

I came to believe these things, and I decided that I should become involved in conservation efforts. I joined the Vermont chapter of The Nature Conservancy (TNC) and served as a trustee from 1990–1995 and as Vermont chapter president for the last three of those years. I volunteered to be the pro bono litigator for TNC-Vermont, and one of the cases that I handled for the organization, which never made it to court, was a righteous one that gave me some pleasure.

One of TNC-Vermont's goals was to acquire and set aside land for preserves, open to the public with prior permission for nonmotorized recreational activities, but each of which has a distinct conservation role. One of these is the Bat Cave Preserve in Dorset, which includes a deep cave where bats live and hibernate during the winter. Bats in the Northeast are scarce now due to a disease from a European fungus called "White Nose Syndrome," which has rendered many bat varieties threatened or endangered. The Dorset Bat Cave Preserve is surrounded by a buffer of more than two hundred acres of hardwood forest, including oak, maple, beech, and ironwood. TNC has posted the land with yellow metal signs attached to trees with wire, marking the boundaries and prohibiting trespassing. There is no mistaking these signs, which are everywhere, every 50 feet or so, at eye level.

Sometime around 1990, TNC land stewards discovered that the Bat Cave Preserve had been logged. They investigated by speaking with local loggers and sawmills, and they learned that the owner of forty adjoining acres of raw land had done this. The wrongdoer was a local guy whose hobby was playing polo.

Vermont has a "timber trespass" law that provides for an award of three times the fair market value of wood unlawfully cut, but the amount of money involved didn't come close to covering the damage to the land in its role as a TNC preserve, including the ecological need for a mature wooded buffer around the bat cave.

After extensive legal research, I learned that federal courts faced with damage to ecologically sensitive areas occasionally will award what are called "restoration damages," that is, the money necessary to rehabilitate the land to its former condition, even when the cost of that exceeds the land's fair market value. With that doctrine in mind, I asked TNC's forester to make a list of every tree unlawfully cut, noting its species and, by counting the rings on stumps, how old each tree had been.

Armed with that information, TNC at my request developed an estimate of the cost to remove all the stumps and fill each hole with a new tree of the same kind and age. This came to well over a million dollars. I wrote a demand letter to our neighboring landowner, complete with case citations and the estimate, promising that TNC was prepared to bring litigation that would seek restoration damages if we weren't able to come to terms forthwith.

My letter set forth a nonnegotiable settlement proposal: that the neighbor convey the entirety of his forty adjoining acres to TNC. This would expand the amount of land buffering the bat cave. Moreover, the forty acres had a market value of at least ten times that of the treble damages authorized by the Vermont timber trespass statute. Our trees (and his, which would become ours) would grow back eventually. He agreed to the deal.

The next time I encountered this (by now) former TNC neighbor was on a freezing winter morning inside an office suite in Manchester Village that I shared with two other lawyers. With a smile he asked me to make a tax-deductible contribution to his "nonprofit" polo club. I figured that my donation would be used to fund the feeding, housing, exercising, and grooming of polo ponies, as well as the hiring of appropriate "help" to shovel manure from the horse stalls and do other work deemed too low-caste for the jet-setter membership to do themselves. I knew this guy was baiting me, but I politely told him no thanks and left the office for a court date, waving him a long and permanent goodbye.

The Lamb Brook Case: Bears and Birds Versus Forest Service Clear-Cutting

The more I learned about forests as critical habitat for animals, as places where humans experience the gift of wild Nature, and as guardians against climate change via conversion of carbon dioxide to oxygen, the more I came to believe that The Nature Conservancy's approach, though worthy, wasn't enough. When I attended TNC conferences, I was able to meet the trustees of the national organization. Except for figureheads like General Norman Schwarzkopf, a garrulous fellow (now deceased) who seemed out of place except at the nightly cocktail parties, at which he drew crowds and was all smiles, TNC's national trustees were mostly executives working for polluters like car manufacturers, bent on "greenwashing" their company images. Their money bought us land, but reliance on polluter largesse troubled me.

The book *Clearcut: The Tragedy of Industrial Forestry* (1993), published by Sierra Club, propelled me into greater activism. I was surprised to learn that the entity most responsible for the abominable desecration that is clear-cutting is the United States Forest Service, an agency that promotes the removal of trees on publicly owned lands by selling them at below cost to timber companies, a form of corporate welfare that continues to this day. A study by the Center for Sustainable Economy found that, in FY 2013 through FY 2017, the government lost between $1.6 billion and $1.8 billion per year from the commercial logging of forests owned by the American people.

My belief that the clear-cutting of forests is a crime against Nature, and that our government is wrong to wreck essential wildlife habitat, led me to file a case against the U.S. Forest Service that took four years out of my life and ultimately cost me my job. But we won the litigation and saved the habitat, and that was far more important than any personal consequences of the battle.

In the spring of 1994, I called Jasper Carleton, head of the Biodiversity Legal Foundation, to ask about opportunities to sue the Forest Service in Vermont. Jasper told me that Mat Jacobson, a member of Earth First! (whose motto was "No Compromise in Defense of Mother Earth"), was attacking timber sales on the Green Mountain National Forest by filing administrative appeals of agency logging projects. Working on his own, without legal counsel, Mat had been successful in stopping timber sales temporarily, but he was looking for a lawyer willing to help him take the next step by filing suit on the worst of those sales. I called Mat, and we met at a Manchester restaurant that no longer exists, The Mucky Duck.

Mat had been working under the banner of a regional conservation group, Preserve Appalachian Wilderness (PAW), but he was in the process of forming a new Vermont-oriented organization, Green Mountain Forest Watch. He gave me a preliminary overview of what he considered to be the most environmentally destructive of the Forest Service logging projects in the state, known as Lamb Brook. Mat gave me a copy of the agency's Environmental Assessment (EA), setting forth in detail the Forest Service plan for roadbuilding and logging this section of the Green Mountain National Forest.

Mat impressed me because, even though he had no legal training, he had been able to use the administrative appeals process to stymie the Forest Service bureaucracy in Vermont. As well as being a very bright guy, he had a sense of humor, an asset when attacking the federal government head-on, which is serious business and difficult and exhausting given the huge advantage the government has in money as well as the army of lawyers and expert witnesses it has on tap to crush the opposition. Mat told me about his recent graduation from Tufts University, where he went on the stage to receive his undergraduate diploma wearing a pair of enormous clown shoes. To the delight of almost everyone except his parents.

Fair warning: my account of the Lamb Brook litigation against the U.S. Forest Service is lengthy because the administrative record was interminably dense, and the litigation took four years from start to finish. The discussion is sometimes technical because of the plethora of scientific issues in the case. Please stick with it; I promise that it will be worth your while.

To BEGIN, Lamb Brook is a remote: 5,561 acres of wildlife habitat in the Green Mountain National Forest in the Town of Readsboro. It's bordered on the west by Vermont Route 8, which leads from the Town of Searsburg south to the Massachusetts border and the Town of Monroe.

The Forest Service proposal called for logging a total of 984 acres, clear-cutting 311.5 of those acres, thereby ripping away 3.033 million board feet of wood. That amount of wood is equivalent to a single board measuring 1 foot wide, 1 inch thick, and 574.4 *miles* long, stretching from Lamb Brook to the city of Raleigh, North Carolina.

The Forest Service plan also included an extension of Forest Road 266 (FR266), a 30-plus-foot-wide, heavily graveled road specifically designed for tons of commercial logging equipment, complete with deep ditches crisscrossed by huge culverts, for 1.3 miles straight into Lamb Brook's core wildlife area.

The Lamb Brook project would have destroyed an important area of black bear habitat. The Vermont Fish & Wildlife Department's Habitat Management Guidelines, with which Forest Service personnel were familiar and were placed into the project administrative record, made clear that the black bear "is close to what is considered a wilderness species" that is intolerant of human presence and that "needs vast undeveloped forestland for concealment and solitude." The Forest Service EA reacted by noting: "Numerous American beech trees within the project area exhibit bear claw scarring. The broad distribution of this scarring suggests that bears find security throughout the entire area. The State [Vermont Department of Natural Resources] has described the project area as having significant value to bears. Species sensitive to human disturbance, such as the black bear, would be negatively impacted by increased human presence and loss of remoteness."

The distinctive claw marks on the beech trees in Lamb Brook meant that bears were climbing them and feeding on beech nuts—a critical food source for the species during the fall and without which they are unable to reproduce. Bears climb the beech trees and pull their branches toward them, stripping them of nuts with their prehensile lips. In the process of doing that, they leave behind what are called "bear nests," made up of the branches they break as they sit in the trees and feed.

Neotropical migratory songbirds, including my personal favorite, the scarlet tanager, spend most of their lives in Central and South America. They fly north annually to the United States and Canada to breed and raise their young during summer before returning home, an astonishingly hazardous and difficult round trip. These are "deep woods" species, which require large blocks of undisturbed forests to reproduce.

In the year 2000, after the conclusion of the Lamb Brook litigation, the U.S. government adopted the Neotropical Migratory Bird Conservation Act, which includes a congressional finding that these birds "provide invaluable environmental, economic, recreational, and aesthetic benefits to the United States" and that they are "are in decline, and some have declined to the point that their long-term survival in the wild is in jeopardy; *and the primary reason for the decline in the populations of those species is habitat loss and degradation*" (emphasis added).

The Forest Service project would have had a devastating effect on the ability of neotropical migratory songbirds to reproduce successfully in Lamb Brook. Industrial-scale roads like FR266 serve as corridors for cowbirds and racoons to reach the nests of the neotropicals. Cowbirds lay their eggs in the nests of songbirds and abandon them to their care. Cowbird young are larger and stronger than the neotropical babies, who do not survive the competition for food. Raccoons climb the trees, find the nests, and eat the eggs.

Roads also hurt neotropicals by creating forest "edges," which act as a haven for the predators and lessen the area available for migratory songbirds. The wider the road, the more efficient and devastating it is as a predation corridor, and the resulting "edge effect" is similarly severe.

Thus, the extension of FR266, the 30-foot-wide truck road into the forest core of songbird breeding habitat, represented a "double whammy" to neotropical migratory songbirds. Moreover, the clear-cutting of more than 300 acres, as the agency proposed, would have killed outright many breeding pairs of birds and eliminated their breeding habitat.

THE FOREST SERVICE CALCULATED that its timber sale would lose $34,600, a tab that the taxpayers would have to pick up. The agency's lowball expense estimate did not include the overhead costs associated with the activities of scores of Forest Service employees or of the hyper-aggressive legal defense of the project, provided on the taxpayer's dime by the Vermont United States Attorney's office and the chief of its Civil Division, Helen Toor, a highly skilled and extremely intelligent graduate of the University of Chicago Law School.

There is no law (except in cases involving officially designated wilderness areas) that provides a means to stop a terrible project like Lamb Brook on the merits, no matter how awful its impacts. The National Environmental Policy Act (NEPA) doesn't deal with substance—only procedure. If a federal agency honestly and fully divulges all the destructive aspects of a proposal, it has complied with NEPA.

Yet there is an understandable bureaucratic incentive to conceal the bad. Full disclosure of environmental problems may generate widespread opposition, leading to defeat of the project through public and political pressure. Agencies are known to succumb to the resulting temptation to lie and cover up, and when they get caught doing this, it sometimes provides public-interest organizations with the ammunition needed to win a NEPA case in federal court.

Here is how this procedural statute works. If the Forest Service's Environmental Assessment of an action reveals no environmental problems of any import, NEPA permits the agency to issue what is called a Finding of No Significant Impact (FONSI), along with a Decision Notice (DN), and the project may go forward.

If, however, the EA reveals the existence of significant impacts, the law requires and the judiciary will sometimes order that the agency conduct a full Environmental Impact Statement (EIS), a much more detailed, time-consuming, and expensive study, before it may proceed. Sometimes an agency will abandon a project rather than expending the time and energy needed for an EIS. From our perspective, at the very least an EIS would result in delay, during which public and political opposition to the project could be organized.

To stop a project under NEPA in federal court, plaintiffs must prove that the agency's decision to issue a DN and FONSI instead of doing an EIS is "arbitrary, capricious, and contrary to law." These strong words create a tough and exacting evidentiary burden, one that few plaintiffs are able to meet, especially given the federal judiciary's historical reluctance to interfere with decisions made by the executive branch.

One of the first decisions required in litigation such as this is, Who are the willing plaintiffs best suited to carry the environmentalist flag into battle?

The choice of plaintiffs also has legal significance in a case against the federal government. To establish what is called legal "standing" to sue, we needed plaintiffs who would suffer actual harm were the Lamb Brook logging and roadbuilding to go forward; mere disagreement on policy grounds isn't enough.

In 1972, in the book *Should Trees Have Standing? Law, Morality, and the Environment*, Christopher D. Stone contended that the standing rule should be modified to allow courts to give Nature the "standing" necessary to defend herself. The only United States Supreme Court Justice ever to endorse this approach was the late William O. Douglas, a lover of Nature who in dissent in the case of *Sierra Club v. Morton* (1972), said that "there should be a federal rule that allow[s] environmental issues to be litigated before federal agencies or federal courts in the name of the inanimate object about to be despoiled, defaced, or invaded by roads and bulldozers and where injury is the subject of public outrage. Contemporary public concern for protecting nature's ecological equilibrium should lead to the conferral of standing upon environmental objects to sue for their own preservation." (Justice Douglas also said in his dissent that the U.S. Forest Service "has been notorious for its alignment with timber companies.")

To prove legal standing under current law, we recruited as plaintiffs several local people who hiked, birdwatched, and hunted in the area who truthfully could assert that the Lamb Brook project would harm their customary use of the land. Enlisting the support of environmental organizations, who get standing by proving that their individual members will be harmed by a project, was also key. A lawsuit of this kind carries more weight and credibility with the federal judiciary when the lead plaintiffs are well-known groups with large memberships who are viewed generally as responsible.

Mat and I scrambled to get agreement from several conservation nonprofits to become plaintiffs. I thought that the best approach was to pick the National Audubon Society as the first named plaintiff because of its 500,000 members and reputation for reasonableness. The public doesn't think of Audubon members, usually older folks armed only with binoculars, as bomb-throwing radicals. Mat and I spoke to Brock Evans, then an Audubon vice president who at this writing is still active in the conservation world, and he agreed to allow us to place Audubon at the top of the plaintiff list. Members who frequented Lamb Brook would suffer "actual harm" because the population of songbirds they watched there would be decimated or eliminated. Such "actual harm" would confer legal standing on their organization.

The Wilderness Society, Sierra Club, as well as Mat's new group, Green Mountain Forest Watch, and a few lesser-known organizations were among the other plaintiffs we included. The shorthand title of the case became *National Audubon Society v. Hoffman.* Named defendant Terry Hoffman was the supervisor of the National Forest when the Lamb Brook project was conceived. We also sued James Bartelme, who replaced Hoffman as Forest Supervisor, Michael Schrotz, the district forest ranger for Lamb Brook, and the agency's regional boss, Floyd "Butch" Marita, based in Milwaukee.

A big issue for us was how to fund the litigation. I was working as lead counsel for no money up front. If we won the case, and the court were to find that the Forest Service's defense of the project was "substantially unjustified," there was a possibility that I could recover a legal fee from the government under a statute, the Equal Access to Justice Act. But Mat had to be paid something for his time, and Green Mountain Forest Watch had overhead in the form of rent for a tiny, down-and-out office whose entrance was an outdoor stairway in an alley next to a loading dock, plus other day-to-day expenses.

Mat and I met with Frank Hatch, of Boston and Rupert, Vermont, to ask for help. Frank had been the Republican minority leader of the Massachusetts House of Representatives, and in retirement he devoted his life to giving away family money of his own and that of his wife, Serena "Bambi" Merck Hatch. Frank became very liberal politically in his later years, supporting organizations on the left such as the National Abortion Rights Action League. He served on the board of the Natural Resources Defense Council as well.

Through a nonprofit family foundation, Frank funneled us the seed money needed to survive while we sued the Forest Service. It took guts for this life-long Republican to fund Green Mountain Forest Watch, which advocated "zero cut" of trees on public lands, a position then and now considered radical by the political establishment even though the goal is an excellent one—to restore large swaths of old-growth forests, so beautifully described by Henry David Thoreau in his book *The Maine Woods* (1864). There exist only miniscule remnants of old growth in New England today, and old-growth forests elsewhere, including the remaining majestic redwoods, which live in a narrow strip between Big Sur in California to southern Oregon are targets for powerful forest products corporations.

Eventually Mat was able to get other funding, from Ben and Jerry's ice cream, which was then a Vermont company, the Foundation for Deep Ecology, the Haymarket People's Fund, and from individual Vermont supporters and nonprofit businesses such as the Brattleboro Food Co-op.

The big national environmental groups gave us only token amounts. They then publicized the litigation and used it to raise money for themselves. But their names added legitimacy and weight to the case, and that was worth a lot to us, so Mat and I didn't object to being used in this fashion.

IN JUNE 1994, WE FILED OUR COMPLAINT in *National Audubon Society v. Hoffman* in the United States District Court for the District of Vermont. Our first Judge was Franklin S. "Bill" Billings Jr., from Woodstock, Vermont, who sat in Rutland. The son of a former Vermont governor, he was a Republican who had served as House Speaker in the Vermont legislature, then as an Associate Justice of the Vermont Supreme Court, then as its Chief Justice, after which President Reagan appointed him in 1984 to the federal bench. Judge Billings was of the "good old boy" school; he was tight with his Rutland lawyer friends, and in my experience he was hostile to civil rights.

In one case I had before Judge Billings, I sued a dog owner who lived next door to the Evergreen Inn, a summer resort in my hometown of Sandgate that catered to "Bubbies," elderly Jewish women from New York City. The defendant, Cliff Ferris, owned a dog he had trained to attack. One afternoon, two witnesses overheard Ferris yell to his dog to "Go get those damn Jews!" Cliff's hound obediently raced across his lawn onto to the Evergreen Inn property and bit my Jewish "Bubbie" client in the leg.

Dog bites can result in serious complications, including persistent infections and pain, and my client, who was in her mid-eighties, never fully healed. I sued Cliff Ferris, and I sought compensation for the bite, including my client's medical bills and pain and suffering, plus further damages based on the defendant's antisemitic motivation and his grotesque violation of my client's civil rights.

On the day of trial, just before jury selection, Judge Billings called counsel into his chambers, and he asked "good old boy" opposing counsel, the veteran Rutland insurance company lawyer John "Zawie" Zawistoski, if he had a motion to make. Zawie obliged by asking Judge Billings to throw out the civil rights violation, even though I had won a previous written motion to dismiss the case on that issue filed by Zawie. I argued to Judge Billings that he had already decided this legal point in our favor, and I told him that I had two witnesses present and ready to testify that they saw and heard Cliff Ferris order his dog to "Go get those damn Jews!" But to no avail. Billings granted Zawie's oral motion without citing a basis for his ruling, and he suggested that we make further efforts to settle the case before assembling the jury.

Antisemitism was the heart of our case, and Judge Billings had at the eleventh hour scuttled it, for no legal reason that he was willing or able articulate or that I could fathom, though I suspected that a reluctance to delve publicly into the existence of hatred of Jews in his beloved Vermont, as well as his long relationship with Zawie, were factors. I had to return to the room set aside for plaintiffs, and I tried to explain to my client what had happened: that antisemitism had prevailed due to Judge Billings's ruling excluding all mention of it from her case. She tearfully agreed to a lowball settlement offer from Zawie rather than going through a trial, then appealing Judge Billings's order, and then enduring a second trial—assuming appellate success and further assuming she were still alive when it came time for a new hearing before a jury.

I was leery of Judge Billings given his ruling in my antisemitic dog-bite case, but the federal court system has exclusive jurisdiction over litigation against the Forest Service. There were only two federal judges in Vermont, and the court clerk assigned cases to them based on geography. Ours was a southern Vermont case, so it went automatically to Rutland and Judge Billings.

ALONG WITH OUR COMPLAINT, we filed a motion for a preliminary injunction to stop the Forest Service from going ahead with clear-cutting and roadbuilding in Lamb Brook while the case was pending. In support of that motion, we filed affidavits of former Forest Service employees and our own bear and songbird experts, detailing the "significant impacts" resulting from the project, which should require the agency to prepare an Environmental Impact Statement.

Litigating this case was a paper chase of gargantuan proportions. In a federal court case under the National Environmental Policy Act, there are no live witnesses and no trial. The court's scrutiny is often limited to the "administrative record," meaning all the paperwork generated by or on file with the agency leading up to the issuance of its FONSI and Decision Notice.

The administrative record on Lamb Brook consisted of entire file drawers of boring and repetitive documents, every page of which we had to read carefully, because there is sometimes a diamond hidden within the spoiled honeypots of odoriferous bureaucratic goo.

Our 10-carat flawless diamond consisted of documents proving that Forest Service administrators had decided to go forward with Lamb Brook *before studying its environmental impacts* and that they had held a scam school on how to commit this deliberate and flagrant violation of the National Environmental Policy Act without being caught.

The documents showed that the agency had already decided to go forward by May 1992, seven months before the agency issued its Environmental Assessment (in January 1993) and eight months before the Decision Notice and Finding of No Significant Impact (in February 1993).

Meetings were held at the Forest Service headquarters in Rutland in the spring and summer of 1992, at which agency moguls from the Milwaukee office (which supervises the Green Mountain National Forest) taught the Vermont staff to work in reverse: to prepare its Decision Notice and Finding of No Significant Impact first, then draft the Environmental Assessment in such a way as to justify the decision already reached, without proper regard for the project's true environmental consequences.

In addition to written minutes of meetings contained in the files, which revealed the reverse-engineering technique of creating a sham EA, a courageous whistleblower came forward. She was Shelley Hight, the agency's architect for the Lamb Brook project. The fact that she had left the Forest Service for a job with a different agency, the U.S. Fish & Wildlife Service, provided her with some protection from retaliation. We filed Ms. Hight's affidavit describing the Lamb Brook scam school, which was created to evade NEPA's requirement of full disclosure of negative environmental impacts.

Under oath, Ms. Hight exposed the Lamb Brook fraud. She wrote:

> The trainers made it clear that they were not interested . . . in full disclosure of the possible impacts of the Lamb Brook Project. Instead, they described the NEPA process as an exercise in preparing paperwork that can withstand legal challenge. They taught us that we should draft and tailor NEPA documents to support a result that has been predetermined within the agency. . . . The purpose and function of the EA, they said, should be to support a Finding of No Significant Impact (FONSI), rather than to disclose potentially adverse environmental impacts.

The Forest Service trainers told the Lamb Brook staff to accomplish this goal by omitting from their EA potential significant environmental impacts which might upset the result desired by the Forest Service and lead to an EIS. They also suggested how, in preparing NEPA documents, we might need to mask the true purpose of logging (i.e., to produce a certain number of board feet of timber for the marketplace), by devising euphemistic and misleading purposes designed to mute public opposition. . . . [W]e should claim in the NEPA documents that the agency's reason for cutting trees at Lamb Brook was "habitat creation."

Ms. Hight was "so upset by what I considered the unethical nature of this training that tears came to my eyes. I was particularly shocked that there were two Forest Service lawyers present in the room, and that they failed to speak out or take any action, even though the training seemed to be specifically designed to evade the law." Ms. Hight also disclosed in her affidavit that the "staff discussed Lamb Brook's importance as a bear nursery" but intentionally omitted that fact from the Environmental Assessment.

DURING THE FOREST SERVICE'S LAMB BROOK administrative process, a state of Vermont bear biologist, Douglas Blodgett, opposed the extension of FR266, the 30-foot-wide logging road, into the core of Lamb Brook's bear habitat. In obedience to their training, the Lamb Brook team omitted mention of the state's official opposition.

Our lawsuit asked the court to issue a preliminary and permanent injunction against the project, and it included a supporting affidavit from Mr. Blodgett detailing what he had told the Forest Service: that Vermont's black bears are "intolerant of human presence and disturbance" and that, on behalf of the State, he had asked the Forest Service to forego the Lamb Brook project because it risked a "significant harmful impact" on bears or even total "abandonment" of the area by them.

We also hired outside bear experts who testified for us via affidavit. Professor Michael Pelton of the University of Tennessee, widely regarded to be the most distinguished black bear expert in the world, had written or supervised over a hundred peer-reviewed wildlife studies, worked for the U.S. Fish & Wildlife Service on bears, and was chief of the International Association for Bear Research and Management. Dr. Pelton hiked through and studied Lamb Brook, and he testified that the place "is critical for bears as a fall feeding area," that "the disturbance created by a road immediately adjacent to this site would put the bears . . . in jeopardy," and that the area's "carrying capacity . . . for bears will be significantly compromised calling into question its ability to support a population into the future."

Dr. Albert Manville, director of the Adirondack Mountain Club and former senior staff wildlife biologist for Defenders of Wildlife, testified that during his career "I have never seen such a heavily bear-utilized [beech tree] stand as this one in the Lamb Brook area," and if the extension of FR266 is built, "bears will abandon this prime feeding area."

On the bird issue, we filed written testimony from Dr. Kenneth V. Rosenberg, chief scientist in the Department of Bird Population Studies at the Cornell Ornithology Laboratory and a former postdoctoral fellow at the Smithsonian Institution.

Dr. Rosenberg made clear in his affidavit that the proposed logging and habitat destruction at Lamb Brook would kill outright between twenty and fifty breeding pairs of "most species" of neotropical migratory songbirds. Of even greater concern to Dr. Rosenberg was his conclusion that Lamb Brook is one of the last remaining large "source areas for forest-interior species" of birds in the Northeast, which are suffering "disproportionate" population declines. Were roadbuilding and clear-cutting to proceed, the result would be "direct loss of breeding habitat . . . over an area larger than the land actually cleared." He added that "altering the undisturbed character" of Lamb Brook "calls into question the long-term commitment of the U.S. Forest Service to assure the protection of forest bird populations."

Another of the major environmental issues arising from FR266 and its proposed extension deep into the forest core was the unlawful use of all-terrain vehicles (ATVs) there and the threats their loud noise and human intrusion posed to bears. The Forest Service wrote in the Lamb Brook EA that many ATVs were unlawfully using the existing road but that this problem could be dealt with by "mitigation" in the form of construction of earthen mounds designed to stop these motor vehicles from blasting their way into bear habitat. But the EA neglected to cite any evidence that such "mounding" would be an effective mitigation measure.

We filed with the court a raft of photographs and affidavits showing that the mounding already in place on the existing portion of FR266 had proven totally ineffective. As Mat Jacobson testified, based on his own observations at Lamb Brook, ATV riders "are amused and attracted by the opportunity to drive over" obstacles. "The ability of ATVs to ride over mounds of earth and other difficult to traverse terrain is their primary selling point." Other persons, including people who were not plaintiffs, filed affidavits detailing the extensive use of ATVs in the Lamb Brook area.

At the injunction hearing, Helen Toor, head of the U.S. Attorney's Civil Division for Vermont, told Judge Billings that the agency would voluntarily refrain from going forward while the litigation was pending, so that no injunction would be necessary. Judge Billings ordered the parties to submit legal memoranda and further evidence on bear and bird habitat. The Forest Service filed its paperwork first.

The agency submitted affidavits on the environmental issues that contradicted its own prior statements in the Environmental Assessment, without mentioning the existence of its changes of position or of any scientific evidence that arguably might justify its about-face.

The agency presented written testimony on bear impacts from two men with no academic degrees in bear biology and who had never visited Lamb Brook. They claimed that the logging and road extension would not "preclude the use" by or "negatively effect" (with the error in the original) black bears. Their statements were directly contrary to the Forest Service admission in the EA for Lamb Brook that "[s]pecies sensitive to human disturbance, such as the black bear, would be negatively impacted by increased human presence and loss of remoteness."

The agency also claimed in its filings that 62 percent of Vermont's land area is bear habitat, an outlandish overstatement that evaded the real issue: that Lamb Brook's habitat is a critical feeding area on which the survival of the bears in that large section of the Green Mountain National Forest depends.

The agency also filed an affidavit from one of its own employees to the effect that interior forest bird species, including neotropical migratory songbirds, are *not* experiencing population declines and that it is only bird species that thrive in "early successional habitats" (such as clear-cuts) who need government help. In other words, the "edge effect" that results from the Forest Service's roadbuilding and clear-cutting is actually *beneficial*.

This new, scientifically unsupported claim contradicted the EA, which had recited as fact that "[r]ecent studies have shown that certain species of [neotropical migratory] forest songbirds" are suffering "disproportionate population declines" due to loss of deep-woods habitat. This would become a formal factual finding by Congress when it passed the Neotropical Migratory Bird Conservation Act a few years later.

The Forest Service also untruthfully represented to the court in affidavits it filed that the environmentally destructive FR266 would be only a "temporary" logging road. The agency's EA had disclosed that FR266 would be maintained and utilized for periodic logging and clear-cutting for at least forty years and perhaps much longer.

Even worse, the Forest Service reversed itself on the issue of outlaw ATV use. While in the EA the agency acknowledged that ATVs are a problem and had proposed a solution of mounding FR266 to stop them, it now claimed in its court submissions that ATV use in Lamb Brook was minimal or nonexistent.

It's difficult to express in words how shocking and depressing it was for me to deal with the lies and unethical conduct perpetrated by our government in its defense of the Lamb Brook project. Mat Jacobson, whose work on scientific, strategic, and public relations issues was incomparable and essential to our victory, felt the same way.

Here we were, two guys from little Vermont, trying to save a bit of critical wildlife habitat necessary for the survival of forest creatures in a state and a country we love. A veritable army of people, employed by two powerful arms of the federal government—the Forest Service and the Department of Justice—had made the decision to smash us and our efforts into smithereens by any means necessary, no matter how underhanded or unscrupulous those means might be.

Why were they doing this? What had happened to these men and women, who after all were public servants supposed to be working for the public good? And why had they abandoned any semblance of personal honor and fairness to further a destructive and immoral cause? And where, in heaven's name, was their compassion for black bears and songbirds, who have as much of a right to live as humans, but who cannot speak for themselves, and who depend on us speak for them and to do the right thing on their behalf?

It's the same unanswerable question I would ask myself when I worked on serious criminal cases. Why do people do such horrible things?

In response to the Forest Service's distortions and outright lies, I filed on April 26, 1995, a fifty-page memorandum, on which I spent a few hundred hours doing the legal research and writing. We also filed supplemental affidavits countering the Forest Service's new positions on birds, bears, and the road extension and all-terrain vehicles. We argued that there exists overwhelming evidence that the Lamb Brook project is replete with significant environmental impacts and that the court should order the preparation of a full Environmental Impact Statement.

Because the National Environmental Policy Act is a procedural rather than a substantive statute, courts are not allowed to resolve disagreements between the parties on environmental impacts. Nonetheless, our sworn testimony on those impacts was probative and appropriate for judicial consideration because disagreements on a project's effects may reveal the existence of a genuine scientific "controversy" on environmental problems. Such a controversy is often dispositive evidence that the agency's deliberative process was not sufficiently complete and objective and that an Environmental Impact Statement is needed. The case law in the Second Circuit, which governs Vermont (as well as Connecticut and New York), supported our view that the court had the right and the responsibility to consider our evidence in that specialized, strictly procedural NEPA context.

In a 1983 case titled *Sierra Club v. U.S. Army Corps of Engineers*, involving the impacts of a proposed landfill on striped bass in the Hudson River, the Second Circuit held that where there is evidence that the agency has "swept under the rug" environmental problems and failed to take a "hard look" at them in an Environmental Assessment, which is sufficient as a matter of law to require the agency to conduct a thorough Environmental Impact Statement. The same case requires that the government agency conduct its environmental inquiries and analyses "in objective good faith."

There is also Second Circuit case law, first set forth in the 1977 case *County of Suffolk v. Secretary of Interior*, which was a dispute over the adequacy of an environmental study of the impacts of offshore oil and gas exploration, allowing plaintiffs in a NEPA case to expand the administrative record with additional evidence in cases where the agency's EA "has neglected to mention a serious environmental consequence . . . or otherwise swept 'stubborn problems of serious criticism . . . under the rug."

It was obvious to us, at least, that our affidavits and photographs were strong evidence of the lack of any thorough or objective "hard look" by the Forest Service at the environmental problems associated with Lamb Brook, so that expansion of the administrative record to include our evidence was required as a matter of law. Moreover, the affidavit of Shelley Hight, which exposed the Forest Service's scam school on ways to cover up environmental impacts and avoid the preparation of an EIS, went straight to the issue of bad faith. As did the Forest Service EA's intentional failure to mention that the Vermont Department of Fish and Wildlife had officially opposed the project due to its impact on bears.

Despite this clear law, Judge Billings on July 19, 1995, excluded every bit of the scientific evidence provided by our expert witnesses, as well as our testimony on the Forest Service's bad faith scam school. At the same time, he admitted into the record all the Forest Service's newly filed materials on bears and birds, which the agency had created for the sole purpose of rebutting our side's evidence, which Judge Billings was now refusing to consider.

To me, this made no logical sense. But I knew there was a way to deal with this decision, which at first appeared to some of our supporters as a death blow to our case. It wasn't that bad, for if we were to lose the case, we could attack the legality of Judge Billings's ruling to higher courts on appeal. In order to make a cogent appellate argument, we would be entitled to highlight and analyze our expert testimony as reasons for our position that Judge Billings was wrong to exclude it.

This is what lawyers call "getting evidence in through the back door," and I believed we could do that and it would be a legitimate winning strategy.

To his credit, Judge Billings did admit into the record some of the fact evidence on the issue of the ineffectiveness of Forest Service mounding FR266 to mitigate the impact of ATV traffic on the extension of that road into critical bear habitat. Judge Billings noted that, while the EA "clearly recognized that ATV use in Lamb Brook is a problem," the agency "in its recent filings . . . alters its position and contends there is little ATV use in the Lamb Brook area."

Judge Billings was "perplexed" by this contradiction. In his decision, he wondered why the Forest Service was proposing and defending the effectiveness of mounding at the terminus of FR266. Mounding, he noted, was proposed by the Forest Service as "a mitigation measure to counter a problem that the Forest Service now contends does not exist. In this vein, we believe that the Forest Service may be ignoring evidence as to illegal ATV use in Lamb Brook and 'sweep[ing] stubborn problems or serious criticisms . . . under the rug.'"

After issuing this order, Judge Billings took what is known as "senior status," with a lesser workload, and the case was transferred to his successor, Judge J. Garvan "Gar" Murtha of Brattleboro, a Bill Clinton appointee.

I HAD LITIGATED AGAINST Gar Murtha when he was in private practice, and I respected his ability. In one case in which we were opponents, Gar took the deposition of my client's trusted and beloved chief business helper and bookkeeper. He solemnly confronted her with documentary evidence he had found that she was altering company records and embezzling large sums, gross misconduct that my client had never suspected. At least in that regard, Gar knew more about my client's business than he did. I was impressed. My client was devastated. He fired the thief. The case settled.

In *National Audubon Society v. Hoffman*, the parties and Judge Murtha agreed that the case was ripe for a final decision given the extensive briefing already on file. Each side filed a motion for summary judgment, a procedural device enabling Judge Murtha to take the case under advisement and issue a ruling without any need for further proceedings. While we waited, there would be no clear-cuts, no dead songbirds, and no starving bears.

During this time, the managing partner of my law firm became progressively more concerned about the amount of time I was devoting to the case.

Because we would get attorney's fees only if we won, and only at the end of the litigation, which wouldn't be soon given that the loser surely would file an appeal, my unpaid time was affecting the firm's cash flow.

He was correct in that regard, but I told him we had a strong case, and it isn't unusual for a law firm to have to wait to be paid. Contingent fees in personal injury cases are a good example of that phenomenon. We had a line of credit with a local bank, from which we drew when needed and repaid when we were flush. But my partner wasn't optimistic about our chances, and he was unhappy that I'd taken it on in the first place. It didn't help that I did significantly more free and low-pay work than the other lawyers in the firm. Was I a drag in that respect? Yes, I'm afraid I was. I was never an effective "rainmaker" as a lawyer. I'm basically a shy person, and I was terrible at "schmoozing" prospective clients in social situations. To the extent that wealthy people knew about my cases, they often disagreed with what I was doing and wouldn't consider hiring me.

When a firm breaks up, or one lawyer splits, it's almost always due to conflicts over money. But penumbras emanate from the money thing in the form of personal issues. My partner hailed from a working-class family in a small Texas town. I grew up near Harvard Square in Cambridge, and my father was a lawyer whose father was a banker. My partner went to Yale on scholarship, and I went to Harvard primarily on my parents' dime. My partner had labored hard to get out of the working class into a position of prominence, and he'd succeeded, by election to the office of State's Attorney, then to the state legislature, where he chaired the House Appropriations Committee, and now he was president of the Vermont State Colleges Board of Trustees. I'd had many advantages as a kid, but I'd abandoned Boston, where I might have parlayed my family connections into social status and wealth. Instead, I'd opted for giving the establishment a hard time. We were opposites. I know that I got on my partner's nerves, and to my regret, I didn't do enough to deescalate the rift.

Then in December 1995, six months after we filed our memorandum on bear and bird habitat, Judge Murtha decided that the Forest Service EA itself proved our case, issued an injunction stopping the project, and ordered the agency to prepare a full EIS.

The ruling was definitive in its language: "[T]he the Court finds that, had it taken the requisite 'hard look' at the context and intensity of its proposal . . . the Forest Service would have decided to prepare an EIS. Therefore, its failure to do so is arbitrary and capricious. On its face, the proposed action, which includes clearcutting of over 300 acres and its admitted attendant effects such as intrusion into bear and neotropical bird habitats, is 'significant' under any reasonable construction of the term."

On the issue of mounding as a way to stop ATV traffic into the core area of Lamb Brook, Judge Murtha found that "[t]he record does not support a conclusion that any of these mitigation measures will actually work to cut down unauthorized use of FR266 or to protect the bird and bear habitats." Judge Murtha concluded: "The cumulative effects on Lamb Brook's black bears and neotropical birds of the road extension, the proposed clearcutting, timber sales of uncertain duration, and the admitted but unquantified additional ATV use, require the Forest Service to prepare an EIS analyzing such effects."

IN ORDER TO APPEAL JUDGE MURTHA'S DECISION to the United States Court of Appeals for the Second Circuit in New York City, Department of Justice procedure required Helen Toor to seek the approval of the United States Solicitor General, Drew S. Days III. Unfortunately, General Days gave Toor the green light in late June 1996, during the last month of his otherwise distinguished tenure.

In an effort to explain the basis for the appeal, Forest Service press aide Kathleen Diehl told the *Rutland Herald* that she expected that the Forest Service would "take issue with the language" of Judge Murtha's decision. "[F]or example, the meaning of the word 'clearcut.'"

The problem with that approach is that the term is self-defining. It means cutting down all the trees. For me, Diehl's effort at semantic dodgeball was reminiscent of President Clinton's assertion that whether he lied when he denied a sexual relationship with Monica Lewinsky "depends on what the meaning of the word 'is' is."

I told the *Herald* reporter that "the Clinton administration has shot itself in the foot politically" by approving the appeal and that "[i]f the Forest Service wins the appeal and succeeds in clearcutting Lamb Brook and exterminating its black bears, Vermonters will be outraged."

This was one of my occasionally provocative statements to the press, but I think there was a lot of truth in it. Even the habitually cautious U.S. Senator Patrick Leahy had written the named defendant "Butch" Marita, asking him to do an EIS on Lamb Brook.

We weren't going to let the Forest Service beat us. I spent eons drafting a 60-page brief, one of the best I've written, and filed it with the court of appeals on October 7, 1996. The court scheduled us for oral argument on February 4, 1997. I spent most of January reading and rereading the decisions I cited in our brief and trying to anticipate and prepare for every possible question that the panel of judges might ask me. I did a couple of dry runs of the argument with one of my law partners, Rob Woolmington, "presiding." Rob also critiqued the brief and suggested excellent changes to it, which I adopted.

During this interim period, the Forest Service, without informing Judge Murtha or asking his permission, quietly allowed members of a snowmobile group, the Vermont Association of Snow Travelers (VAST) to widen (by cutting down trees) and grade the "Old Stage Road."

The Old Stage Road is a historic one-lane thoroughfare that was used by horse and buggy on the route from Albany, New York, to Boston. In Lamb Brook, the remnants of that once heavily traveled dirt road lead east from FR266 to the banks of Harriman Reservoir in Wilmington, Vermont. The tree-cutting and grading were substantial. The work exposed and partially destroyed the visually striking and fragile ancient "corduroy," slabs of wood similar to railroad ties sunk horizontally across the road surface designed to enable stagecoaches to operate without getting stuck, especially during Vermont's "mud season" in April.

Judge Murtha's order had specifically provided that "the defendants are hereby ENJOINED from conducting any further timber harvesting or road-building activities in Lamb Brook." We filed a motion to hold the Forest Service in contempt of the order.

An evidentiary hearing was held. The Forest Service's defenses consisted of half-truths: that the work had been done by VAST, not the agency; that cutting down trees to widen a road isn't the same as "timber harvesting;" and that the Forest Service considered the Old Stage Road a "trail," not a road, despite its name, and thus it was not covered by the injunction.

We proved that the Forest Service had given the go-ahead to VAST to do the work and that the president of VAST was also a Forest Service employee, so that in context VAST was essentially an *alter ego* of the agency. I argued that the agency's remaining defenses, on the definitions of "harvesting" and "road," were specious and dishonorable.

Judge Murtha was obviously angry with the Forest Service, but he decided that we had failed to meet our heavy burden of proof by "clear and convincing evidence" that their violation of his order was intentional and contemptuous. Murtha made it clear, however, that he would not look kindly on any further violations of his order. Our appeal went forward.

THE UNITED STATES COURT OF APPEALS for the Second Circuit building, named after the late Justice Thurgood Marshall, is set in Lower Manhattan in Foley Square, near the Chambers Street subway station and a short walk from Chinatown. Mat Jacobson and I rented rooms a couple of days before the argument in a nearby fleabag hotel. I had a room to myself, to study and practice my argument, and Mat's was the designated "war room," where he met with supporters and used the internet (as best he could in those dial-up days) to schmooze with the press and otherwise publicize the proceeding.

Mat arranged for the Bread and Puppet Theater to travel 350 miles from its communal headquarters in Glover, Vermont, to stage one of its arresting and unique performances in front of the federal courthouse. On the morning of the argument, a troupe of twenty Bread and Puppet artists formed a "forest" of handmade, 10-foot-tall papier-mâché puppets of trees topped with humanoid heads with branches sprouting upward from them. These sentient-being trees were menaced by life-size, axe-wielding, skeleton-faced Forest Service puppets. Mat managed to persuade fifty forest activists to travel from Vermont to attend the court proceeding. It never hurts to have well-behaved spectators on your side; this is something that judges always notice, and a large audience tends to make them more attentive and to treat the case (one of hundreds argued during every year in that court) more thoughtfully.

The seventeenth floor courtroom, built in 1936, is divisible by eleven. I wonder if there is a hidden, magical meaning here, or if it's simply an architect's inside joke. The room is 66 feet long and 33 feet wide, with cherry-stained wooden walls carved with Ionic columns. The 22-foot-high white ceilings are ornate, bejeweled with circular, octagonal, and rectangular gold- and copper-colored art nouveau decorations and ancient Greek carved patterns, from which hang Tiffany-style lamps.

Our panel of Judges consisted of a former Yale Law School professor, Ralph K. Winter; the liberal Jose A. Cabranes, a native of Puerto Rico appointed by President Clinton and the first Judge of Latin descent to serve on the court; and the environmentally conscious Richard J. Cardamone, a Reagan appointee who had written the striped bass fishery NEPA decision, on which we had relied heavily in our brief.

I don't remember the argument. But I trust Susan Smallheer's front page report in the February 5, 1997, edition of the *Rutland Herald*:

Senior Judge Ralph Winter took the offensive from the start, questioning [Helen] Toor why the government had conceded what he considered to be a major point—that the forest plan of the Green Mountain National Forest already had an umbrella environmental impact statement, and thus a second one dealing with Lamb Brook issues wasn't needed.

Why aren't you arguing that? he asked Toor.

Toor acknowledged that there was already an environmental impact statement, but it didn't go into any detail about the specific impacts on wildlife that were raised by the environmental groups.

With those kind of questions, the environmentalists who filled several rows in the ornate courtroom, smiled.

But when it was Saltonstall's turn to explain the legal virtues of his case, the smiles faded.

Does every logging job in the forest need an environmental impact statement, Judge Winter wanted to know. The issue involved a road that was only 1.3 miles long, he noted.

The second environmental impact statement was needed, Saltonstall argued, because the earlier environmental assessment "swept serious environmental problems under the rug."

Judge Richard Cardamone questioned whether Murtha, from the judicial branch of government, had the authority to order an agency in the executive branch, to complete an environmental impact statement.

Saltonstall gently reminded him that there were two decisions on just that point—written by him.

Judge Jose Cabranes, who's been mentioned as a possible United States Supreme Court Justice, questioned Toor why the government didn't want to do a full environmental review. "They take time," Toor said.

In front of the massive U.S. courthouse, a mock forest was being threatened by skeleton-faced Forest Service employees. By the end of the skit, the trees were still standing, and the skeletons were flat on their backs.

All considered, I thought that the argument had gone well. Susan Smallheer's decision to end her account of the hearing with a description of the Bread and Puppet Theater performance, with its giant papier-mâché trees winning a decisive battle against Forest Service ghouls, was a hopeful sign.

It took almost a year for the Court of Appeals to decide the case, but on December 22, 1997, it issued a narrowly drawn decision in our favor, written by Judge Cardamone. While refusing to consider our expert testimony and evidence of bad faith in the preparation of the EA, the court decided that the Forest Service violated NEPA by failing to present any evidence to support its contention that mounding the end of the proposed FR266 extension would stop outlaw ATV traffic. Because the agency had failed to take a "hard look" at the efficacy of mounding, its Finding of No Significant Impact on Lamb Brook's environment was arbitrary and capricious. The court held: "The Forest Service's failure to weigh the factors related to its project's environmental impact is a flaw that precludes a definitive determination as to whether the project may have a significant impact." It added that what "the Forest Service's proposed action will have on the birds, the bears, and the existence value of Lamb Brook is not clear because the scope of current and future ATV use is unknown."

Instead of forcing the Forest Service to prepare an Environmental Impact Statement, however, the court remanded the matter to the agency for further study and reconsideration of all the project's potential impacts on Lamb Brook's bears and neotropical songbirds. It directed the agency to study and revisit "the issues which we have held were inadequately addressed in its initial environmental assessment, and it should also address additional possible shortcomings raised by the district court which we have elected not to explore here. After doing so, it should reconsider its finding of no significant impact in light of its additional investigation and the applicable legal standard."

The court's approach, which departed from its earlier decisions ordering the preparation of a full EIS, nonetheless put the Forest Service in a bind from which even the most adept bureaucratic Houdini could not escape.

Were the agency to begin anew and analyze all the issues, it would have to take into account and disclose publicly the opposition of the State of Vermont's Fish & Wildlife Department to the project, as well as the expert testimony on wildlife impacts that we had presented. In other words, reconsideration and further study meant that the Forest Service would have to expand the administrative record to include and analyze the same damning information it had persuaded the courts to suppress.

Rather than going back to the drawing board, the Forest Service dropped the Lamb Brook project, which was the exact result that we were seeking. This was a total victory for the bears and songbirds.

CHAPTER 17

⚖

The Lamb Brook Aftermath

By the time the Second Circuit decision came down, I had left my Bennington law firm of fifteen years and was in the process of spending an unhappy annum working for the Conservation Law Foundation in Vermont's beautiful, Tinkertoy-scale capital city, Montpelier. It was a five-hour round trip to and from the office in good weather, and I often slept on a chair in my office instead of driving home.

I managed to help save some more bear habitat by opposing a proposed land swap between the state of Vermont and a Stowe ski resort. The land that the state had agreed to give the ski area contained a large grove of beech trees heavily scarred with bear-claw marks. Not wishing to go through a reprise of the Lamb Brook case on the losing end, the state backed down and cancelled the land deal the day before a scheduled administrative hearing.

I also was able to force the owner of a large commercial dock jutting out into Lake Champlain to open it up to use by the community for free, including for sunbathing and swimming, citing the public trust doctrine, which holds that if you use a state-owned resource (in this case the lake) you have to give something to the people in return.

Despite these small victories, I missed Ellen and my Sandgate home too much to continue my commute. Moreover, I had policy differences with the

Conservation Law Foundation, especially its failure to endorse or publish a fifty-three-page report I wrote on Forest Service timber sales in New England, titled *Chainsaw Logic.* The report demonstrated conclusively that nonextractive activities on national forests, such as birdwatching, fishing, hunting, hiking, and camping, generate far more in the way of jobs and income for local people than logging. From a purely economic as well as an environmental perspective, it makes good sense to adopt a zero-cut policy on National Forests and allow the trees to revert gradually to old growth.

In the executive summary of *Chainsaw Logic,* I pointed out that in New England only about 4 percent of the land base is publicly owned, while the amount of industrially owned forest land is twice the national average. Yet the Forest Service doggedly pursues a counterproductive agenda of clear-cutting and other intensive and destructive modes of industrial forestry and selling the wood off to private industry at a loss, compromising the welfare of wild creatures who depend on the willingness of humans to protect them. I noted that this is something that "isn't widely known outside of the environmental community, for after all, who could think of an agency that uses Smokey Bear as its mascot as anything but benign?"

Why does the Forest Service act so irresponsibly? The answer, I wrote, may be found in financial incentives: "Congress gives the Forest Service money to log *and* permits the agency to skim large sums of money 'off the top' of its timber sales, *even when those sales are conducted at a net loss to the U.S. Treasury.*" It continued: "This strange system fosters a Forest Service culture that is hooked on 'getting the cut out,' with little regard for environmental or economic consequences or the will of the public that the agency is supposed to serve. Like the house in a permanent floating crap game, the Forest Service always wins, no matter how much the American people lose."

In the fiscal year closest to the release of *Chainsaw Logic,* the net loss to the U.S. Treasury from Forest Service timber sales in New England's national forests was $725 for every acre cut. Yet the agency pocketed more than $1,000 for each acre logged.

I argued that we should allow publicly owned forests to revert to the natural state they were in when Henry David Thoreau described the landscape in his classic work *The Maine Woods* (1864). Thoreau saw forests with "a wild damp and shaggy look" with "countless falling and decaying trees" covered with a "thick coat of moss." Northern New England was still a place "full of silver birches and watery maples . . . with innumerable lakes and streams, peopled with trout and . . . salmon." The woods rang with "the scream of the fish hawk and the eagle, the laugh of the loon, and the whistle of ducks." They were a refuge for the now extirpated panther, as well as a "home of the moose, the bear, the caribou, [and] the wolf."

I wrote in *Chainsaw Logic* that Thoreau had prophesied correctly that the timber industry would soon destroy New England's ancient forests through clear-cutting. People, he noted, had begun to view trees as mere commodities: "[T]he pine is no more lumber than man is, and to be made into boards and houses is no more its true and highest use than the truest use of a man is to be cut down and made into manure."

The Conservation Law Foundation's New Hampshire Advisory Board was steadfastly opposed to release of my report. In fact, they hated it and hated me, and they dressed me down for presuming to write it. CLF's internal politics were such that, given the opposition of its New Hampshire advisers, the report would never be released under the CLF banner, though Vermont's Green Mountain Forest Watch publicly endorsed it. The New Hampshire contingent was dominated by members and allies of an organization called the Society for the Protection (some might say "Destruction") of New Hampshire Forests, which advocates for Forest Service–style timber policies under the glittering rubric of "working forests."

"Working forests" is a misleading, Madison Avenue slogan used by pro-logging interests, cleverly designed to obscure the fact that forests are already "working" a full-time job: supporting and maintaining an ecosystem. Unfortunately, this catchphrase has become gospel with some land trusts and environmental organizations, and given the New Hampshire Advisory Board's attitude toward me and my zero-cut agenda, it was clear that I had no future at the Conservation Law Foundation.

While I had been willing to endure a long commute for a righteous cause, the drive between Sandgate and Montpelier was tiring and dangerous in bad weather. The alternative—sleeping in my office after eating a sandwich from Subway washed down with Diet Pepsi—was a lonely and depressing way to live. One Friday night around midnight, driving home through a snowstorm, I turned on the radio and listened to Susannah McCorkle singing Jimmy Van Heusen and Johnny Mercer's 1939 standard, "I Thought About You," which ends with one of her amazing signature blue notes—"and every stop that we made / I thought about you . . . and what did I do / I thought about you." And I realized that I love my wife too much to work 120 miles away from her in another town.

Sierra Club Legal Defense Fund offered me a job in Hawaii, but I decided that Honolulu was too far away from family and friends and prohibitively expensive. Even more important, Ellen loved her students in the Dorset School, and she was making a statewide impact with a Holocaust unit she had developed for middle-school kids. I moved back to Sandgate full time and hung out a shingle on Union Street in Manchester Village.

Mat Jacobson's reward for his work on Lamb Brook was a high-ranking job with the militant environmental organization Greenpeace in its Washington, D.C., headquarters. Government lawyer Helen Toor's consolation prize for losing Lamb Brook was her appointment by Governor Dean in 1999 as a judge on the Vermont Superior Court.

Judge Helen Toor sits primarily on civil cases in Burlington, and she is highly regarded, with one glaring exception. Judge Toor alarmed the Vermont criminal defense bar when in 2004 she found attorney Lorin Duckman in contempt and confined him in the Middlebury District Court prison lockup for a period of forty-five minutes, the first time in Vermont history that a judge had summarily jailed a lawyer. The reason? Duckman had refused to obey her verbal order from the bench that he take his client outside the courtroom and give him certain legal advice that she, but not Duckman, considered appropriate. A former New York City criminal court judge himself, Duckman believed that Judge Toor had no right to order him how to advise his client or how he should practice law, and he unwisely presumed to tell her so.

The Vermont Supreme Court by a vote of 4–1 affirmed the contempt citation in 2006 in a case titled *In Re Duckman*, albeit noting critically that "Judge Toor appears from the videotape to have become upset and angry" and that "[p]erhaps her state of mind was demonstrated by her order to have attorney [Duckman] taken away in shackles, an order that was never implemented, and one that she regretted."

From time to time, I would run into Judge Toor at Vermont Bar Association continuing legal education seminars. She'd been as hard-boiled as a Dashiell Hammett character when she marshaled the Forest Service Timber Beasts and led what I'd called their "Assault on Truth," and she'd been angry with me for calling her out on that. But now she was relaxed and cordial, basking in the warmth of her high position and the reflexive deference that lawyers pay to judges even out of the courtroom, a cultural norm that most robed ones seem to enjoy.

I didn't have to pay homage to Helen. We had been warriors against one other in an all-out battle lasting the better part of four years, and I had beaten her fair and square, and so in that limited sense we would always be equals despite her elevated station. One morning between classes, I managed to make her laugh when I told her privately the nickname I'd given her during Lamb Brook: "Helen of Toor, the face that launched a thousand logging trucks."

IN TERMS OF POLICY, I believe, based on what I learned in the litigation, that the United States Forest Service must be abolished. This rogue agency has shown over the years that it is little more than a tool of the logging and forest product industries, subsidizing their environmentally destructive activities at a prohibitive cost to the taxpayer and the environment. We need to preserve the forests owned by the American people and let them revert naturally to old growth, not cut them down or crisscross them with mile after mile of logging roads. There is plenty of private land available for growing and selling timber in an environmentally sustainable way.

Our publicly owned forests are valuable, and not just because they turn carbon dioxide into oxygen, prevent erosion and flooding, and provide critical habitat for nonhuman creatures. They are an important source of economic well-being, by providing jobs for the recreation sector, including camping, fishing, hunting, hiking, and birdwatching. They are an irreplaceable cultural resource, allowing people to experience the calming force of Nature, while providing inspiration for naturalists like Edward O. Wilson, and for writers, from John Muir to Edward Abbey, as well as artists, including the great landscape painter Albert Bierstadt and the entire Hudson River School, and preeminent photographers like Ansel Adams and Eliot Porter.

We should either consolidate the U.S. Forest Service with the U.S. Park Service or replace it with a much smaller agency, perhaps called the "National Forest Preservation Service." Its statutorily redefined jobs should be wilderness creation and protection, scientific research, and environmentally benign actions, such as making safe and nondestructive trails for hiking, stopping the theft of trees, ending motorized traffic (except for emergency rescues and humanitarian relief), conserving pure rivers and lakes, and training and employing nature guides, field biologists, and teachers—all for the benefit of the American public and for the wildlife that depend on us for survival.

It will take a couple of centuries for our forests to recover fully from the damage done by the Forest Service, but in my opinion zero cut is the only rational and moral policy course.

CHAPTER 18

⚖

Political Cases

The Lamb Brook case was essentially political in the sense that it involved an attack on government policy and the operations of a government agency in the executive branch. It wasn't my only political case. I enjoyed representing people who, motivated by their conscientious beliefs on political issues, committed acts of civil disobedience. I'd done this myself, both as a student at Exeter and as a foot soldier in the civil rights struggle in Selma, Alabama, when I was arrested and jailed for parts of two days for the "crime" of walking with a Black man on a public sidewalk in the neighborhood of Mayor Joe Smitherman. For me these were fun cases, and I became known in Vermont as a lawyer who would represent defendants in political prosecutions pro bono.

Antinuke Cases

In 1972, the Vermont Yankee nuclear power plant opened, supplying about a third of the state's electricity. The plant, which closed in 2014, is located on the Connecticut River in Vernon, Vermont, only a thousand feet away from the town's public elementary school. Had there been a serious accident, such as the one at Chernobyl in 1986, most or all of the school's students and teachers would have suffered agonizing deaths from the explosion or radiation burns and poisoning. But the plant's property taxes covered half of the town's annual budget, so it was popular.

Vermont Yankee was the subject of protests even before it opened. The organization primarily responsible for organizing the movement to close the plant is Citizens Awareness Network (CAN), sometimes called "Nukebusters," led by Deb Katz. After the plant experienced a series of problems, including the total collapse of one of its cooling towers in 2007 and the discovery in 2010 of more than thirty-seven times the allowable federal level of radioactive tritium in the groundwater, relentless public opposition and state political and regulatory pressures became so great that the plant's owner, Entergy Corporation, of New Orleans, decided to close it.

Even if advanced technology were able to eliminate the danger of catastrophic accidents posed by nuclear power, there is the unsolved (and possibly unsolvable) problem of what to do with the high-level radioactive waste such plants generate, which according to a study by the National Academy of Sciences remains lethal for at least *one million years*. No safe disposal site has been located. (Yucca Mountain in Nevada, a former volcano that at this writing is the only site still under consideration, has been shown to leak water into the cavern that was built to store the waste.)

Assuming that a safe disposal facility were found and constructed, how would it be possible to warn future generations of humans to stay away from it for a million years? Recorded human history goes back only 5,000 years. Languages change and are lost. A warning composed of symbols carved into rock, or rocks arranged in a fashion designed to convey a warning, even if understandable to future beings, wouldn't physically last anywhere close to the length of time that high-level waste continues to be deadly.

In the summer of 1998, Citizens Awareness Network held an "action camp" near the Vermont Yankee plant and planned another in its annual series of nonviolent demonstrations against it, which usually included a sitdown on plant property, including in the parking lot directly in front of the gate to the reactor. A Brattleboro lawyer, Jonathan Block, and I teamed up to represent those who would be arrested for unlawful trespass.

Jon and I had two goals. The first was to get the prosecutions dismissed before trial in such a way that would make it impossible or unpalatable for the state to bring future prosecutions. In the event of a jury trial, we wanted to flip the proceeding and make the nuke plant and nuclear power the defendants, using the testimony of those arrested and expert witnesses on nuclear safety and pollution.

Deb Katz of CAN organized the Thursday, August 20, demonstration to minimize inconvenience to the Town of Vernon and its residents. She scheduled the action to begin at 4:00 p.m., after the elementary school across the street from the plant had closed for the day and the kids had been bussed home. She arranged with school officials to allow demonstrators to park their cars at the school, so that the highway wouldn't be clogged, inconveniencing motorists and hindering the ability of Vermont State Police to arrest and transport protesters to Town Hall for booking.

In a show of goodwill toward the police, CAN bought pizzas for them. A CAN volunteer, dressed in formal waitstaff coattails and a bowler hat, delivered the pizzas on roller skates to the smiling cops, who, I can attest because I was there, ate all of them while processing and citing into court the twenty-one people they'd busted. Jon and I gathered contact information from the "VY 21" and obtained their written permission have us represent them.

David Dellinger, then 83 and living in Peacham, Vermont, was one of the VY 21 arrested for trespassing on the nuke plant's parking lot along with his wife and fellow activist, Elizabeth Petersen. Dave died at age 88 from Alzheimer's disease.

I considered it a special honor to represent Dave, a lifelong civil rights and antiwar activist who was a defendant in the "Chicago Eight" conspiracy trial in Chicago following the 1968 Democratic National Convention, at which the cops beat and arrested hundreds of peaceful demonstrators in Grant Park. Outside the convention hall, demonstrators chanted "The whole world is watching!" as they were attacked by Chicago policemen. On the floor of the convention, Chicago Mayor Richard J. Daley screamed "You fucking kike!" at U.S. Senator Abraham Ribicoff of Connecticut, who was making a speech criticizing the police. My brother Tom, a staffer for the antiwar presidential candidate, Senator Eugene McCarthy, became a victim of the police violence when cops invaded McCarthy campaign headquarters, beating people and trashing the place. One of their number deliberately broke Tom's hand by slamming it in a glass door.

The Department of Justice responded to the Chicago "police riot" (as the National Commission on the Causes and Prevention of Violence later called it) by indicting eight opponents of the Vietnam War, including Dellinger, Abbie Hoffman, Jerry Rubin, Tom Hayden, and Black Panther Bobby Seale. The charges were for conspiracy and crossing state lines to incite the riot, for which the brutal Chicago cops were solely responsible. During the trial, Judge Julius Hoffman shackled and gagged the only Black defendant, Bobby Seale, when he insisted that the trial be delayed so that the lawyer of his choice, Charles Garry of San Francisco, who was ill and hospitalized, could represent him.

The defendants' convictions were reversed on appeal. At the conclusion of the trial, Judge Hoffman sentenced the defendants and their lawyers for contempt of court, including a four-year jail term for lead defense counsel William Kunstler. On appeal, the contempt sentences were also set aside.

David Dellinger had been flanked by the much younger Youth International Party (Yippie) leaders Abbie Hoffman and Jerry Rubin at their trial in the Chicago federal court. Thirty years later, Hoffman and Rubin were dead, but David was still around and making good trouble. I watched as he was handcuffed and arrested at Vermont Yankee with his wife. Dave was lucid and committed but sufficiently frail that I worried about him. When Dave learned that I was going to represent the protestors in court, he gave me one of his calling cards, my only client ever to do so.

After the arraignments of the protestors in Brattleboro, Jon Block and I divided up the written work. Jon filed a motion for pretrial discovery, and I filed a motion to dismiss the case based on the First Amendment right of free speech and the related right of the people peaceably to assemble.

Jon requested, and we believed that we had the right to obtain, all police reports, video tapes, details on the use of confidential informants inserted within the ranks of protesters, and the means of intelligence-gathering as well as the substance of all communications between Vermont Yankee employees and law enforcement. Jon and I figured that the state and Vermont Yankee would never want to give up this information and that the State's Attorney might well opt for dismissal of the cases rather than disclose it.

On the issue of free speech, the problem I faced was that the United States Supreme Court had decided in *Pruneyard Shopping Center v. Robins* (1980) that pro-union organizers do not have a First Amendment right to pass out leaflets on the grounds of a shopping mall. In *International Society for Krishna Consciousness v. Lee* (1992), the Court reached a similar result with respect to a religious group that was seeking converts and soliciting contributions indoors in an airport. The Court reasoned that the First Amendment generally does not apply to activities conducted on private property.

I argued in my motion that office property owned by the nuclear industry is sui generis, legalese for "unique," different from all other types of commercial private property. Nuclear power is the most highly regulated industry in America, to the point where industry can do zilch without the permission and active oversight of the Nuclear Regulatory Commission. I wrote that the interrelationship between the two is so great that the Vermont Yankee office grounds should be viewed as "federalized" for the purposes of the First Amendment.

I added that Vermont Yankee had on at least three occasions in the past welcomed CAN protesters onto their property, even passing out apple cider and cookies to them, and by doing so they had waived their right to claim that a trespass had occurred. Moreover, Vermont Yankee management's total ban on protesters in the parking lot was patently unreasonable under the *Krishna Consciousness* case, which allowed for some limited First Amendment activity on airport property, subject to "reasonable" regulations by the airport's owners, as long as it is conducted outdoors.

Winning this motion would mean that antinuke demonstrators would have free reign to conduct protests on Vermont Yankee property outside its office and in the parking lot, in front of the plant gate. This would have been an unacceptable result for the owners of Vermont Yankee, and nuclear plant owners elsewhere in the country, because of the bad precedent it would set.

State's Attorney Dan Davis understood what was at stake. He decided to dismiss the VY 21 cases.

The *Brattleboro Reformer* edition of November 6, 1998, quoted State's Attorney Davis explaining his dismissal: "'If Saltonstall's motion was successful, it would have limited the ability of the power company to arrest protesters,' he said. 'The dismissal of charges stops action on the motion,' Davis said."

Faced with the reality that Jon Block and I would refile the same motions after every demonstration and arrest, Davis stopped prosecuting these types of cases. When people were arrested at the Vermont Yankee plant and showed up in court for their arraignments, they found that either no charges had been brought or that the State's Attorney had filed but dismissed them. Neither I nor Jon Block had much to do in terms of real legal work after the 1998 Vermont Yankee plant demonstrations, though we attended many later ones to offer support and advice to the activists there.

My LAST INVOLVEMENT with antinuke demonstrators was a freedom of speech case, representing them in a civil rights lawsuit against the Brattleboro police chief, Eugene Wrinn. The case arose in 2009, while Republican Governor James Douglas, a supporter of nuclear power and the Vermont Yankee plant, was giving a speech at the Latchis Theater in downtown Brattleboro. I was in the audience.

Douglas was in the process of speechifying on the penurious wonders of his fiscally conservative administration to this most far left of Vermont towns, when four antinuclear protestors stood up, holding an antinuke, anti-Douglas sign. A few people whose views of the governor were blocked briefly by the sign asked the protestors to sit down, but Douglas continued with his speech without interruption.

Taking it upon themselves to squelch and censor this silent expression of dissent, members of the Brattleboro Police Department, led by Chief Wrinn, handcuffed the protesters, Eesha Williams, Elizabeth Wood, Amy Frost, and Jonathan Crowell, all of whom lived locally, and arrested them for disorderly conduct.

When I arrived at the Brattleboro District Court to represent the four at their arraignment, I learned that the new State's Attorney, Tracey Shriver, who had taken over from the retiring Dan Davis, had declined to prosecute them.

Under the ACLU-Vermont banner, I sued Chief Wrinn in federal court for violation of the civil rights of the protestors. I was confident of victory. In a January 19, 2010, Vermont Public Radio interview, a day after I filed the complaint, I said: "The law is absolutely clear in my opinion that the police had no right to arrest these folks. They were peacefully and quietly expressing their views against Vermont Yankee and Governor Douglas and his support of Vermont Yankee."

The insurance company lawyer representing Chief Wrinn knew that I was correct in that view, and we settled the litigation in May 2010, near-record time to conclude a federal civil rights case. As a general matter, insurance companies set aside a cash "reserve" to cover their liability in each meritorious lawsuit, then drag the cases out with endless duplicative discovery requests and depositions while investing and earning substantial income on that reserve. But here, delay would mean more bad publicity for the cops, and anyway this wasn't a big-money case with a large reserve.

The settlement agreement awarded each protestor $2,500 in compensatory damages, not so bad for a couple of hours in the pokey; even better, my clients were local heroes.

The most important victory, though, was a stipulation in the agreement mandating that the Brattleboro police, including Chief Wrinn, must undergo extensive training on the First Amendment rights of freedom of speech and assembly, as well as the state and federal constitutional prohibitions against arresting peaceful protesters. I had wanted an ACLU lawyer to conduct that training, but that was too bitter a pill for the town to swallow, and so I agreed that State's Attorney Tracey Shriver would be the police department's teacher.

The Brattleboro cops needed a civics lesson, and I'm happy to say that I helped them get it.

The Rosemarie Jackowski Case

During March and April 2003, the United States Air Force and its Coalition allies conducted a bombing campaign over Baghdad, Iraq, known as

"Shock and Awe." The bombing was conducted at night and recorded and broadcast by American television news cameras stationed directly across the Tigris River. From that vantage point, the explosions looked like a spectacular Fourth of July display, worthy of those made by the Zambelli Fireworks Company. Buildings blew up, with enormous fireballs, and burning shrapnel was propelled into the night sky, without any apparent impact on the city's human population.

The stated purpose of the bombing was to paralyze and destroy the will of enemy forces to fight and thereby to bring a quick end to the war. Shock and Awe did not accomplish that goal. However, according to Iraq Body Count, a project of the British nonprofit Oxford Research Group, the three weeks of Shock and Awe bombing killed more than 6,700 civilians.

On a typically cold morning in spring 2003, a crowd of antiwar protesters, eventually swelling to several hundred citizens, marched up and down Main Street in Bennington and wound up at the Four Corners, the town's main intersection, filling and blocking the sidewalks and the road as well. Traffic was backed up for a half-hour. Bennington police headquarters was a block away; they cleared the crowd, but a dozen protestors refused to leave the intersection and were arrested.

One of these was Rosemarie Jackowski, a senior citizen who carried a sign with antiwar slogans and a grisly photograph of a little Iraqi girl whose head had been partially blown off by an American bomb. Rosemarie was an Air Force veteran and a former teacher who had also worked in low-level positions in the defense industry.

In her old age, Rosemarie had fallen on hard economic times. She was disabled and unable to work because a fully loaded logging truck had rear-ended her car, causing serious injuries that made it painful for her to walk or sit. Her less-than-talented lawyer had lost her personal injury suit, even though it's almost impossible to lose a "rear-ender" case. She was surviving on a small Social Security pension, Medicare, and food stamps.

As Ms. Jackowski wrote in her book about the March demonstration, *Banned in Vermont* (2010), "It was my 66th birthday," but it was "no time to celebrate."

"As I stood holding my sign most of my thoughts were about the Iraqi children. . . . I could feel the heat from the engine of the eighteen-wheeler that was inching closer and closer to my back. I did not turn to look at it. I kept my eyes cast down and remained focused on the job I had to do that day. I stood perfectly still and silent. I often refer to those moments as the most solemn of my life."

A Bennington police officer walked Rosemarie to the nearby headquarters and put her in a cell. The other arrestees arrived, and eventually everyone was booked and given citations to appear in the district court for arraignment on the criminal charge of disorderly conduct.

After several hours, the police released the twelve, and they were greeted by fellow protestors in front of the station, who asked Rosemarie to make a speech.

"I was not really prepared for this but still remember my exact words to the group. I said, '*Bring the troops home now. We need them here to protect us from the government.*' There was approval and cheering from the crowd."

At the Bennington District Court arraignment on April 21, the State's Attorney's office offered the protesters the diversion program, which would result in dismissal of the disorderly conduct charge after completing a community service assignment. Eleven defendants accepted this offer. Rosemarie Jackowski elected to go to trial. This was the lead story in the next day's *Bennington Banner*.

The reporter, John LeMay, asked me how I intended to conduct Rosemarie's case. Wasn't it obvious that she was guilty? I responded: "I believe that Rosemarie has a viable defense, and we'll let a jury decide. Our defense is going to be . . . that this was an act of conscience, not a criminal act."

The disorderly conduct statute under which Rosemarie was charged reads as follows:

§1026. Disorderly conduct
(a) A person is guilty of disorderly conduct if he or she, with intent to cause public inconvenience or annoyance, or recklessly creates a risk thereof: . . .
(5) obstructs vehicular or pedestrian traffic.
(b) A person who is convicted of disorderly conduct shall be imprisoned for not more than 60 days or fined not more than $500.00, or both.

The prosecutor's information (the name given to the charging document in the case) accused Rosemarie of obstructing traffic "*with intent* to cause public inconvenience or annoyance," even though the statute gave the State's Attorney the option of charging that she "recklessly created the risk" that this would occur. Our defense was simple: that Rosemarie's intent was to protest the bombing and killing of Iraqi children, not to cause public inconvenience. Rosemarie knew that she had obstructed vehicular traffic, but her *intent* was different: it was to raise public consciousness about the evils of the Iraq War.

Rosemarie testified with sincerity and eloquence to that effect. During the demonstration, she was thinking of the fate of the children of Baghdad, and she intended to oppose the indiscriminate bombing that was killing those children and thousands of adult civilians. She told the jury that the underlying motivation for her action was her Catholic faith and the Catholic Church's opposition to unjust wars.

In addition to Rosemarie's testimony on the intent issue, we relied on her protest sign, on which she had placed the photograph of the dead Iraqi child and antiwar slogans and statements, including former Attorney General Ramsey Clark's allegation that the United States had committed various war crimes.

We might have had an outside chance to win the case, but rulings by Judge David Suntag made that impossible. Over my objections (which I stated on the record up at the bench at least three times to provide a clear record in the transcript for appeal purposes), Judge Suntag instructed the jury that they should convict Rosemarie if the state proved beyond a reasonable doubt that she knew that her actions made public inconvenience "virtually certain." But there is a difference between *intending* that something will happen and *knowing* that it will likely occur. As charged, the statute, by its express language, required proof that the defendant *intended* the forbidden result.

I knew that Suntag's instruction was wrong. In effect, it directed the jury to return a verdict of guilty. Everyone present at the Four Corners that morning *knew* that traffic was being obstructed.

Although he had admitted Rosemarie's sign into evidence, Judge Suntag also ruled that he would not allow it in the jury room during their deliberations, on the basis that the photograph of the dead Iraqi girl was too "prejudicial." Maybe it was prejudicial to the state's ability to prove its case, I argued, but the sign was the best documentary evidence of Rosemarie's intent, which was to protest the bombing of civilians. Moreover, I had never heard of a judge refusing to allow the jury to consider in the jury room an exhibit that had been admitted into evidence. But Judge Suntag wouldn't budge on that issue either.

Given Judge Suntag's wrongheaded rulings, the jury had little choice but to find Rosemarie guilty. They deliberated for only fifteen minutes before returning with that verdict.

At the sentencing, I called several witnesses who affirmed Rosemarie's sincerity of belief, which was based largely on her interpretation of the teachings of Catholicism on the issue of unjust wars.

I told the court that during Rosemarie's childhood in Pennsylvania coal country amid the Great Depression, when her hard-working father made only 50 cents an hour, she got a job in a sweatshop at age 10 to help support the family. At age 30, she was a rape victim, and even though she named the perpetrator, the police did nothing about it, telling her that "this is just the kind of thing that men do every Saturday night," and "you don't want to hurt this guy, do you?"

I stressed that Rosemarie had no criminal record, was physically disabled, and indigent to boot; in fact, the court had previously granted my motion to allow her to proceed in forma pauperis.

Arguing that she should be required to attend a "Reparative Board" and perform 200 hours of community service, the prosecutor compared Rosemarie to white supremacists while conceding sourly that a racist defendant with prowar views would not "have the same amount of people coming up here and testifying for leniency." The prosecutor argued, "If this were a true case of civil disobedience," Rosemarie would have pled guilty "and taken the sentence that had come to her," which he incorrectly claimed is what Martin Luther King Jr. did. "This is not true civil disobedience. This is just a means to get media attention and to create a buzz."

I responded that the prosecutor erred when he "compare[d] Rosemarie to white supremacists," who "stand for hate and division in our society." In contrast to such racists, Rosemarie "was, in her view, standing up for people of color, children in Iraq, and to compare someone who's dedicated her life to peace organizations to white supremacists I think is more than over the top. I think it's grossly inappropriate." I added: "Martin Luther King and his followers went to trial many times and appealed many convictions, and they made some good law. The Deputy State's Attorney is just wrong about that." And: "To say that Rosemarie Jackowski did this just to create some media attention for herself is also wrong. She wasn't the only one who got media attention. The Deputy State's Attorney got plenty of media attention, and I didn't see him running away from the news cameras after he won the trial."

Rosemarie testified that she would refuse to comply with a sentence of community service, because in her mind she had done nothing to hurt the community. On her behalf I asked the court to sentence Rosemarie to "time served," the one day she had already spent in the Bennington police lockup.

Instead, Judge Suntag sentenced Rosemarie to zero to two days in jail, with credit for the one day she'd served, and with the second day in jail suspended on probation, along with a condition that she complete the Reparative Board program. Suntag knew when he imposed that sentence that Rosemarie would violate the terms of her probation by refusing to participate in the program or do community service and thus that she would be required, after going through yet another needless court hearing, to do the extra day of jail time and possibly face a separate contempt of court charge.

I appealed Rosemarie's conviction to the Vermont Supreme Court, which agreed that Judge Suntag's "virtually certain" instruction was wrong and that he should have instructed the jury that the state must prove criminal intent. It also directed Judge Suntag to reconsider the issue of Rosemarie's sign in the event of a retrial.

There would be no second jury trial. The prosecutors in the State's Attorney's office were thoroughly disheartened by the Vermont Supreme Court's ruling. They threw in the towel and dismissed the case. A retrial would have wasted state resources, and—who knows?—the jury might have returned an embarrassing not-guilty verdict.

For Rosemarie, this was a huge win. She went on to run twice (unsuccessfully) for Attorney General as the nominee of the democratic socialist Liberty Union Party, where Senator Bernie Sanders got his start before switching his registration to Independent. In the 2016 election, the party's gubernatorial candidate was Bill "Spaceman" Lee, the former southpaw Red Sox pitcher, whose campaign slogan was "We're so far left, we're right." Lee identified himself during the campaign as a socialist and a fan of Eugene Debs and fellow Vermonter Bernie Sanders.

Bill Lee was never elected governor, but during the 2011 season, at age 55, he became the oldest baseball player ever to appear professionally, pitching a complete nine-inning game for a minor league team, the San Rafael Pacifics of the independent Pecos League, held to raise funds for victims of Lou Gehrig's disease. Lee drove in a run with a homemade bat, and he beat the opposing professional squad from Hawaii by the score of 9–4.

During this time, I continued to serve as a volunteer for the American Civil Liberties Union of Vermont, both as a board member and as a cooperating attorney. My last judicially reported case for the ACLU set a legal precedent that continues to protect the right of millions of public school students to express their political views in school without fear of censorship or punishment by school boards or educational administrators.

⚖️

CHAPTER 19

A Precedent-Setting Case for Student Freedom of Speech

First Amendment hero Zachary Guiles is an accomplished professional musician who has performed with the Boston Symphony Orchestra. He became principal trombonist for the Richmond (Virginia) Symphony, where he met his wife, Ayano, who was the orchestra's acting principal trumpet player. Both were laid off due to the coronavirus, which has resulted in widespread unemployment for performing artists in every discipline. Zach and Ayano moved to Japan (Ayano grew up in Yokohama), hoping to find steadier work there in the classical music field.

I met Zach in the spring of 2004, the year that President George W. Bush was running for reelection. In March, Zach attended an antiwar rally held on the Vermont statehouse lawn in Montpelier. The Vermont Green Party was "tabling" the event and selling anti-Bush T-shirts for five bucks. Zach bought one of them because, as he testified on his own behalf as the first witness at the trial of his civil rights case in the United States District Court in Burlington, "I wanted to have a shirt that expresses my political view."

The shirt describes President Bush as the "Chicken Hawk in Chief" who is engaged in a "World Domination Tour." It accuses Bush of being an "AWOL draft-dodger," a "crook," a "lying drunk driver," and a "cocaine addict."

Crude illustrations enhance and dramatize the text, including a large caricature of a helmeted and chicken-bodied President Bush, drawings of gushing oil wells, dollar signs, liquor bottles, a Revolutionary War minuteman drinking liquor, martini glasses, razor blades, lines of cocaine, and straws for inhaling the cocaine.

In 2004, Zach was only thirteen and a seventh-grader in Williamstown Middle High School, a Vermont public school just south of Montpelier, which houses grades six through twelve in the same building. Relatively speaking, Williamstown schools rank low on the achievement scale. Statistics I found online show that just 21 percent of students met state standards in math, and 32 percent reached that standard in English.

Zach's father, Tim, had home-schooled Zach the previous year. Looking backward, Zach recently described his seventh-grade experience in Williamstown by saying that "I wasn't particularly popular, nor did I have any real problems there. I never really felt concerned about what other students would think of what I was doing or saying." A kid after my own heart!

Zach wore his provocative T-shirt to school once a week for approximately two months without incident, until Ashley Anderson, one of Zach's Bush-supporting classmates, complained to teachers. They told her that the shirt was protected by the First Amendment.

Ashley refused to let it be. She enlisted the support of her mother, the school cheerleading coach, who complained twice to the vice principal, Seth Marineau. Her specific complaint, and that of her daughter, was that the shirt violated the school's dress code. Under pressure, Mr. Marineau decided to take action against Zach.

Mr. Marineau called Zach into his office and told him that the shirt violated the school dress code, which prohibited students from wearing clothes "displaying alcohol, drugs, violence, obscenity, and racism." Marineau gave Zach three choices: remove the shirt, wear it inside-out, or cover the word "cocaine" and the illustrations of alcohol and drugs with tape.

Zach called his father, and together they went to the office of the superintendent of schools, Douglas Shiok, to protest this decision. Shiok supported the school administration's decision and brushed them off.

The next day, Zach defiantly and courageously wore the shirt to school uncensored, knowing that trouble from the administration would follow. He did so because, as he testified later at his trial, "it was concerning my free speech, and I think free speech is a very important aspect of life."

Seth Marineau, whose duties included student discipline, saw Zach wearing the shirt and escorted him to his office. Zach noticed that there was a Holocaust Remembrance Day poster on Mr. Marineau's wall depicting a Nazi swastika with a line drawn through it, and he pointed out that the poster would violate school policy if it were clothing, because the swastika is a symbol of racism. Marineau's answer to Zach's assertiveness was to rip the poster off his wall, crumple it up, and throw it into his trash can.

The vice principal gave Zach the same three choices that he had listed the day before: take off the shirt, wear it inside-out, or cover with tape the offending symbols and the word "cocaine."

Zach refused to comply with Marineau's ultimatum, citing his right to freedom of speech.

While Zach sat there, Mr. Marineau filled out a disciplinary form, which would become a part of Zach's permanent school record. He suspended Zach forthwith from school for the remainder of the day and sent him home.

Zach's response was to tape over the forbidden word and illustrations as ordered by Mr. Marineau. In protest, however, Zach wrote the word "censored" on each piece of tape, and he again wore the shirt to school. Zach's father, Tim Guiles, called ACLU-Vermont and spoke with its executive director, Allen Gilbert, who telephoned me. I agreed to represent Zach, and we asked my friend and ACLU cooperating attorney, David J. Williams of Montpelier, to be my cocounsel. David's home office (his kitchen) is close to where Zach lived, so we were able to hold client meetings there.

I drove to Montpelier immediately, and Zach and his father authorized David and me to file suit against the school administrators.

Within a few days, I filed a complaint in the United States District Court in Burlington, alleging violations of section 1983 of the federal Civil Rights Act. When a plaintiff is a minor, a civil action must be brought with the permission and participation of a custodial adult or, in archaic but still-used legal language, a "next friend." So our side was set forth in the court pleadings as "Zachary Guiles, by his father and next friend Timothy Guiles, and by his mother and next friend Cynthia Lucas."

We asked the court to rule that Zach has a constitutional right under the First Amendment to wear his T-shirt in class without any censorship and also to order the school to expunge his disciplinary record. We decided as a tactical matter to refrain from asking the court to award money damages, to make this a pure freedom of speech case, with no possible taint based on criticism from the public or the press that Zach and his parents were motivated by a desire to profit financially from the lawsuit.

To ensure that an injunction and order from the court would be binding legally on everyone, we had to name all the responsible school administrators and executives of Williamstown Middle High School as parties. The defendants were Vice Principal Seth Marineau, Principal Kathleen Morris-Kortz, School Superintendent Douglas Shiok, and Rodney Graham, a local dairy farmer and chair of the Williamstown School Board, who now serves as a Republican state representative.

Attorney Anthony Lamb entered his appearance for the defendants. According to Lamb's website at this writing, Tony has "a lifelong commitment to the rights of the underprivileged. Tony has argued expansively in federal court before such leading jurists as current Supreme Court Justice Sonia Sotomayor. His long experience in the region's highest court provides the expertise and confidence to win."

David Williams and I tried the case against Tony before Chief Judge William K. Sessions III, who had been the campaign manager for Senator Patrick Leahy, who sponsored his appointment to the federal bench by President Clinton. Sessions was a member of and later chairperson of the U.S. Sentencing Commission, the powerful and prestigious body responsible for drafting the federal sentencing guidelines.

David prepared and examined our two witnesses: Zach (who testified on the facts and made an excellent impression), and Charles Phillips, the principal at Montpelier High School, who'd received an award as Vermont's "Principal of the Year."

Phillips testified that his school's dress code bans only clothing that promotes alcohol and drug abuse. In his opinion, the sole function of the drug and alcohol illustrations on Zach's T-shirt was to make "a clear political statement" about President Bush's fitness for office and that there was "no way" that a student could interpret them "to be a positive statement about the use of drugs and alcohol."

Phillips concluded that, in his opinion as an educational expert, a ban on all drug symbols in school without regard to context is counterproductive because it "creates a climate where you can't talk about these things or [are] not as apt to talk about them."

As part of the Montpelier High School curriculum, Principal Phillips had students design antidrug and anti-alcohol posters that included visual depictions of these substances, which he found "more effective in many ways than the canned responses that come down from various publishing companies and things of that sort. It's something that the student himself or herself has created . . . has put some thought into."

I dealt with the defense witnesses.

Williamstown school administrators testified that they had required students to remove student clothing such as Budweiser hats and shirts, which advertise alcohol use. They admitted that Zach's antiwar, anti-Bush shirt was the first item of clothing with political content that they had ever banned or censored. They conceded that the school allows students to wear T-shirts with a prowar, pro–Bush administration slant with slogans such as "Go Army," "U.S.A. No. 1," "Don't Mess with the U.S.A.," and "These Colors Don't Run."

The school witnesses also admitted that the dress code did not apply to verbal messages or take context into account. So whereas a shirt emblazoned with the slogan "Take Heroin" in six-inch block letters passes literal muster under school policy, a shirt with the message "Just Say No to Alcohol," enhanced with an illustration of a beer can with the international "No" symbol drawn through it, would trigger disciplinary action.

To support its case for censorship, the school relied primarily on the pretrial deposition testimony of Carol Rose, who was the Vermont state official responsible for youth drug and alcohol programs.

In her testimony, Rose endorsed the Williamstown School's dress code because, in her opinion, the context in which illustrations of drugs and alcohol are displayed is irrelevant, and the mere viewing of them is intrinsically harmful to students. Her term for the banning of all images of drugs and alcohol was the "environmental approach" to substance abuse education and prevention.

On cross-examination, Ms. Rose unwaveringly affirmed her counterintuitive and absolutist idea that a T-shirt *opposing* substance abuse using images of drugs or alcohol is just as bad as one that explicitly *promotes* such use. Ms. Rose admitted that she knew of no scientific or psychological research to support that opinion or that the mere viewing of a political T-shirt like Zach's makes a student more prone to engage in drug or alcohol abuse.

I asked Ms. Rose if the gist of her testimony is that "the way to stop drug abuse is to make sure that students don't see any depictions at all of drugs," and she responded, "It would help." I then asked her "how would they know what drugs are if they don't see pictures of them? How would they know what to avoid?" She answered, "They wouldn't have to worry about it until they became of age."

Before the trial, I sent a copy of the Rose deposition to William J. Reedy, Esq., the general counsel of the Vermont Department of Education, Ms. Rose's employer. I had on other occasions dealt with Bill, who is the son of the late George Reedy, President Lyndon Johnson's press secretary, who resigned because he disagreed with Johnson's Vietnam War policy.

During a subsequent telephone conversation, Bill seemed surprised and embarrassed by the content of Carol Rose's deposition, which the parties had agreed could be considered by the judge in lieu of her live testimony. Bill wrote me a letter, which Judge Sessions admitted into evidence, stating that Rose's testimony "was not intended to draw any conclusions with respect to the outcome of the case or any substantive legal issue therein. To the extent that it did, it did not reflect an official position of the Commissioner or the Department." Which was a polite way of saying that Rose had no authority to speak on behalf of Vermont schools. In legalese, Ms. Rose's unapproved education policy positions were a "frolic and detour."

I thought that Bill Reedy's letter would win the case for us, but I was wrong. Judge Sessions issued a mixed opinion, holding that the First Amendment protected the words on Zach's T-shirt but not its illustrations. The school was wrong to require Zach to cover the word "cocaine" on his shirt, but it was fully justified in censoring the drawings of cocaine lines and liquor bottles.

Zach told me recently that, at age 13, he was "disappointed and a bit surprised" when he read Judge Sessions's opinion and that it "seemed very curious for him to draw the line that speech was protected in a school, but that it only applied to the printed word." Zach was a very smart kid, and when his case finally ended, it turned out that he'd been right all along.

We appealed Judge Sessions's decision to the United States Court of Appeals for the Second Circuit in New York City, where I had argued Edwin Towne's "ex-con with a gun" no-parole sentence and the Lamb Brook case. The school filed a cross-appeal with the court on the issue of the text on Zach's shirt, asking it to rule that it has the right to ban its messages in totality.

I was surprised that Tony Lamb, the school's lawyer, would go that far. But this was part and parcel of an extraordinary effort that the school made to justify and uphold the punishment of a seventh-grader for the sin of expressing opposition to George W. Bush and his administration's war policy in a colorful and attention-grabbing way.

I thought then, and I believe now, that a major reason for the school's authoritarian stance was that most school board members and townspeople disagreed with Zach's political views. Williamstown's leaders seemed to favor spending their time and energy squelching freedom of speech and catering to the whims of the school's cheerleading coach and her daughter over the need to improve the exceedingly poor academic achievement of the students in their care.

Our legal argument on Zach's behalf rested heavily on a case that arose out of students protesting the Vietnam War, *Tinker v. Des Moines Independent Community School District*, which the United States Supreme Court decided in 1969. In that case, Mary Beth Tinker and John Tinker, her brother, had been suspended from their public schools for wearing black armbands to express their opposition to the Vietnam War.

Des Moines schools had in the past allowed students to wear political buttons, and even the German Iron Cross, a symbol widely associated with Nazism. Stressing that the wearing of the antiwar armbands had neither interfered with the rights of others nor disrupted school activities in any way, the Supreme Court by a 7–2 vote held that the protest was constitutionally protected. Writing for the Court's majority, Justice Abe Fortas, a Lyndon Johnson appointee, proclaimed that "state-operated schools may not be enclaves of totalitarianism. School officials do not possess absolute authority over their students. Students in school as well as out of school are 'persons' under our Constitution. They are possessed of fundamental rights which the State must respect, just as they themselves must respect their obligations to the State." He continued: "In our system, students may not be regarded as closed-circuit recipients of only that which the State chooses to communicate. They may not be confined to the expression of those sentiments that are officially approved."

There are two narrow exceptions to *Tinker*. Schools have a right to censor student speech made in school-sponsored activities (especially where the public might infer the school's endorsement of its content), if such censorship is "reasonably related to legitimate pedagogical concerns." In *Hazelwood School District v. Kuhlmeier* (1988), the Supreme Court determined that the school principal acted reasonably by banning from a journalism class newspaper an article on teen pregnancy from which the identity of pregnant students might be gleaned from the text.

The second exception, set forth by the Supreme Court in a 1986 decision, *Bethel School District No. 403 v. Fraser*, involved disciplining a student for making a speech to his high-school assembly that was laced with "pervasive sexual innuendo." The Court determined that permitting students to engage in "vulgar and lewd speech" would "undermine the school's educational mission."

Fraser is the case on which Judge Sessions relied when he approved the censorship of Zach's T-shirt. Sessions deemed images of drugs and alcohol as inappropriate, "plainly offensive," and the equivalent, from a constitutional perspective, of using obscene language. In his opinion, images have less protection than text under the First Amendment because only the "manner" of speech is implicated when illustrations are censored.

We argued in our brief and at oral argument that Judge Sessions was wrong to put Zach's T-shirt into the *Fraser* box for several reasons. First, unlike the student's sex-laced address to his peers in a high-school assembly, Zach's T-shirt was a form of political speech, which traditionally is deserving of the highest possible protection under the First Amendment.

Second, we noted that the Supreme Court has limited the *Fraser* exception to lewd and obscene speech; thus, Judge Sessions was wrong to equate what he termed "inappropriate" images with "plainly offensive" speech under *Fraser*.

Third, we argued that Judge Sessions's opinion erred when it gave less constitutional protection to images than to the written word. The Supreme Court had in a 1985 commercial free speech case, *Zauderer v. Office of Disciplinary Counsel*, decided the contrary, holding that the illustration of a Dalkon Shield in a lawyer's advertisement was entitled to the same level of protection as the text that accompanied it, which asked the reader, "DID YOU USE THIS IUD?" The Supreme Court reasoned that "the use of illustrations or pictures . . . serves important communicative functions" by "attracting the audience's attention" and by "serv[ing] to impart information directly." The Court's opinion made clear that visual images are deserving of the same First Amendment protection as text because they "are a primitive but effective way of communicating ideas . . . a short-cut from mind to mind."

I argued the case for Zach at the Thurgood Marshall Federal Courthouse in New York City on October 28, 2005, with Tony Lamb on tap for the school. Our Second Circuit panel was a good one in the sense that it included no right-wing zealots. Richard Cardamone, the environmentally conscious Reagan appointee who had written the appellate decision in the Lamb Brook case, was the senior jurist of the three. I thought he was on our side, because from the bench he restated arguments from my brief in the form of pithy questions to me, beginning with "Are you saying that?" and "Do you mean that?" Judge Rosemary Pooler, a Clinton appointee with a background in consumer law and energy regulation and no apparent experience in First Amendment cases, asked most of the questions, and she seemed undecided. Judge Sonia Sotomayor, appointed by President Clinton to the court of appeals in 1998 and elevated by President Barack Obama in 2009 to Associate Justice of the Supreme Court, didn't say much during the oral argument, and when it was over I had no idea what she was thinking, but it seemed pretty clear from her silence that she had already made up her mind.

On August 30, 2006, the court of appeals issued a decision in favor of the freedom of speech of Zachary Guiles and that of the more than 3.1 million public school students in New York, Connecticut, and Vermont. Judge Richard Cardamone wrote the unanimous decision.

The first sentence of Judge Cardamone's opinion, like the rest of his writings, has a distinctly literary flavor, reminiscent of the humanistic writing style of Justice William O. Douglas. "This case requires us to sail into the unsettled waters of free speech in public schools," Judge Cardamone began, "waters rife with rocky shoals and uncertain currents."

The Second Circuit decision, since cited in more than a hundred other cases and law review articles and memorialized with its own Wikipedia page, navigated perfectly through those rocks and calmed those waters by explaining how the three leading United States Supreme Court cases should be viewed and applied to Zach and his shirt.

Judge Cardamone, joined by Judges Sotomayor and Pooler, agreed with our analysis: that *Tinker*, the black armband case holding that schools "may not regulate such student speech unless it would materially and substantially disrupt classwork and discipline in the school," is the touchstone. *Fraser* and *Kuhlmeier* delineate the two narrow exceptions to the *Tinker* rule. This way of looking at student speech is of great import for civil liberties because it elevates *Tinker*, the case with the most expansive view of the First Amendment in the school context, to the role of basic rule.

Applying the law to Zach's case, the court's opinion began by analyzing the *Tinker* exceptions to see whether they were applicable to Zach's T-shirt and justified its censorship.

Kuhlmeier, the court held, had no application to the Guiles case; that exception to freedom is triggered only in fact patterns involving a school-sponsored activity, such as a school newspaper. The court spent more time on *Fraser*, the decision that permits restriction of "lewd, vulgar, indecent or plainly offensive" speech. Clearly Zach's T-shirt was neither lewd nor vulgar or indecent, as those adjectives have purely sexual connotations. Were the illustrations of drugs and alcohol plainly offensive, as Judge Sessions held?

No, as a matter of law, they were not. The court ruled: "What is plainly offensive is not susceptible of precise definition," but it is "something less than obscene but related to that concept, that is to say speech containing sexual innuendo and profanity." It added, "The term plainly offensive cannot be so broad as to be triggered whenever a school decides a student's expression conflicts with its 'educational mission.'" The interpretation of "plainly offensive" adopted by Judge Sessions would "eviscerate" *Tinker* by allowing administrators to censor student speech whenever they disagree with it.

More Cardamone poetry: "While the exact contours of what is plainly offensive are not so clear to us as the star Arcturus is on a cloudless night, they are evident enough for us to hold that the images of drugs and alcohol on Guiles's T-shirt are not offensive, let alone plainly so, under *Fraser*. We believe this is especially so given that these images are presented as part of an anti-drug T-shirt, and, moreover, a T-shirt with a political message." And a flourish: "Indeed the *Fraser* court distinguished its holding from *Tinker* in part on the absence of any political message in Fraser's speech."

In sum, the court determined that the T-shirt is protected from school censorship by *Tinker*. Zach's repeated wearing of it did not cause any disruption at all. "Only when a fellow student's mother—who had different political views from plaintiff—protested did defendants direct Guiles to cover the drug and alcohol illustration."

Finally, the Second Circuit summarily disposed of Judge Sessions's legally unsupported view that illustrations have less First Amendment protection than words. Judge Cardamone wrote, "The pictures are an important part of the political message Guiles wished to convey, accentuating the anti-drug (and anti-Bush) message. By covering them defendants diluted Guiles's message, blunting its force and impact. Such censorship may be justified under *Tinker* only when the substantial disruption test is satisfied."

WHEN PRESIDENT OBAMA nominated Sonia Sotomayor for the Supreme Court, Republicans on the Senate Judiciary Committee attempted without success to make *Guiles* an issue during her confirmation process in a tendentious written question they posed to her:

Q: In *Guiles v. Marineau*, . . . you endorsed the First Amendment rights of a student to wear a shirt containing images of cocaine and alcohol, as well as the word "cocaine." Do you believe that a student's First Amendment right to wear a shirt displaying images of drugs and alcohol is stronger than the right of a private law-abiding citizen to participate in a political campaign?

Sotomayor deftly responded, in a way that provided her with some political distance from *Guiles*, by noting that she was not the author of the court's opinion:

A: In *Guiles v. Marineau*, . . . the court unanimously concluded that the school's decision to discipline the student for wearing a t-shirt that criticized the President violated the First Amendment. The basis for the court's decision is set forth in its opinion, which was written by Judge Cardamone. *Guiles* did not present the question whether the student's First Amendment rights were "stronger" than the right of a citizen to participate in a political campaign.

The Second Circuit's decision should have ended the case, but it didn't. The relentless Tony Lamb filed an attempt to appeal, by way of what is known as a "petition for certiorari," with the United States Supreme Court. On average, the Supreme Court hears only eighty of the 8,000 "cert petitions" each term. It takes the vote of four Justices for the Court to hear this form of appeal, which by statute and court rule is discretionary.

I filed a brief in opposition to Tony Lamb's cert petition. It began as follows: "The school administrators who have petitioned this Court for certiorari in this case have gone to extraordinary lengths to justify punishing a student for wearing a political T-shirt that criticized President Bush for allegedly engaging in the very thing that they understandably oppose: the abuse of alcohol and drugs."

I had done my best to encapsulate the case in a single sentence, and as I hoped, the Supreme Court denied certiorari. But it did decide to hear a cert petition that had been pending at the same time as *Guiles*, which presented a closely related student free speech issue. The Supreme Court granted the petition from a decision of the Ninth Circuit Court of Appeals and arising out of school discipline in Juneau, Alaska, titled *Morse v. Frederick*.

While standing across the street from his Juneau high school during a school-sanctioned parade, student Joseph Frederick, along with some classmates, held up a large banner emblazoned with the slogan "BONG HiTS 4 JESUS." When a school administrator ordered the students to pull down the banner, only Fredrick refused. The school punished Frederick by suspending him for ten days.

In an opinion by Chief Justice John G. Roberts, the Supreme Court affirmed the right of the school administration to impose that discipline. The Supreme Court's opinion cited the *Guiles* decision with approval, noting that the Second Circuit had taken pains to contrast Zachary's T-shirt with the "Bong Hits" emblem: one opposed drug abuse, while the other, in the words of Judge Cardamone, was "a clearly pro-drug banner."

Chief Justice Roberts also adopted the same method of analysis used by the Second Circuit in *Guiles*. He first determined that neither *Kuhlmeier* nor *Fraser*, which set forth the exceptions to the rule of *Tinker*, applied to the facts.

Although the parade in Juneau was a school-sponsored event, Justice Roberts found that no viewer reasonably could interpret a sign endorsing the marijuana high-inducing inhalation of "Bong Hits" as carrying the school's endorsement, unlike articles in the student newspaper in *Kuhlmeier*. So that case isn't applicable.

Neither is *Fraser* on point, Chief Justice Roberts continued, because the slogan "BONG HiTS FOR JESUS" isn't "plainly offensive" in a constitutional sense. Echoing Judge Cardamone's view in *Guiles* on the limited connotation of the term "plainly offensive," Justice Roberts said: "We think that stretches *Fraser* too far; that case should not be read to encompass any speech that could fit under some definition of 'offensive.' After all, much political speech . . . might be perceived as offensive to some."

The Supreme Court went on to hold that *Tinker* is the case that applies. Although the banner didn't create a "substantial disturbance" in a physical sense, its display undermined the school's educational mission and compelling interest in conveying to kids that illegal drug use is harmful and wrong. Moreover, unlike the black armbands in *Tinker*, which were worn to protest the Vietnam War, the "Bong Hits" slogan was not a form of political speech deserving of heightened protection under the First Amendment.

MY OWN VIEW OF *Frederick* is that it unwittingly stands for the proposition that a majority of the Justices lack any sense of humor. Mr. Frederick's banner was intended to be funny, but they didn't get the joke.

From the standpoint of continuing a line of clear First Amendment precedent, the Supreme Court would have done better to grant certiorari in *Guiles* and affirm the Second Circuit decision, while laughing off the "Bong Hits" case as a silly outlier. But from the standpoint of the Court's prestige and image, it was necessary for it to refrain from approving in any way the messages on Zach's T-shirt: that George W. Bush is a hypocrite and an imperialist. The marijuana-loving bong-hitter Joseph Frederick became a convenient whipping boy, and his case was a safe way for the Supreme Court to allow the school to punish him while sticking with the precedent of *Tinker*, which allows students broad latitude to express their opinions in public schools.

In late June 2021, in the case *Mahanoy Area School District vs. B.L.*, the Supreme Court reaffirmed that *Tinker* is the lodestar for deciding student free speech cases. In *Mahanoy*, a student cheerleader who was passed over for the varsity squad and for the position she wanted to play in softball sent an internet video message to a group of friends while she was in an off-campus convenience store. The video showed the student raising her middle finger with the caption: "Fuck school fuck softball fuck cheer fuck everything."

Justice Stephen Breyer wrote the Court's opinion, with only Justice Clarence Thomas dissenting. (In my opinion, Breyer, now retired, was the best writer on the Supreme Court; unlike other Justices, whose prolix, intellectual showoff styles often confuse and annoy, he never uses footnotes, a practice that promotes clarity and readability. I think that Justice Breyer's way is particularly important for nonlawyer readers, for whom court decisions ought to be readily understandable.) Justice Breyer acknowledged that, while schools have the power to discipline some limited forms of off-campus speech, such as internet bullying or threats directed at specific students or teachers, the idea that everything that a student says or writes "during the full 24-hour day" is subject to school discipline would "mean that the student cannot engage in that kind of speech at all."

Public schools are the "nurseries of democracy," and as such they have the responsibility for "the protection of unpopular ideas," and they must ensure that "future generations understand the workings in practice" of the First Amendment's guarantee of freedom of speech. In B.L.'s case, her criticism of the school was "the kind of pure speech to which, were she an adult, the First Amendment would provide strong protection."

The Court then applied the "demanding standard" of *Tinker*, finding that there was no evidence that her video (despite its bad language, which might be offensive to some) had caused a "substantial disruption" of a school activity or its mission. Thus, under *Tinker*, the student's social media message was constitutionally protected and the school had no right to discipline her.

The Supreme Court's reliance on *Tinker* as the ultimate guide means that the Second Circuit's opinion in *Guiles v. Marineau* lives on in full force, and at this writing it continues to be legally binding and the leading case on First Amendment protection of student speech in the states of New York, Connecticut, and Vermont.

After the Supreme Court denied certiorari in *Guiles*, Tony Lamb called me and asked if David Williams and I would either forego or vastly reduce our claim to attorney's fees, to which we were entitled as a matter of law as the winners of a civil rights case. Tony explained that the school's insurance policy had a combined limit of $100,000 on damages and legal fees for a covered occurrence; the policy benefits had been exhausted, or nearly so, by paying his law firm for representing the school. To cover our legal fees, the municipality would either have to raise taxes or cut the school budget.

"Tony," I said, "you must be joking. In effect, my man, what you are telling me is that my law firm, as well as David Williams's law firm, should take a huge financial hit for challenging your clients' unconstitutional conduct, while you are paid in full for defending that bad behavior. The answer is no, Tony, and in my opinion, it is important that the taxpayers of Williamstown be made to understand that there will be a financial downside associated with violating the First Amendment rights of its students."

THE ZACHARY GUILES CASE wasn't the only First Amendment issue that I litigated in Vermont's public school arena. The other involved the academic freedom of a veteran, dedicated high-school teacher, Jay VanStechelman. The Green Mountain Union High School Board, in Chester, wrongfully fired Jay for showing the graphic, uncompromising, antiracism film *American History X* (1998) to a senior U.S. history class. After two narrow-minded parents complained about the film's content, the board furiously consigned Jay to a garbage dumpster. I settled the case for $70,000, and Jay resumed his distinguished teaching career elsewhere.

Clients almost never thank or remember me, but in December 2020, Jay kindly wrote me to say that my advocacy "meant more than I can put into words and was so helpful in my transition to my new life. I can't say I rolled in shit and came out smelling like a rose, but the experience educated me as much as it hardened me. Made me also realize that what is hard to say is also hard to hear and that our words mean everything when trying to reach a certain outcome, even if we feel we stand strong on the right side of an issue."

In other words, there are significant personal and professional costs associated with the exercise and defense of First Amendment rights. We should admire and support those with the gumption to stand up to authority when those rights are violated.

CHAPTER 20

⚖

Foiling a Frame-Up

I tried my last jury case as a criminal defense lawyer in 2013, around the time I noticed that something was wrong with me. My left thumb had developed a tremor that sometimes spread to my entire hand. I was having trouble keeping my work schedule accurately, and it was taking me longer to spot legal issues that might be helpful to my clients and to follow up with the legal research necessary to combat the state.

My client, a young man named Larry, of Shaftsbury, had been charged with two criminal counts of aggravated domestic assault for allegedly slashing his brother Keith with a knife and for causing a serious wound to his arm. The maximum penalty for these offenses was imprisonment for thirty years. Larry was innocent, but if I lost the case he would probably go to prison for a long time. This is every decent criminal defense lawyer's worst nightmare, one that thankfully I hadn't experienced in my career—yet—but which is a kind of Golem that always looms out there, on the verge, waiting in the shadows.

The personalities involved in the trial aren't what stick in my mind the most. Instead, it's the realization that the case brought home to me: that decades after I started my law practice, the criminal justice system hadn't changed much. The prosecutors and the cops and judges were still part of the same buddy-buddy "it's just us chickens against those low-life defendants" culture that presumes guilt and cuts corners to railroad the poor and those with brown or black skin.

In all criminal cases, under the United States Supreme Court case *Brady v. Maryland* (1963), prosecutors are required to turn over to the defense any "exculpatory" evidence they have in their file. This means any and all material that might bear on the defendant's innocence, reduce the degree of guilt, or be helpful to the defense at sentencing in the event of conviction.

Prosecutors often delegate to support staff the boring task of assembling this "Brady material" and making it available to the other side. Overworked or lazy prosecutors, or ones who aren't terribly interested in the truth, will occasionally withhold exculpatory evidence. Sometimes they sloppily prepare for trial without realizing that it's there, or they pretend that it doesn't exist when they present their case to a jury, hoping that the defense won't find out about it.

Negligent private defense lawyers, or public defenders who are so overwhelmed with their heavy caseloads that they can't possibly spend the time they would like on each case and are forced to go to trial and "wing it," sometimes overlook a priceless nugget of exculpatory evidence that is buried in the piles of police reports, witness statements, criminal record checks, arrest sheets, and meaningless forms that the prosecutor's office has turned over—along with a bill to reimburse them for their efforts.

In this case, State Trooper Lewis Hatch, who arrested Larry, had drafted and signed under oath two separate affidavits stating that Larry, while being processed in the police lockup, had "taken responsibility for" stabbing his brother. In other words, he had supposedly confessed to the crime.

Hiding in the large stack of discovery materials that I received from the Bennington County State's Attorney's office was a computer disc inside a blank envelope. I wasn't sure what the disc contained, but as soon as I was able, I slid it into my computer drive and played it.

It was a video recording of Larry being placed in the lockup and interrogated by Trooper Hatch.

The conversation between Trooper Hatch and Larry, while he was being processed and then when he was behind bars in a cell, was extensive. The video of it made it clear and beyond dispute that Larry had never confessed to the crime, as Trooper Hatch had claimed. In fact, Larry denied stabbing his brother. Trooper Hatch had not told the truth in his affidavits, and he did not tell the truth when I took his pretrial deposition. Was Hatch's erroneous statement that Larry had "taken responsibility" for the injury to his brother a simple mistake? That was hard for me to believe, given that it was Hatch who conducted the interrogation and he who made a video of it, and I was hoping that the jury would agree.

Neither had the prosecutor disclosed to the defense everything that the cops who had investigated the case either knew or should have known about the psychological problems of their complaining witness, Larry's brother Keith. Fortunately, I had uncovered a great deal about him from speaking with Larry and his mother.

Three Vermont State Police troopers took the stand. I have the official transcript of the trial, and so I'm not relying on memory here. On cross-examination of the officers, and through other witnesses, I brought to the jury's attention that:

WHEN THE POLICE ARRIVED, they met Keith in the driveway, obviously under the influence of alcohol, bleeding from a slash wound to his arm. Initially, Keith told the police that he had not seen Larry stab him and that he had not seen a knife and didn't know what had caused his injury. On further prompting, when asked to describe the knife that cut him, Keith said, "I don't know. Probably a black handle and a silver blade." The officers left out of their reports the fact that Keith initially told them that he had not ever seen a knife. In my opinion, this was a deliberate omission.

Trooper Hatch interviewed Larry's mother, Cheryl, and her boyfriend, Burt, and they told him that Larry had been with them all evening and that they knew he had not stabbed his brother. It was only after Keith had left the trailer home, walked down the road with his new girlfriend, and returned to the trailer a half-hour later that Keith was bleeding from a wound. When Larry saw that his brother was injured, he called 911 to request emergency help for Keith.

The police searched the surrounding area outdoors but never found a bloody knife or other weapon, such as a box cutter, that could have been used to cause a slash wound. Moreover, and the officers never saw even a single drop of blood on Larry or his clothing, highly unusual for the perpetrator of a stabbing; usually the stabber is splashed with blood. And the next morning, Burt (Cheryl's boyfriend) found and photographed large congealed pools of blood 465 feet down the road, where Keith had walked with his girlfriend. Burt also testified that Keith owned a box cutter, a device utilizing a razor blade that could have caused Keith's wound.

The troopers knew that Keith had taken Larry's car without permission and drove to pick up his girlfriend in another town, even though Keith was drunk to the point of being "hammered." Keith testified that he was so drunk at the time that he had no memory of the incident. Keith admitted that he had also taken the antidepressant drug Effexor, which he knew he shouldn't have done because he had been drinking. The evidence was that Keith had made two suicide attempts in the recent past, one of them by taking an overdose of drugs. (However, the trial judge refused to let me establish through Keith's mother that the other suicide attempt was with automobile exhaust and that he had been an inpatient in a mental hospital after the suicide attempts.)

Despite all of this, police chose to accept uncritically the word of the grossly intoxicated Keith that his brother had stabbed him, and they refrained from charging Keith with any offense, though they could have done so: for operating a motor vehicle without the owner's consent, driving while his license was under suspension, and driving under the influence of alcohol. Instead, they arrested only Larry and charged him with the crime of aggravated domestic assault.

The prosecutor called Trooper Hatch to the stand. He asked Hatch whether Larry had made any statements while he was being questioned in the police lockup. Hatch's response was that Larry had confessed and that he had done so by saying "something to the effect that I really screwed up this time" and that this was "mumbled under his breath."

I knew this to be untrue, and it was essential that I expose that untruth on cross-examination. I asked Hatch: "And you have also testified that [Larry] essentially admitted the offense when you took him into custody?"

Hatch knew what was coming, and he didn't like it. "Can you clarify that one more time, please?"

DEFENSE: "You took Larry into custody. You took him to the barracks, right?"
HATCH: "Correct."
DEFENSE: "And you processed him?"
HATCH: "Correct."
DEFENSE: "He was in a cell there for a period of time?"
HATCH: "Correct."
DEFENSE: "And I think you testified that you read his release conditions to him."
HATCH: "Yes."
DEFENSE: "And it was while you were doing that that he took responsibility for the offense; is that right?"
HATCH: "In a small nature, yes."
DEFENSE: "Actually, didn't he tell you that he never hurt his brother?"

At this point, the prosecutor objected, on the nonsensical ground that my question called for inadmissible hearsay, even though the prosecutor had himself asked Trooper Hatch on direct examination what Larry had told him. The judge overruled the objection.

DEFENSE: "Now, didn't [Larry] tell you, while you had the conditions of release in your hands and you were going over them, that he never hurt his brother?"

HATCH: "He did mention that throughout the night. I'm not sure if he did at that exact time."

DEFENSE: "Would looking at the video help refresh your recollection in that regard?"

HATCH: "It may. If it—"

DEFENSE: "Well, if the video—there is a video camera in the lockup there, right?"

HATCH: "Correct."

DEFENSE: "—in the interview room."

HATCH: "Yep."

DEFENSE: "And there's a microphone, right?"

HATCH: "Uh-huh."

DEFENSE: "Yes?"

HATCH: "Correct."

DEFENSE: "And what happens there is recorded, right?"

HATCH: "Yes."

DEFENSE: "So if the recording and the video are accurate, wouldn't it help you to refresh your recollection about what actually happened?"

HATCH: "Yes."

The judge then excused the jury so that Trooper Hatch could watch it in private, although I had wanted to play the video while the jurors were present so they could see and hear for themselves what actually transpired. The prosecutor then renewed his objection to the video, but the judge correctly ruled that "if you introduce a part of a statement then the other side is entitled to introduce the rest of the statement." The prosecutor continued to object, and I responded, "I don't understand why the deputy—the state's attorney doesn't want the truth to come out."

The prosecutor eventually lost it, angrily telling the judge, "Your Honor, Mr. Saltonstall is now calling my officer a perjurer and a liar." I thought, *If the shoe fits, wear it*, but I said nothing.

The judge brought the jury back in and allowed me to resume my cross-examination.

> DEFENSE: "Now, isn't it true that you asked [Larry] if he understood the release conditions, correct?"
> HATCH: "Yes."
> DEFENSE: "And he said no, I really don't?"
> HATCH: "Correct."
> DEFENSE: "And then he said that I didn't do anything to him, meaning his brother?"
> HATCH: "Correct."
> DEFENSE: "And then he said his brother must have been depressed and gotten ahold of something?"
> HATCH: "Correct."
> DEFENSE: "And then he said, you guys have got me now, right?"
> HATCH: "Correct."
> DEFENSE: "And he said, my brother has gotten me into a doo-doo load of trouble?"
> HATCH: "Yes."
> DEFENSE: "Right? He didn't use the word *doo-doo*, though, right?"
> HATCH: "He used the word *shitload*. Your Hon—"
> DEFENSE: "All right. I was trying to avoid that, but you're right. And then, he asked you if it was a felony, correct?"
> HATCH: "Yes, he did."
> DEFENSE: "And you responded in the affirmative?"
> HATCH: "I said yeah."
> DEFENSE: "That's not the same as admitting guilt; is it?"
> HATCH: "No, he asked a question."

Hatch hadn't told the truth on direct examination. Larry had never confessed or "taken responsibility" for the stabbing. I looked at the jury. I could tell that they understood.

Defendants almost never testify at their trials, for two reasons. Either the defendant is guilty, and if he lies about that on the witness stand after admitting guilt in private to his defense lawyer, the lawyer is ethically bound to move to withdraw from representation (which often results in a mistrial). Or the defendant decides not to testify for tactical reasons, because a skilled cross-examination by the prosecutor might prove detrimental to the defense case, even when the client is innocent.

Larry wanted to testify. It was his constitutional right to do that, and he was innocent, and I agreed with his decision. He did well, telling the jury through genuine tears that he loved his brother very much and that he had not stabbed him. When he saw that his brother was hurt, he called 911 for help. Larry's mother and her boyfriend corroborated his account. The only witness at the trial who claimed that Larry had stabbed Keith was Keith himself. No one other than the "hammered" Keith blamed Larry for his injury.

After the evidence is closed in a criminal case come final arguments. The prosecutor goes first, then the defense has its say, then the prosecutor is allowed to get up and rebut the defense lawyer's closing.

I couldn't believe what I was hearing from the prosecutor in his argument. He actually reiterated Trooper Hatch's untruthful claim that Larry had confessed. Even after Hatch had been forced to weasel out of that falsehood. Had the prosecutor been listening to the testimony? Did he think that the jurors were complete idiots? Or perhaps he was relying mistakenly, and in harried good faith, on final argument notes he'd made before the trial started. Or maybe the prosecutor hadn't been getting enough sleep and he'd been zoned out during the proceedings.

It was my turn to speak to the jury. I began by thanking them for their service, something that the prosecutor had failed to do. I said:

[F]or many of you, it's a financial sacrifice. It's a sacrifice of your time. But . . . this jury system is one of the things that distinguishes America from other countries that we wouldn't want to live in like red China or Iran or Nazi Germany. If we didn't have this system, it would be a system where the executive would decide who is guilty or not guilty. And thank God that we have this jury system and that you folks are here today.

This was a less-than-thorough police investigation. I think that's understandable. It was late at night on a weekend. The police have a hard job. We all know that to be true. But they apparently took the work [sic] of Keith—who was drunk and on Effexor, which is a powerful drug—that his brother cut him. Now, what did Keith say when he was first asked about this? He said that he didn't see what had cut him. And then, on further prompting, I would suggest by the police, he said I guess it was a knife with a black handle and a silver blade. And later on at the hospital, he goes back to well, I didn't see it because it was too dark. . . .

And who was it that found the blood the next day? Well, it wasn't the police. It was Burt, who did some detective work on his own. He took those photos, which you'll have in the jury room, of all that blood . . . 465 feet away from the house. . . .

And take a look at Keith's eyes [in the police photographs]. He is really hammered. And you heard testimony that he had been suicidal. He's a very troubled young man. . . . Keith had made a couple of recent suicide attempts. He was, by his own admission, so drunk that he had some sort of blackout. He can't remember anymore what happened. Nevertheless, he took Larry's car and drove it. . . . Someone like that is capable of almost anything. And frankly, you know, he's taking a medication that he knows shouldn't be taken with alcohol. You know, we don't really know what happened. Maybe he cut himself since he had done suicidal acts before with his mixture of Effexor and alcohol. . . .

Now, there was no evidence that the police frisked Keith. . . . There was no testimony that they actually frisked him to see if he had anything. He was—basically, the testimony . . . [was] that he was taken to the hospital. Of course, if there was a boxcutter, which we know he owned, he could have chucked it somewhere or somehow gotten rid of it, maybe under a car. We just don't know.

Now, why did he blame his brother? Well, that is also somewhat of a mystery. We know that he was drunk and he was drugged up and that Keith was not making sense and he wasn't rational or reliable. Maybe he was hiding something. Maybe he was concerned that, if it came out that he cut himself, he was going to be hospitalized again and didn't want that to happen. We just don't know. But remember, the defense doesn't have the burden to prove anything. . . .

Now, contrast these . . . prosecution witnesses with Cheryl, Burt, and Larry. They told you what happened from their perspectives. And I submit to you, and you're the judges, but I submit to you that they were sincere and they were candid. You can consider the witnesses' demeanor and how they seem to you. And I suggest to you that they were worthy of belief and that their testimony had the ring of truth. And they all told you—Burt and Cheryl told you that Larry did not have a knife that night and that Keith wasn't wounded [by Larry]. . . .

Now, Larry . . . he didn't have to take the witness stand. But he had the courage to get up and tell you folks what happened. And once again, I suggest that he was candid and truthful. I think you can tell when someone is being truthful and when they're not. Larry called 911 when . . . he saw that his brother was injured. What does that tell you? He was concerned about his brother. Did he run away? No.

I had decided to save the best for last, without using the loaded word "perjury" that the prosecutor had suggested at a bench conference:

And what did [Larry] say in the lockup? My memory's different from what the prosecutor said.

You may recall that Trooper Hatch initially said that Larry had said something to the effect that he was guilty. Then Trooper Hatch had the opportunity to watch the video again, the video in the jailhouse there. And he came back and said, No. Larry said he'd done nothing to his brother. He must have gotten ahold of something. Now he's telling a story, he's gotten me into deep doo-doo and you've got me now. That's not an admission of guilt. It's just the opposite.

Now, you don't have to agree with everything I've said here. But if the evidence leaves you with this lingering doubt, you're scratching your heads and saying to yourselves, you know, I really don't know what happened, well, that's a reasonable doubt. And if you have a reasonable doubt, it's your duty—the Judge will tell you when he instructs you to return a verdict of not guilty.

Why do we have that burden of proof beyond a reasonable doubt? It's to protect the innocent. It's so that innocent people aren't convicted of crimes that they haven't done, and the consequences of a wrong verdict. I'm sure all of you have read about wrong verdicts and people are exonerated years later and the tragedy that has happened. I'm sure you've all read about cases like that.

Larry did not commit any crime, and the state has utterly failed to prove that he's guilty of anything beyond a reasonable doubt. So I'm asking you, please, to return a verdict of not guilty. Thank you.

In his rebuttal argument, the prosecutor failed even to mention, much less defend, Trooper Hatch and the change in his testimony about a supposed "confession" by Larry after viewing the video, which had established the truth: that Larry had denied hurting his brother.

The judge then instructed the jury on the law, and the jury retired to deliberate. Forty minutes later, the jury returned. They did not look at my client, which is supposed to be a very bad sign.

The judge said, "I'd ask the foreperson to stand for the verdict. And I'd asked the defendant to stand. Mr. Foreman, has the jury reached a verdict?"

JUROR: "We have."
THE COURT: "Is your verdict unanimous?"

JUROR: "It was."
THE COURT: "What is your verdict?"

The foreman paused for a few heart-stopping seconds. Then he proclaimed in open court the two most cherished words in the criminal defense lawyer's lexicon:

"Not guilty."

The outcome was the correct one, and I was both relieved and disgusted. The way I saw it, a police officer had testified untruthfully, in his paperwork and on the witness stand, in a wrongful effort to convict my innocent client, and the prosecutor appeared to accept and even endorse Trooper Hatch's baloney. The judge had done nothing to punish summarily this uniformed, badge-toting witness; neither did the judge direct or suggest that the State's Attorney's office bring charges against him or report him to his superiors for potential discipline.

It was just another day in the criminal justice neighborhood.

Trooper Hatch's behavior in a different case came back to bite him shortly after Larry's trial—and with a vengeance. Hatch had achieved, among some Vermonters and their lawyers and even his supervisors in the Vermont State Police, a reputation for racially profiling motorists and stopping people of color without cause to search them and their vehicles for drugs. Hatch finally did that once too often, to a young man who was willing to stand up for himself, and who had the ACLU-Vermont in his corner, ready to expose this officer and do battle against his misconduct.

The case involved Gregory Zullo, a 21-year-old African American man driving home to Rutland from his job in Killington, down a dangerously steep mountain. Trooper Hatch stopped Mr. Zullo in cold, snowy, late-winter weather for no reason other than his skin color. Hatch claimed that he had detected a "faint" smell of marijuana when the Black "subject" rolled down the driver-side window on command.

Hatch seized the car and had it towed to a police lot, abandoning Mr. Zullo, who was forced to walk and hitchhike 8 miles in the freezing dark to his home. A search of the car turned up a pipe with a tiny amount of marijuana residue, but that wasn't enough to support a criminal charge, even assuming that the pipe actually belonged to Mr. Zullo, rather than being planted or stashed there by someone else.

The ACLU sued Hatch in Superior Court for violation of Mr. Zullo's civil rights. Judge Helen Toor (the Forest Service's lawyer in the Lamb Brook case) dismissed the litigation on legal issues before trial, but the Vermont Supreme Court reversed her decision in an opinion issued in January 2019, and the ACLU then settled the case against Hatch for the sum of $50,000.

THE STATE POLICE FIRED Trooper Lewis Hatch in 2016, three years before the issuance of the Vermont Supreme Court's opinion upholding the civil rights of Gregory Zullo.

Mark Davis, in an article published in the May 4, 2016, edition of the Vermont weekly newspaper *Seven Days*, set forth the reasons for Hatch's termination. His reporting is based on his reading of the Trooper's personnel file, which had been released to the public after Hatch appealed his sacking to the Vermont Labor Relations Board. According to Davis, "Hatch had a history of conducting drug searches with no legal justification. Often, his targets were black men." Davis added that "Hatch's superiors were so concerned about his pattern of behavior that they eventually required him to call a supervisor, describe the situation he was in and obtain permission in advance of any search. But Hatch refused to follow those protocols on at least two occasions, according to the documents, and referred to such supervision as a 'fucking monkey game.'"

It's gratifying that the state of Vermont fired Trooper Lewis Hatch for his "monkey game" racial profiling and illegal searches. In my opinion, however, the state should have prosecuted him for his false testimony in Larry's case. I will never forget what this man tried to do: convict an innocent, powerless, low-income trailer-home resident and send him to prison.

In the 1978 book *Mocking Justice*, the journalist Hamilton Davis chronicled the Vermont career of a crooked cop named Paul Lawrence, whose perjury sent many young counterculture kids to prison during the late 1960s, Vermont's "back to the land" hippie era. Lawrence's phony drug busts, including one that snared a friend of mine, always occurred when he was alone, with no other cops around to vouch for what he was doing. The marijuana that Lawrence claimed to have seized from the multitude of longhaired victims whom he busted turned out to be the property of Paul Lawrence himself, a stash he'd obtained somehow from a New York State drug lab.

Ultimately, Paul Lawrence was caught and sent to prison. Hamilton Davis warns at the end of his book, however, that frame-ups, including those engineered by a single bad cop, "could happen again, in Vermont or elsewhere."

Trooper Lewis Hatch charged Larry with a crime he hadn't committed, and he claimed falsely under oath, both before and during the trial, that Larry had confessed. I was never able to fulfill my ambition to do something great that would be instrumental in bringing about systemic legal change, but in a sense this last jury trial was a fitting end to my career as a renegade for justice. At least on a small-town level, I had helped to foil the ethically bankrupt attempt of a police officer to convict an innocent man, a happy ending to my career as a trial lawyer.

CHAPTER 21

⚖️

Epilogue

From Lawyer to Water-Truck Driver

The end came soon after Larry's stabbing case. In the late spring of 2014, I finally got around to seeing Kim Fodor, MD, my primary care physician in Bennington, to tell her about puzzling symptoms that I was experiencing—a tremor in my left thumb, reduced intellectual acuity at times, night sweats, and persistent nightmares—to find out what it all meant. She had me stand with my eyes closed and arms outstretched. I started to fall backward, but she was there behind me. She watched me walk up and down a hallway and felt my left hand. She told me she thought I had Parkinson's disease, and she sent me to Stephen Lee, MD, a neurologist and movement specialist at the Dartmouth–Hitchcock Medical Center in Hanover, New Hampshire, for a workup. A doctor named Stephen Lee was going to diagnose a patient named Stephen Lee Saltonstall, a funny bit of synchronicity, I thought.

Dr. Lee measured my tremor, using a special app he'd invented, by simply resting his cell phone underneath my left hand. He ordered a bunch of other tests, including a set of scratch-and-sniff cards. I was supposed to identify the smell on each card. I flunked that, and I also learned that my IQ test result had plummeted from the 150s to the 130s, primarily because I was unable to duplicate from memory a series of line drawings. I could still remember numbers and count them backward as well as forward, which was some consolation, but the IQ drop was embarrassing and frightening.

Dr. Lee privately told Ellen that he was concerned that I might have an aggressive form of Parkinson's disease called "Lewy Body," the illness that afflicted the actor Robin Williams and that typically causes death within a year or two. Williams hung himself rather than waiting to become totally demented and a terrible burden on his wife and family.

In the fall of 2014, Dr. Lee ordered an MRI, under anesthesia so that the test wouldn't be affected by tremors. When I emerged from the electronic tube, Ellen and I waited for Dr. Lee to come to see us with the result.

After an hour, Dr. Lee arrived in our waiting room and gave us the good news. "You have the common form of Parkinson's disease, he said. You're lucky. With onset at age 70, drugs will slow the symptoms of your Parkinson's long enough so that you'll die of something else. Moving to a warmer clime will lessen those symptoms, and I recommend that you do that."

I closed my law practice. Ellen retired from teaching. We sold our house in Sandgate and moved to Tucson, Arizona.

WHEN I THINK BACK to my three years at Phillips Exeter Academy, I realize now that, bad as it was—with the hazing, forced Christianity, WASP white privilege, and loneliness—that it served a purpose, though not the purpose that my father or the school had intended.

Without the Exeter experience, I might have settled into a comfortable life in the Cambridge intellectual establishment, perhaps as an academic, teaching a course on the Hudson River School of landscape artists or tutorials examining the impact of technology on American culture.

Instead, my rebellion against Exeter's elitist, Social Darwinist culture thrust me into a new universe. I walked the walk of the shoeless in their dirt-floor homes. I shared the fears and nightmares of the hopeless and the lumpen, crushed by circumstance of birth or by exploitation or cruelty or racial prejudice. I lived among wild animals who can't speak for themselves or save the forests they need to survive. I became a street-level guerrilla warrior, defending the defenseless in an outlaw world run by the apologists and enablers of the wealthy and powerful. I won a few skirmishes here and there, but never the war; I couldn't change the system. My battle scars are the stories I told here, and the lives of my clients, which won't leave me. I wake up with them, live with them, and sleep with them. Their world defines my world, though my life as a lawyer is no more.

In retirement, I am a volunteer water-truck driver for Humane Borders, a Tucson-based relief organization dedicated to saving the lives of migrants fleeing their home countries from political oppression, torture, sexual exploitation, and murder, crossing our southern border without papers.

These wretched and defenseless people, including unaccompanied adolescents and mothers with tiny babies, desperately attempt the ultra-hazardous trek on foot across the Sonoran Desert to urban Arizona, their only chance for freedom and safety. Many expire from dehydration and exposure. They experience horrible deaths. Hungry, thirsty, their feet covered with blisters, and delirious from the 110-degree heat, they will sometimes strip themselves naked, trying to cool off but increasing their suffering instead.

An average of 150 bodies are found each year in the Tucson sector; in 2020 the number was 225. As many as ten times that number don't make it, but their bodies are never located in the desert wilderness. It takes only two weeks for predators to skeletonize the dead; then coyotes scatter their bones.

Humane Borders has fifty water stations in the Sonoran Desert, consisting of 55-gallon plastic drums with spigots and mounted sideways on cradles, marked by thirty-foot-high blue flags, and filled with Tucson city water.

We test the water with meters for particulate matter, check it visually for algae, and taste it ourselves to make sure the water is okay to drink. We place our barrels strategically where we know that migrants walk, either from consulting our own "death maps" where bodies have been found, or seeing pathways in the brush, footprints in the sand, or finding artifacts such as discarded clothing, backpacks, cell phones, and empty water bottles. Sometimes the artifacts are themselves troubling, such as a baby's sock I picked up under a mesquite tree where a family had slept, and a pair of worn-out ballet slippers that someone, likely a young girl, had left behind in a wash (a seasonally dry riverbed). In November 2021, I picked up a green plastic baby spoon in the dirt within a few feet of one of our water stations.

It's rare that we encounter a migrant alive, because they run and hide when they see or hear us, not knowing that our purpose is to be of help, not to arrest or injure or kill them. Migrants must deal not only with the ever-present U.S. Border Patrol but also armed vigilante gangs who will beat and even shoot them. I have seen a photo of a migrant wounded by bullets fired by vigilantes. One of our volunteers has overheard them bragging about capturing a migrant group, raping the women, and then forcing everyone in the band to undress, taking away their clothes and leaving them nude in the sun to die. The vigilantes also vandalize our water stations by shooting the water barrels with guns of every caliber, puncturing them with screwdrivers, removing the spigots, stealing the equipment, and smashing our flagpoles.

A few years back we started putting locks over the holes used to fill the barrels, because vigilantes were pouring gasoline and turpentine into the water. What amazing commitment these misguided people show in pursuing their cruel mission, and what pleasure they seem to derive from it. Vigilantes try their best (unsuccessfully) to terrorize us volunteers as well. One hot afternoon, I drove our beat-up old pickup truck, with a 300-gallon water tank mounted on the back, to service a water station on a high ridge called Cemetery Hill near Arivaca, Arizona, and our team was greeted by a missing spigot, an empty, vandalized barrel, and the sad sight of a dead coyote dumped at the station, doubtless courtesy of one of the local militia groups.

On another day I was driving a different route, through the Buenos Aires National Wildlife Refuge, with fellow volunteer Jorge Soto, a brave United States Army veteran whose job in Afghanistan was to deactivate roadside bombs. We found a teenage migrant lying exhausted and debilitated under a tree, unable to go any farther. His name was Norberto, and he was from a town called Margarita in the state of Chiapas, near Mexico's southern border. Norberto was trying to reach his brother, who lives in Gadsden, Alabama, more than 1,700 miles east–northeast from where he'd crossed the border into Sasabe, Arizona. Norberto had no idea how far he'd have to travel, assuming that he made it alive as far as the road to Tucson, a forty-mile hike in the desert heat.

Norberto had been trekking with a group of six, which the Border Patrol deliberately scattered by hovering over it with a helicopter. Officers chased him through the cactus-filled desert landscape through the night, using all-terrain vehicles, horses, and dogs. Norberto had no money and was very hungry, so we gave him some food and all the cash we had on us (both dollars and pesos). But he wanted to give himself up, so I walked a mile, flagged down a Border Patrol SUV, and after five Border Patrol and sheriff's cars converged on the scene, officers handcuffed him and drove him to detention in Tucson, later to appear in federal court for sentencing to a term of imprisonment for the crime of unlawful entry before being deported. We telephoned Norberto's brother in Alabama to let him know what had happened.

Spending a day driving a Humane Borders water truck through the Sonoran Desert and checking and filling our water barrels isn't heroic; it's a rewarding routine that I'm honored to be able to perform. On the day of each water run I get up at 3:30 a.m., get myself together, do household chores, leave the house at 4:45 a.m., and drive through the empty city of Tucson, down 22nd Street, over a bridge and across railroad tracks into South Tucson, an independent municipality that's home to a large community of brown-skinned people, to our truck lot. It's early, and the only other beings in sight are the homeless dogs who populate the neighborhood, existing on scraps. I go through a couple of locked gates, check our Chevy

250 truck, with its 300-gallon tank of water weighing more than a ton, for safety issues, especially the tires and wheels. Not long ago someone broke in and loosened all the lug nuts on one wheel, which nearly caused a fatal accident with three volunteers headed to Ajo and the west desert water run, which ends on Devil's Highway. I picked them up on the roadside, freaked out, with one wheel off the truck.

MY FRIEND AND COPILOT Guillermo Jones arrives, and we head south to the borderlands and Arivaca, where we have eight water stations to service, mostly in remote desert areas where migrants walk, with roads so bad that we seldom see the Border Patrol. Some of the water stations will have been used, with 20 gallons of water or more gone. Others will have been vandalized, and we will replace the bullet-scarred barrels (we have two spares on the truck) and crushed flagpoles. Our ten-hour drive through beautiful, treacherous desert killing fields is automatic now, a kind of meditation. We know that, if our water saves even one of the wretched migrant souls who are so despised and so denigrated by so many, then we have succeeded.

This is my last, best cause. It feels better than law practice. There is something wonderful and pure about trying to help people I don't know and will never meet. The work is love made visible, with no money or thanks either asked for or given in return.

Though on one winter morning, with the sun just coming up, as I opened a water barrel, I found a five-peso coin that a migrant had left on it: a gesture that brought tears to my eyes and renewed my faith in the power of compassion and the need to continue, even in a small way, defending the defenseless in an outlaw world.

Relevant Cases

Arrington v. M.B.T.A., 306 F.Supp. 1355 (D.Mass. 1969)

Associated General Contractors of Mass., Inc. v. Altshuler, 490 F.2d 9 (1st Cir. 1973)

Attorney General v. Massachusetts Interscholastic Athletic Association, 378 Mass. 342 (1979)

Bethel School District No. 403 v. Fraser, 478 U.S. 675 (1986)

Black Voters v. McDonough, 421 F.Supp. 165 (D.Mass. 1976)

Blair v. Blair, 154 Vt. 201 (1990)

Boston Chapter, N.A.A.C.P., Inc. v. Beecher, 504 F.2d 1017 (1st Cir. 1974)

Brady v. Maryland, 373 U.S. 83 (1963)

Coffin v. United States, 156 U.S. 432 (1895)

Commonwealth v. Colon-Cruz, 393 Mass. 150 (1984)

Commonwealth v. DiStasio, 294 Mass. 273 (1936)

Commonwealth v. Franklin, 376 Mass. 885 (1978)

Commonwealth v. Gilfedder, 321 Mass. 335 (1947)

Commonwealth v. Long, 485 Mass. 711 (2020)

Commonwealth v. McInerney, 373 Mass. 136 (1977)

Commonwealth v. McInerney, 380 Mass. 59 (1980)

Commonwealth v. Millen, 289 Mass. 441 (1935)

Commonwealth v. Min Sing, 202 Mass. 121 (1909)

Commonwealth v. Soares, 377 Mass. 461 (1979)

Commonwealth v. Tucker, 189 Mass. 457 (1905)

Commonwealth v. Walker, 370 Mass. 548 (1976)
Commonwealth v. Webster, 59 Mass. 295 (1850)
County of Suffolk v. Secretary of Interior, 562 F.2d 1368 (2nd Cir. 1977)
Custody of a Minor 375 Mass. 733 (1978)
Custody of a Minor, 378 Mass. 732 (1979)
District Attorney for the Suffolk District v. Watson, 381 Mass. 648 (1980)
Estelle v. Williams, 425 U.S. 501 (1976)
Gideon v. Wainwright, 372 U.S. 335 (1963)
Green v. Truman, 459 F.Supp. 342 (D.Mass. 1978)
Griswold v. Connecticut, 381 U.S. 479 (1965)
Guiles v. Marineau, 349 F.Supp.2d 871 (D.Vt. 2004)
Guiles v. Marineau 461 F.3d 320 (2nd Cir. 2006)
Hazelwood School District v. Kuhlmeier, 484 U.S. 260 (1988)
In Re Barney's Will, 70 Vt. 352 (1898)
In Re Duckman, 2006 VT 23
In Re Estate of Raedel, 152 Vt. 478 (1989)
In Re O'Dea, 159 Vt. 590 (1993)
International Society for Krishna Consciousness, Inc. v. Lee, 505 U.S. 672 (1992)
Jacobson v. Massachusetts, 197 U.S. 11 (1905)
Livingston v. Page, 74 Vt. 356 (1902)
Matter of Erdmann, 333 N.Y.S.2d 863 (1972), *reversed* 33 N.Y.2d 559 (1973)
McCulloch v. Maryland, 17 U.S. (4 Wheat.) 316 (1819)
Mooney v. Holohan, 294 U.S. 103 (1935)
Morgan v. Hennigan, 379 F.Supp. 410 (D.Mass. 1974)
Morse v. Frederick, 551 U.S. 393 (2007)
National Audubon Society v. Hoffman, 917 F.Supp. 280 (D.Vt. 1995)
National Audubon Society v. Hoffman, 132 F.3d 7 (2nd Cir. 1997)
Nichols v. Mudgett, 32 Vt. 546 (1860)
Nuclear Energy Institute v. EPA, 373 F.3d 1251 (D.C. Cir. 2004)
Oses v. Commonwealth of Massachusetts, 775 F.Supp. 443 (D.Mass. 1991)
Oses v. Commonwealth of Massachusetts, 961 F.2d 985 (1st Cir. 1992)
Police Comm'r of Boston v. Lewis, 371 Mass. 332 (1976)
Prince v. Massachusetts, 321 U.S. 158 (1944)
Pruneyard Shopping Center v. Robins, 447 U.S. 74 (1980)
Sierra Club v. Morton, 405 U.S. 727 (1972)
Sierra Club v. U.S. Army Corps of Engineers, 701 F.2d 1011 (2nd Cir. 1983)
State v. Gates, 2016 VT 36
State v. Jackowski, 2006 VT 119
State v. King, 131 Vt. 200 (1973)
State v. Pinsince, 105 N.H. 38 (1963)
State v. Kenneth Sargent and Corina Reagan (Vt.S.Ct. unpublished entry order
    11/17/1989)
State v. Waters, 2013 VT 109
Tinker v. Des Moines Independent Community School District, 393 U.S. 503
    (1969)

United States v. Kamin, 136 F.Supp. 791 (D.Mass. 1956)

United States v. Towne, 870 F.2d 880 (2nd Cir. 1989)

Vermont Women's Health Center v. Operation Rescue, 159 Vt. 141 (1992)

Vermont Yankee Nuclear Power Corp. v. Natural Res. Def. Council, 435 U.S. 519 (1978)

Walker v. Butterworth, 457 F.Supp. 1233 (1978)

Walker v. Butterworth, 599 F.2d 1074 (1st Cir. 1979)

Zauderer v. Office of Disciplinary Counsel, 471 U.S. 626 (1985)

Coda and Notes on Sources

In a December 1882 letter to her friend Elizabeth Holland, Emily Dickinson wrote that "Memory is a strange Bell-Jubilee, and Knell." And so it is with this book, this artifact from the annals of the obscure, my epitaph in a bottle. Perhaps it will survive the wild surf of history and be of some value to those minds struggling many years from now to understand American life after Little Boy and Fat Man.

The process of recall is different for everyone. For me, when an event from long ago rises to the surface of consciousness, I see a series of still photographs, some vivid, others curled and faded like expired Polaroids. They emanate past feelings, swirling emotional dust devils, untamed and unerasable from heart and mind.

But memory isn't enough or always correct, so I have relied in part on newspaper, magazine, and web articles. Many that I extricated from the commercial research website newspapers.com were helpful, and I used them to supplement my own frayed and crumbling collection. I read material from the *New York Times*, *New York Times Sunday Magazine*, *New York Times Book Review*, *Time* magazine, *Life* magazine, *Newsweek*, *The Guardian*, *Dissent*, *Salon*, *Washington Post*, *Boston Globe*, *Boston Herald*, *North Adams Transcript*, *Hartford Courant*, *Selma Times-Journal*, *Harvard Crimson*, *Exonian*, Wikipedia, and the following Vermont newspapers: the

Bennington Banner, *Rutland Herald*, *Brattleboro Reformer*, *Burlington Free Press*, *Barre Time-Argus*, *Seven Days*, and *VT Digger*. Where my memory of events is faulty, and I've gotten the facts wrong, I apologize.

I studied copies of appellate briefs and trial memoranda that I filed with the courts on behalf of my clients. The ones that I thought worthy of saving have been archived and are available in the Saltonstall family collection of papers at the Massachusetts Historical Society in Boston. For the benefit of lawyers and law students and courtroom wonks, I've included below the official citations to a raft of reported decisions to make them readily accessible.

Going through this book sequentially, here are some of the sources that I found useful, along with commentary on them.

Chapter 1: Prelude: Suicide Notes and Golden Hits on the Way to the Bar

The best work on King Philip's War, in which Nathaniel Saltonstall fought, is titled *The Name of War* (1998), by the Harvard professor and *New Yorker* writer Jill Lepore. Bridget Bishop's conviction and death sentence, after which Judge Saltonstall resigned in protest, rested primarily on spectral evidence. Her sparse extant trial record, including a summary of testimony (Salem court personnel destroyed official documents out of embarrassment and shame), is contained in a slim volume edited by David Levin, *What Happened in Salem? Documents Pertaining to the 17th-Century Witchcraft Trials* (1952), 43–62.

Judge Nathaniel Saltonstall is reputed to have said that, if not for the introduction of spectral evidence, Bridget Bishop could have been found guilty only of "wearing scarlet, countenancing shovel board, and getting herself talked about." Marion L. Starkey, *The Devil in Massachusetts* (1949), 156. See Joan Vennochi, "Hunting for Truth, not Witches," in the *Boston Globe*, October 2, 2019, A-10. See also the book by Richard Francis, *Judge Sewall's Apology* (2005), 122. Mr. Francis writes of Saltonstall that, although the death-dealing conduct of the other jurists in the witch trials "can be explained away in terms of prevailing beliefs and assumptions and by reference to precedent, at least one of their number was able to see that the emperor had no clothes."

After Nathaniel Saltonstall resigned from the tribunal, the presiding judge, Samuel Sewall, thought it prudent to write him a note critical of a whispering campaign, which was based on spectral evidence, to the effect that Saltonstall was himself a witch. Said Sewall: "I have sympathized with you and your family, as to the report that went of some being afflicted by a person in your shape, and that I fully believe the Letter [written by Saltonstall] asserting your innocence." See Levin, ed., *What Happened in Salem?*, 131.

I'm proud to be a direct descendant of Nathaniel Saltonstall, but as to some other family members, not so much.

Connecticut Governor Gurdon Saltonstall owned two slave ships, the *Africa* and the *Fox*. He sent his son Dudley on some of their evil voyages as overseer of the captives. Dudley was court-martialed for cowardice for his failure to attack the British fleet during the Battle of Penobscot Bay. This is the subject of *The Penobscot Expedition: Commodore Saltonstall and the Massachusetts Conspiracy of 1779* (2002) by George E. Buker.

Dudley Saltonstall continued his participation in the slave trade after the Revolution; in 1784, Dudley wrote his wife from what was known then as the Gold Coast, now the Republic of Ghana, detailing his effort to buy 300 slaves. See Anne Farrow, "Logging Misery and Death Aboard Connecticut Slave Ships," *Hartford Courant*, June 11, 2014.

Frederick Buechner served as the school minister at the Phillips Exeter Academy from 1958 to 1967. I met him only once after my expulsion, at a nerve-wracking (for me) chichi cocktail party in Dorset, Vermont, where waitstaff in white uniforms served catered canapes to formally attired guests of the old money Republican tribe. I was out of place (they knew who I was—a radical, troublemaking lawyer, unworthy of social acceptability despite my last name), and I proceeded directly to the open bar in search of fortification.

After draining a rocks glass filled with Jack Daniels neat, I buttonholed Fred Buechner and tried to convey to him the pain I experienced as a hazing victim at Exeter. I don't understand why, but Fred immediately ceased to engage at the mention of this apparently taboo subject. His eyes searched the room for a safe harbor of old friends, and he ditched me as soon as he could do so in a manner consistent with the tenets of the revised standard version of the Gospel of Politesse.

The website www.frederickbuechner.com describes Fred Buechner as "an American writer and theologian" who "is the author of more than thirty published books and has been an important source of inspiration and learning for many readers. His work encompasses many genres, including fiction, autobiography, essays, sermons, and other nonfiction. Buechner's books have been translated into twenty-seven languages for publication around the world. Buechner's writing has often been praised for its ability to inspire readers to see the grace in their daily lives."

Albert Bigelow wrote a self-effacing account of his effort to stop hydrogen bomb testing by sailing into the prohibited atomic zone, *The Voyage of the Golden Rule: An Experiment with Truth* (1959).

The New Hampshire Supreme Court case upholding the convictions of the UNH college students who defied the mandatory "take shelter" edict is *State v. Pinsince*, 105 N.H. 38, 39 (1963). The Court's opinion woodenly proclaims its flimsy legal basis for affirmance: "It appears not to be questioned that the Directive which the respondents are charged with violating provided in part: 'Upon receipt of warning Red, sound the take cover signal, (1) Stop all traffic except emergency vehicles . . . (2) Clear streets and sidewalks. Have pedestrians take the nearest shelter.' The Civil Defense Act provides for the arrest of any person violating any order, rule or regulation made pursuant to the Act 'which affect[s] the public generally' RSA 107:19 (supp), and a penalty for such violation. RSA 107:22 (supp)."

The Phillips Exeter Academy's weekly student newspaper ran a front-page story on the Town of Exeter's 1961 Memorial Day parade, headlined "Sign-Bearing Student in Memorial Procession Arouses Town's Anger." It's in *The Exonian* edition of June 8, 1961, 1: "Attempts to bait the Student Peace group backfired May 30 when PEA senior Stuart Russell picketed the town Memorial Day Parade with a sign reading 'Student War Council. Complete Destruction of the World Would Be a Good Thing.' Russell . . . walk[ed] beside a car carrying Gold Star Mothers." The article doesn't mention my presence on the Academy's lawn while holding my "End the Arms Race: Ban the Bomb" sign or my rapid-fire expulsion from the school thereafter.

Photographs of the American Friends Service Committee workcamp in Missouri's boot heel, taken by coparticipant John Engel, a New York City trusts and estates lawyer, are in the inaptly named Stephen L. Saltonstall Photograph Collection (1962) at the Special Collections and University Archives, University of Massachusetts Amherst Libraries. One evening I happened to show a CD of John's photos to Tom Fels, a North Bennington author and professional archivist, who made a copy and donated it to UMass. At my request, Tom tried to have the collection renamed after its creator, John Engel, but he failed in that effort. One of the photos in the archive is of me and my friend Priscilla Pace. I look very young, more like a middle-schooler than a senior in high school.

Roland Thomas "Mick" Micklem, our AFSC workcamp head counselor and our savior from violence by night riders, died in Staunton, Virginia, in 2018 at age 89. An obituary written by the Bear Funeral Home in Churchville, Virginia, notes that Mick was "a follower of St. Francis."

Charles "Chuck" Neblett was one of the four original Freedom Singers,

along with Rutha Mae Harris, Bernice Johnson Reagon, and Cordell Reagon. His Wikipedia entry says that he was arrested twenty-seven times
during his participation in the civil rights movement. In 2014, he performed
at the White House at the invitation of President Obama. A video clip from
that performance is currently available on YouTube: www.youtube.com
/watch?v=hhafyI6-Bp0. In the video, Mr. Neblett is the tall man at stage left,
auditorium right. He sings bass. Beautifully and with conviction.

On the burial of Colonel Robert Gould Shaw beneath the sands of a
Morris Island, South Carolina, beach in a common trench with his soldiers,
see, for example, "The Need for a Tougher Heroism" by J. Anthony Lu-
kas, *Time* magazine (April 29, 1996): "When the Union army asked for his
body, a Confederate officer replied, 'We have buried him with his niggers.'"
General Colin Powell's views on the assault on Fort Wagner by the Massachusetts 54th Regiment are contained in the Foreword to Martin H. Blatt et
al., eds., *Hope and Glory: Essays on the Legacy of the Massachusetts 54th
Regiment* (2001). The quote by William James appears in a speech he gave
at the unveiling of the St. Gaudens bas-relief on May 31, 1897, contained
in the volume *Dedication of the Monument* (1897). Robert Lowell's poem
"For the Union Dead" is from a book by the same title, published in 1964.

Innumerable sources exist on Selma. A seldom-seen video that I recommend above all others is an emotionally gripping *New York Times* documentary short, "A Call from Selma" by Andrew Beck Grace, featuring the
late Reverend Clark Olsen, who was walking with his friend, the Unitarian
minister James Reeb, when a white racist ran up behind them and smashed
the side of Reeb's head with a club. Reverend Olsen held Jim Reeb's hand as
he lapsed into a coma; he soon died. This important bit of primary-source
history is available on the *Times* website: www.nytimes.com/2015/03/06
/opinion/a-call-from-selma.html.

Reverend Olsen tearfully contrasts the starkly different public reaction to
the murders of the white-skinned Reverend Reeb and the Black civil rights
activist Jimmie Lee Jackson. To which I plead nolo contendere. The murder
of Reverend Reeb, who was from Boston, made it mandatory for me and
cars packed with other like-minded souls to leave the city forthwith for
Selma from a Commonwealth Avenue staging area at Boston University. At
that time I was unaware of Mr. Jackson's voting rights work or of his assassination by an Alabama State Trooper in Mack's Café in Marion, Alabama.

For more on John Ballard, in whose cramped Mercury Comet I rode to
Selma, and who was able to remain there long enough to participate in the
march to Montgomery, see "Man Searching for Boy From 1965 Photo" by
Tyra Jackson, *Selma Times-Journal* (February 14, 2015), on the web at

www.selmatimesjournal.com/2015/02/14/man-searching-for-boy-from
-196 -photo.

Vietnam War troop levels are listed by year in a chart titled "Battlefield Vietnam Timeline," available at www.pbs.org/battlefieldvietnam/timeline /index1.html.

On the Defense Department's "Project 100,000," my sources include James Maycock's "War Within War" in *The Guardian* of September 14, 2001, and Myra Macpherson, "McNamara's 'Moron Corps,'" in the *Salon* issue for May 30, 2002. A detailed critique of the program is by Lisa Hsiao, "Project 100,000: The Great Society's Answer to Military Manpower Needs in Vietnam" (1989). at https://digitalcommons.lasalle.edu/vietnamgeneration /vol1/iss2/4. Hsiao writes:

> Project 100,000 assumed the guise of a social program with the primary goal of helping black youth and reconstructing 'the fabric of black society.' In reality, the Johnson administration, the DOD, and the Armed Forces used Project 100,000 to further their own agenda by sending over 100,000 [draftees and recruits] (about 50,000 of them black) to fight and die in Vietnam. The Administration had little time and money to devote to the war against poverty and the campaign for civil rights. But by adopting the paternalistic hypotheses of selected government reports, Johnson and McNamara constructed the pretense of Project 100,000. Not only would the program provide soldiers to produce the body counts on which the Vietnam War focused, it would also temporarily eliminate pressure on the administration to show its support for civil rights.

Professor Neustadt's fear that a debate between McNamara and Robert Scheer would make it difficult for the Kennedy Institute to attract other important government figures is examined in "McNamara's Challenge," in the *Harvard Crimson* edition of November 7, 1966, and in a letter to the editor titled "Shoddy Ploys" in the November 16, 1966, edition. SDS's modest and limited goal, which was to hold a debate on the war between McNamara and Robert Scheer, was the sort of event that later became commonplace at university campus teach-ins. Nonetheless, Neustadt opposed a debate because, in his view, the Harvard SDS chapter's "primary purpose" was "to discredit government policies." See Robert J. Samuelson, "Mill Street: Chronicle of a Confrontation," *Harvard Crimson*, November 15, 2016. See also the excellent account of the McNamara demonstration by Robert Greenstein, "The McNamara Incident at Harvard," *Dissent Magazine*, March 1967, 215. Greenstein was for many years the director of the influential nonprofit Center for Budget and Policy Priorities.

The Peter Simon photograph of Secretary of Defense Robert McNamara surveying the crowd from the roof of his limousine on Mill Street in Cambridge is posted on the web at http://digitaljournalist.org/issue0610/simon 10.html.

Robert Strange McNamara's inaccurate description of the 1966 demonstration, and the apology he received from Harvard dean John U. Munro, are contained in McNamara's book *In Retrospect* (1995), 254–256. Harvard University President Nathan Marsh Pusey's post-demonstration letter to Secretary McNamara reads in part: "Those young SDS students, while worshiping something they call participatory democracy but adopting the tactics of Brown Shirts, must surely be confused." See Morton and Phyllis Keller, *Making Harvard Modern* (2001), 308.

Petitioning the Harvard administration to allow a debate on the Vietnam War, and then holding a nonviolent protest in response to Kennedy School stonewalling, is not a "Brownshirt" or Nazi tactic. President Pusey should have audited the one Harvard College course given on Hitler and the Holocaust when I was an undergraduate there, and which I took, called "Nazi Totalitarianism." Had he done so, he would have learned how the Brownshirts, a nickname for the SA paramilitary group, helped the Nazis achieve power by street-fighting the outmanned and disorganized democratic socialists opposed to Hitler, and of the leading role played by these antisemitic thugs in perpetrating Kristallnacht, the "Night of Broken Glass," which ushered in the Holocaust.

The number of civilian casualties suffered in Vietnam is documented in Nick Turse's *Kill Anything that Moves* (2013), in the chapter "An Operation, Not an Aberration," at page 13. As his title implies, Turse views the appalling number of noncombatant deaths as an intentional goal of U.S. policy. This opinion finds support in Douglas Valentine's book *The Phoenix Program* (1990), which describes the miserable fate of hundreds of Vietnamese civilians whom the CIA branded as political opponents of the Saigon regime and whom the agency kidnapped and interrogated in torture chambers from which no inmate is believed ever to have emerged alive.

The "Save the Sycamores" demonstration is chronicled in an article titled "Underpasses: A Chronology," *Harvard Crimson*, October 3, 1964, and in a photo essay by Charles Sullivan, "Radical Events (and Bad Behavior) in Cambridge," Cambridge Historical Commission, July 20, 2017, 7, which includes a photograph of a MDC police officer and his German Shepherd threatening peaceful Harvard students.

An account of the draft card turn-in on April 3, 1968, on Boston Common's Flagstaff Hill, near the intersection of Beacon and Charles Streets, may be found in Michael S. Foley's book *Confronting the War Machine: Draft Resistance During the Vietnam War* (2003), 262. According to Foley, between 5,000 and 12,000 people attended the rally (depending on who was counting), and "at over sixty similar rallies across the country, more than 1,000 men gave up their draft cards; 235 of them did so in Boston." I was one of those. Foley's book contains photos of the Boston event.

For the full text of the antiwar speech by Eugene V. Debs at Canton, Ohio, on June 16, 1918, see *Debs and the War* (Socialist Party, Chicago, undated), available at https://debsfoundation.org/pdf/canton-and-court.pdf. The quoted passage is at page 19. Debs's allocution at his federal sentencing begins at page 40. On Woodrow Wilson's attitude toward Debs and his case generally, see "When America's Most Prominent Socialist was Jailed for Speaking Out Against World War I," *Smithsonian Magazine*, June 15, 2018.

George King's unsuccessful appeal of his murder conviction is in the Vermont Reports, *State v. King*, 131 Vt. 200 (1973). Neil Moss, Esq., the State's Attorney who prosecuted the case, told me that he is certain that Mr. King was guilty, but I have doubts, admittedly based only on George's behavior and that of his wife when I saw them in public interacting with the children. The fact that the police never bothered to interview me, a next-door neighbor, suggests that their work was less than thorough. Any murder investigation, especially when each of two suspects claims that the other was the perpetrator, ought to include an exhaustive canvass of the residents near the crime scene.

On Ho Chi Minh's surprising connection to Boston's Parker House Hotel, see William J. Duiker's biography, *Ho Chi Minh* (2000), 50–51, and the hotel's internet blurb, "Historic Omni Parker House," at: www.omnihotels.com/hotels/boston-parker-house/property-details/history.

Anchorage criminal defense lawyer Wendell P. Kay, known in the legal profession as the "Silver Fox," was Speaker of the House when Alaska was a territory. In 1970, he lost a race for U.S. Senate to Ted Stevens. See "Wendell Kay Is Candidate for Senate," *Fairbanks News-Miner*, February 13, 1970, 1. He died in 1986 at age 72.

Chapter 2: The Outlaw Road and Its Challenges

Martin Erdmann's censure by the New York judiciary is memorialized in *Matter of Erdmann*, 333 N.Y.S.2d 863 (1972). Erdmann's notorious interview, which gave rise to the censure, is featured in the March 12, 1971, issue of *Life* magazine, 56. Erdmann became a New York City criminal court judge in 1985. See his obituary in the *New York Times*, January 17, 1987,

Sec. 1, 15. See also the comments on the Erdmann disciplinary case in Bruce McM. Wright's "Caveats from the Elders: Warnings and Alarums to Students of the Law as They Learn to Tread Water in its Inconsistent Depths," *North Carolina Central Law Review* 4, no. 2 (1973): 220.

Chapter 3: My First Case: Representing a Serial Killer

The facts underlying the prosecution of Professor Webster for murder and Chief Justice Lemuel Shaw's jury charge are contained in the Massachusetts Reports, *Commonwealth v. Webster*, 59 Mass. 295, 304 (1850). The discussion of premeditation in the *Tucker* case may be found in the decision *Commonwealth v. Tucker*, 189 Mass. 457, 494–495 (1905). The SJC opinion reducing my client Thomas McInerney's conviction to second-degree murder is *Commonwealth v. McInerney*, 373 Mass. 136, 154 (1977).

On Judge Chmielinski's courtroom behavior, the First Circuit decision affirming the United States District Court's scathing issuance of the writ of habeas corpus, *Oses v. Commonwealth of Massachusetts*, 961 F.2d 985 §6 (1st Cir. 1992), is just as damning as the opinion of the trial court: "We can recognize the problems and the strain involved in presiding over this case. These difficulties, however, cannot and do not excuse the trial court's improper conduct during the trial. We agree with the district court that the judge's conduct incited the defendant to misbehave. The trial judge should have realized that his sarcasm and pettiness had the effect of pouring gasoline on a fire."

The SJC's less than collegial affirmance of Judge Chmielinski's denial of my motion to dismiss, which I had argued at Thomas McInerney's resentencing, is set forth in *Commonwealth v. McInerney*, 380 Mass. 59, 69 (1980). Mr. McInerney was represented on that appeal by the renowned and learned Boston defense lawyer Robert L. Sheketoff. I was living in Vermont and working for the Massachusetts Department of Social Services as its counsel for Berkshire County when the appeal was briefed and argued.

Unlike the issue of guilt or innocence, which is still debated by journalists and scholars, Judge Webster Thayer's prejudice against Sacco and Vanzetti is not in dispute. See, for example, "The Danger of Donald Trump: Prejudice Can Fuel Gross Miscarriages of Justice," *Washington Post*, August 15, 2020. ("Judge Webster Thayer, who presided over the trial, made no secret of his loathing for the two men he called 'anarchist bastards.'")

On August 23, 1977, the fiftieth anniversary of the executions of Sacco and Vanzetti in the electric chair, Massachusetts Governor Michael Dukakis issued a proclamation (in English and Italian) urging people "to reflect upon these tragic events and draw from their historic lessons the resolve to prevent the forces of intolerance, fear, and hatred from ever again uniting to overcome the rationality, wisdom, and fairness to which our legal system aspires."

The findings and order of the Commonwealth of Massachusetts Parole Board in Tom McInerney's most recent hearings, are available on the internet at www.mass.gov/doc/thomas-mcinerney-life-sentence-decision-o /download and at www.mass.gov/doc/thomas-mcinerney-life-sentence-deci sion-april-26-2021/download.

Mr. McInerney's two known murders and his violent history were extensively publicized in the press. For example, see the *Boston Globe*, June 17, 1962, 2; "Springfield Youth, 19, Held in Waitress' Slaying," *Boston Globe*, June 18, 1962, 14; and the *North Adams Transcript*, September 27, 1962, 17, "Springfield Youth Given Life for Murder of Waitress." After McInerney's second murder, the *Globe* ran an objective, in-depth piece by the highly regarded late reporter William A. Henry III, "What Went Wrong with the Ideal Risk," December 21, 1985, A-1.

Chapter 4: Representing a Cop-Killer

There are many press accounts of the murders of Boston police officers Walter and John Schroeder and the fates of the perpetrators of those crimes in editions of the *Boston Globe* and *Boston Herald*. The articles on Terrell Walker's post–Walpole Prison arrests invariably mention his cop-killer past and imply or state explicitly that he never should have been released by the criminal justice system.

Singular in that regard is an op-ed by Mike Barnicle, written after Terrell's 1994 bust for armed robbery. Barnicle describes in detail the murder of John Schroeder two decades before. Then, writing in his "working stiff" persona, he misstates the basis on which the United States Court of Appeals for the First Circuit issued the writ of habeas corpus granting Terrell a new trial. According to Barnicle, Newman Flanagan's prosecutorial misconduct was simply a "mistake of semantics in his summation"—he "screwed up his tenses." Barnicle makes no mention of the egregious Fifth Amendment violation or of the prejudice inherent in the use of the prisoner's dock. See "Stumbling in the Courts," *Boston Globe*, August 9, 1994, 29.

I enjoy Mike Barnicle's political insights on MSNBC's weekday television program *Morning Joe*, but this *Globe* opinion piece is the archetype of inaccurate, inflammatory press coverage that can make the profession of criminal defense unduly and unfairly difficult and at times dangerous.

Terrell Walker's postconviction appellate journey is of record in *Walker v. Butterworth*, 599 F.2d 1074 (1st Cir. 1979), which overruled the United States District Court's decision set forth in 457 F. Supp. 1233 (1978), as well as the Massachusetts Supreme Judicial Court's refusal to grant appellate relief, in the Massachusetts Reports at *Commonwealth v. Walker*, 370 Mass. 548 (1976). The Supreme Court's decision on prison clothing and the presumption of innocence is *Estelle v. Williams*, 425 U.S. 501 (1976).

Terrell's final arrest in 2018 is documented by the U.S. Department of Justice website at www.justice.gov/usao-ma/pr/project-safe-neighborhood -sweep-nets-29-individuals-charged-drug-and-gun-charges-brockton. There is nothing further on the web about Terrell, and he is not mentioned in the state or federal prisoner locator websites. Norman Zalkind told me in November 2021 that he thinks Terrell was in bad health at the time of his arrest in 2018 and that he died in custody, but I was unable to confirm that.

The Supreme Court decision authored by Chief Justice John Marshall discussed in connection with the Terrell Walker case is *McCulloch v. Maryland*, 17 U.S. (4 Wheat.) 316 (1819). The case affirming the right under the First Amendment to use birth control is *Griswold v. Connecticut*, 381 U.S. 479 (1965). *Gideon v. Wainwright*, 372 U.S. 335 (1963), established the constitutional requirement that states provide free legal counsel for defendants charged with serious crimes.

Chapter 5: The Chad Green Case: Medicine Versus Quackery

Both Massachusetts Supreme Judicial Court opinions in the Chad Green case are titled (to protect the identity of the child) *Custody of a Minor* and are in the Massachusetts Reports, 375 Mass. 733 (1978) and 378 Mass. 732 (1979). The parents' unsuccessful federal civil rights lawsuit against my client John T. Truman, MD, Chad's pediatric oncologist, is *Green v. Truman*, 459 F. Supp. 342 (D.Mass. 1978).

The shockingly severe punishments prescribed for stubborn children in seventeenth-century Massachusetts are preserved in the *General Laws of the Colony and Province of Massachusetts Bay* (1814 ed.) in Ch. XVIII, Sec. 13, 59 (capital punishment), and Ch. XXII, Sec. 2, 74 (whipping).

The United States Supreme Court cases discussed in the chapter on Chad Green are *Jacobson v. Massachusetts*, 197 U.S. 11 (1905), and *Prince v. Massachusetts*, 321 U.S. 158 (1944).

On Laetrile and its history and dangers, see, e.g., "Laetrile/Amygdalin

(PDQ ®)—Health Professional Version": www.cancer.gov/about-cancer /treatment/cam/hp/laetrile-pdq. This article makes clear that the toxicity of Laetrile was known to cancer physicians at the time Chad's parents abandoned professional medical care in favor of that quack remedy.

Chapter 6: Fighting to End the Death Penalty in Massachusetts

My father's First Amendment case—reversing the criminal convictions of socialists for making a speech and passing out political pamphlets on Boston Common—is *Commonwealth v. Gilfedder*, 321 Mass. 335 (1947). United States District Court Judge Bailey Aldrich's opinion finding Leon J. Kamin not guilty of the crime of contempt of Congress is *U.S. v. Kamin*, 136 F. Supp. 791 (D.Mass. 1956).

The death penalty case in which I participated is *District Attorney for the Suffolk District v. Watson*, 381 Mass. 648 (1980). Citations for cases mentioned in my brief in that litigation include *Attorney General v. Massachusetts Interscholastic Athletic Association*, 378 Mass. 342 (1979) (the ERA protects men from being subjected to harsher criminal penalties than those imposed on women); *Morgan v. Hennigan*, 379 F. Supp. 410 (D. Mass. 1974) (school and housing segregation); *Associated General Contractors of Mass., Inc. v. Altshuler*, 490 F. 2d 9 (1st Cir. 1973) (race discrimination in the building trades); *Boston Chapter, N.A.A.C.P., Inc. v. Beecher*, 504 F. 2d 1017 (1st Cir. 1974) (discriminatory practices in the hiring of firefighters and local police officers); and *Arrington v. M.B.T.A.*, 306 F. Supp. 1355 (D. Mass. 1969) (same as to public transit workers).

The case documenting violent assaults on Black citizens by roaming bands of whites, and police approval of same, is *Police Comm'r of Boston v. Lewis*, 371 Mass. 332 (1976). *Black Voters v. McDonough*, 421 F. Supp. 165 (D. Mass. 1976), deals with attacks on Black candidates and their supporters. The cases on unconstitutional race-motivated juror challenges and selective prosecution are *Commonwealth v. Soares*, 377 Mass. 461 (1979), and *Commonwealth v. Franklin*, 376 Mass. 885 (1978).

Cases that I cited as evidence for my due process argument in *Watson* that the Supreme Judicial Court once approved executions on legal grounds that were later deemed reversible error include *Commonwealth v. DiStasio*, 294 Mass. 273 (1936) (holding that the constitutional prohibition against double jeopardy is not binding on the states); *Commonwealth v. Min Sing*, 202 Mass. 121 (1909) (no error when the trial judge refused to admit evidence that the police had bribed witnesses to testify against the defendant), a position later rejected by the United States Supreme Court in *Mooney v. Holohan*, 294 U.S. 103 (1935) (the knowing prosecutorial use of perjured testimony violates due process of law); and *Commonwealth v. Millen*, 289 Mass. 441 (1935), where three codefendants were shackled together and surrounded by police in the courtroom during their trial.

Here is how I determined the identity of the dozen Massachusetts defendants who were executed in the twentieth century without benefit of an appeal of their convictions: I compared a list of those condemned and electrocuted, as compiled in the essential volume *Executions in America* (1974) by William J. Bowers, at pages 448–449, with the relevant volumes of the Massachusetts Reports, finding them bereft of any record of mention of appeals in the twelve cases.

Commonwealth v. Colon-Cruz, which eviscerated a constitutional amendment purporting to overrule *Watson* and resurrect the death penalty, is published at 393 Mass. 150 (1984). *Commonwealth v. Long*, the decision on race discrimination in traffic stops, is at 485 Mass. 711 (2020).

Chapter 7: Vermont Law Practice

The late Paul L. Olson, PhD, who testified for the defense in Joe Maillet's case, was the author of several editions of a standard reference book, *Forensic Aspects of Driver Perception and Response* (through the third edition, published in 2010), and he was the coauthor of *Human Factors in Traffic Safety* (2002).

Chopper Lake's murder case was the subject of extensive press coverage, particularly in the *Bennington Banner*, including "Bennington Youth Held in Fatal Shooting," October 1, 1984, 1; "Lake Lodges Innocent Plea," October 2, 1984, 1; "Lake Released on Bail," November 3, 1984, 1; "Lake Agrees to Bail Conditions," April 25, 1985, 6; "Hearing Is Today in Lake Case," June 4, 1985, 18; "Lawyers Present Arguments in Lake Murder Hearing," June 5, 1985, 18; "Arguments Honed for Lake trial," July 27, 1985, 1; "Jury Selection Begins in Lake Case," July 30, 1985, 16; "Lake Jury Still Being Chosen," July 31, 1985, 7; "Jury Selection Continues in Lake Case," August 1, 1985, 6; "22 Ruled Out as Jurors in Lake Case," August 2, 1985, 6; "Lake Jury Is Selected," August 3, 1985, 6; "No Contest Plea Entered by Lake," August 6, 1985, 1; "Hearing Opens on Lake Sentencing," September 18, 1985, 6; "Charles Lake Sent to Jail for 1984 Slaying of Father," September 19, 1985, 1; and "Just Who Is the Strongest Man?" April 25, 1998, 9.

Chapter 8: The Cowboy Snodgrass Case

My files in the Cowboy Snodgrass case had long since ceased to exist when I began work on this book, but I retained a copy of my trial brief, from which I took material, and fortunately a helpful story of the litigation appears in the *Rutland Herald* edition of January 9, 1987, 15. This article, "Cowboy Snodgrass Wins Suit," contains verbatim the arguments in Paul Kulig's memorandum of law that I criticize, as well as the dollar amount of the court's verdict.

The Vermont Supreme Court decision *Livingston v. Page* is reported in 74 Vt. 356 (1902). *Nichols v. Mudgett* is at 32 Vt. 546 (1860).

Chapter 9: My Most Troubling Walk-In Cases: The Cleaning Lady and the Doctor and the Gun on My Desk

Dr. Z's effort to have sex with my client Nancy, which included the violent assault on her husband, was the subject of a series of newspaper articles still available on the internet, including "Doctor Will Be Subject of Inquest," *Bennington Banner*, January 9, 1986, 6; "Doctor's License Suspended," *Rutland Herald*, January 14, 1986, 1; "Doctor Pleads Innocent to 4 Charges," *Bennington Banner*, January 22, 1986, 6; "Pediatrician Denies Criminal Charges," *Rutland Herald*, January 24, 1986, 8; "Dr. Avoids Trial," *Bennington Banner*, May 20, 1986, 8; "Board Orders 60 Day Suspension," *Bennington Banner*, August 21, 1986, 1; "Dr. Faces Third License Suspension," *Bennington Banner*, October 3, 1988, 1; and "Judge Mahady Rejects Dr.'s Complaint," *Bennington Banner*, March 2, 1990, 3. At this writing, according to the website of the Vermont Board of Medical Practice, Dr. Z's license remains suspended. See https://apps.health.vermont.gov/CAVU /Lookup/LicenseLookup.aspx at credential no. 0006074.

The Vermont Supreme Court decision describing Nancy's mistreatment by her disabled son is at 2016 VT 36.

Chapter 10: Continuing with Public Defense

The study I cited on lack of education as a predictor of incarceration of young men is by Phil Smith, EdD. It was published in *Disability Studies Quarterly* 25, no. 3 (2005), and is titled "There Is No Treatment Here: Disability and Health Needs in a State Prison System." I found it on the web at https://dsq-sds.org/article/view/571/748.

The case involving Steven Shearer and his assault on his wife's divorce lawyer was the subject of two articles in the *Brattleboro Reformer* by the veteran pro-prosecution journalist Susan Johnson: "Attorney Protections Don't Apply to Lawyer in Office Assault Case," April 1, 2000, 13; and "Judge Rules Lawyer Entitled to Official Protection," May 11, 2000, 13. Ms. Johnson failed to cover Mr. Shearer's favorable plea agreement or his stellar performance on the Department of Corrections work crew. Vermont's obstruction of justice statute that Shearer was charged with violating is 13 V.S.A. § 3001.

The case I cited of a client who spent a year and a half in prison for conduct later determined by the Vermont Supreme Court to be noncriminal is *State v. Waters*, 2013 VT 109. With the assistance of attorney Merrill Bent, who finished the case after I retired, I successfully represented Mr. Waters in a suit for money damages against the state of Vermont for wrongful incarceration.

Chapter 11: Homicides by Auto

Raymond Mohr's plea deal is reported in the *Bennington Banner*, August 12, 1986, 1. On Matthew Wolff's no-jail plea agreement, which did require him to plead guilty to a felony driving offense, see *Bennington Banner*, May 8–9, 1999, 1.

Chapter 12: Representing the Worst Person in Vermont

Edwin Towne Jr.'s federal firearms case, which I argued before the United States Court of Appeals for the Second Circuit in New York City, is reported as *United States v. Towne*, 870 F. 2d 880 (2nd Cir. 1989). There was sparse press coverage of that appeal, limited to squibs such as "Appeals Court Hears Argument on Towne," *Burlington Free Press*, September 20, 1988, 15; and "Towne Conviction is Upheld," *Rutland Herald*, March 24, 1989, 14.

The exhaustive and creative police work leading to Towne's arrest for the murder of Paulette Crickmore, including the hunch-based decision by Leo Blais to X-ray the foundation of Towne's home, which turned up the murder weapon, is lauded by reporter John Dillon in his article "For Sgt. Leo Blais, the Search for Paulette Crickmore Became an Obsession," *Rutland Sunday Herald*, December 14, 1986, 1.

The bizarre psychological evaluation conducted on Mr. Towne by a New Hampshire prison employee, which diagnosed Ed as a regular guy who just needed a little sex, is discussed with appropriate scorn in the article "East of the Jericho Road: The Murder of Paulette Crickmore" by John Philpin, which is available at www.karisable.com/crickmore.

Chapter 13: Getting Rid of a Bad Judge

The Vermont Supreme Court's decision on my appeal of the will-contest trial at which Judge Arthur O'Dea presided is *In Re Estate of Raedel*, 152 Vt. 478 (1989). Hiding in decrepit old sets of the Vermont Reports at 70 Vt. 352 (1898) is the primary case on which I relied in drafting my appellate brief, *In Re Barney's Will*. The case of *Blair v. Blair*, reversed by the Vermont Supreme Court due to misconduct by Judge O'Dea, is at 154 Vt. 201 (1990), and his disciplinary matter, *In Re O'Dea*, is in the Vermont Reports at 159 Vt. 590 (1993).

The Vermont legislature initially defeated Judge O'Dea's retention by thirty-seven votes, but after a recess and two hours of intense lobbying, followed by a motion for reconsideration, he lost by only one vote, which I understand was cast by Senator Jan Backus after the phone call to me from her husband, Steve Blodgett. A later move by the legislature to vest Judge O'Dea's annual pension post hoc, which would have increased his retirement pay from $4,000 to $22,800, also failed to pass. See "O'Dea Denied Reappointment," *Burlington Free Press*, March 26, 1993, 1; and "Judge Denied Extra Benefits," *Burlington Free Press*, April 16, 1993, B-1.

Chapter 14: Operation Rescue Accuses Me of Attempted Murder

Press coverage of McHugh's relentless efforts to shut down Vermont women's health clinics that perform abortions includes "Fifty Arrested at Anti-abortion Demonstration," *Burlington Free Press*, September 23, 1988, 1; "Police Cart Off 97 Abortion Protesters," *Burlington Free Press*, November 30, 1988, 1; "500 March to Protest Abortion," *Burlington Free Press*, January 22, 1989, 1; "Judge Issues Order to Halt Protests of Pro-Life Group," *Bennington Banner*, February 10, 1989, 3; and "Authorities Grow Impatient as Protesters Change Tactics," *Burlington Free Press*, May 20, 1989, 1.

Here is a selection of some of the newspaper articles on Ronald Comeau's case: "Man Attempts Suicide in Jail," *Bennington Banner*, June 23, 1993, 1; "Man, Would-Be Suicide, Breathes on His Own," *Bennington Banner*, August 25, 1993, 3; "Appeal Filed to Save Patient's Life," *Bennington Banner*, November 12, 1993, 1; "Court Orders Food for Patient," *Bennington Banner*, November 13, 1993, 1; "Little Known about Comeau," *Bennington*

Banner, November 16, 1993, 1; "Comeau Case Takes Surprise Twist," *Brattleboro Reformer,* November 17, 1993, 1; "End Near in Life and Death Saga," *Bennington Banner* November 19, 1993, 1; and "Family May Take Comeau Out of State," *Rutland Herald,* November 19, 1993, 1.

The press account quoting Mr. Comeau's sister to the effect that he made "little progress" while bedridden for four years after his suicide attempt is "Ronald Comeau, Center of 1993 Right-to-Die Case, Dies," *Bennington Banner,* July 5–6, 1997, 6A.

Chapter 15: Combatting the War on Drugs

On the flaws of the against the Duquenois-Levine test, see *False Positives Equal False Justice* by John Kelly (2008), available at www.mpp.org/wp-content/uploads/2016/01/falsepositives.pdf.

Regarding the nonspecific nature of the drug test by microscope for presence of cystolithic hairs, see Frederic Whitehurst, "Forensic Analysis of Marijuana and the Kurzman Mystery: A Case Study in Flawed Logic in Determination of Guilt," *Texas Tech Law Review* 41 (2008): 1.

Thin-layer chromatography, like the Duquenois-Levine test, is at best presumptive. For example, it can't distinguish retail products like CBD, which does not contain THC, the chemical that makes one "high," from marijuana. See Lane Harper et al., "An Overview of Forensic Drug Testing Methods and Their Suitability for Harm Reduction Services," which appears in the publication *Harm Reduction Journal,* July 31, 2017, and is available at www.ncbi.nlm.nih.gov/pmc/articles/PMC5537996/.

See also "Drug Screening by Enzyme Immunoassay and Thin-Layer Chromatography," 7 *J. Clin. Chem. Biochem. Clin.* 15 (1977): 275–283 (false positive results using TLC for urine drug tests occur in 48.4 percent of cases, "and it is suggested that thin-layer chromatography is used as a screening test, and to confirm positive results with other methods").

Michael F. Neerman article "Drugs of Abuse: Analyses and Ingested Agents That Can Induce Interference and Cross-Reactivity," *Laboratory Medicine* 37, no. 6 (June 2006): 358–361, is on the internet at https://academic.oup.com/labmed/article/37/6/358/2504490. The article concludes that thin-layer chromatography "requires considerable skill by the technician involved to analyze the results. The relative position of the spot can be characteristic of the specific substance while the diameter and intensity of the spot can be related to the amount of material present in the spot. Although capillary action establishes a distinctive separation pattern for each drug, this test will often produce subjective . . . results."

The *Bennington Banner*'s coverage of the Hugo Nieto trial was the main source on which I relied other than memory. This local daily paper's articles on the case include "Former Janitor Arraigned in Drug Sale Case," May 25, 1999, 1; "Nieto Lawyer Concerned About Bias," October 9, 1999, 3; "Attorney for Middle School Janitor Wants Evidence Banned," November 5, 1999, 2A; "Nieto Marijuana Trial Begins," April 12, 2000, 1; "No Answer: Nieto Trial Jury Hangs," April 14, 2000, 1; and "Charges Against MAUMS Janitor Dropped," April 21–22, 2001, 1. The Pew Research Center poll on racism in the criminal justice system may be found at www.pewresearch.org/politics/2018/10/15/little-partisan-agreement-on -the-pressing-problems-facing-the-u-s.

Chapter 16: Defending Nature

On the concept of biophilia, which argues that there is an innate, genetically determined basis for a love of Nature, see Edward O. Wilson's *The Biophilia Hypothesis* (1990).

Wilson, who died in late 2021, is still considered the world's foremost expert on ants, and his study of the ways that leaf-cutter ants cooperate (including a complex division of labor between individuals, with discreet groups of ants each performing different jobs) documents their survival as a species for millions of years. Their social structure and activities are biologically and chemically driven (ants do not have brains), and Wilson contends that this suggests some human behavior is genetically determined. In this regard, see Wilson's fascinating book *The Leafcutter Ants: Civilization by Instinct* (2011).

In Nicholas Wade, "Scientist at Work: Edward O. Wilson; From Ants to Ethics: A Biologist Dreams of Unity of Knowledge," *New York Times*, May 12, 1998, sec. F, 1, there is this: "Karl Marx, Dr. Wilson once joked when talking about ants, was correct: he just applied his theory to the wrong species. Ant societies, of course, are very different from the biped variety, but one common feature is the inherited nature of social behavior. Like any other feature of an organism, behavior can be shaped by evolution."

Vermont's timber trespass statute, 13 V.S.A. § 3603(a), provides, in relevant part, that in addition to other damages permitted by law the aggrieved party may sue the trespasser for three times the value of the timber that is damaged or cut. Traditionally, courts have capped the amount of "restoration damages" to the land's fair market value. For a review and discussion of cases where courts have awarded restoration damages in excess of the land's value, see "Dump It Here; I Need the Money: Restoration Damages for Temporary Injury to Real Property Held for Personal Use," *Boston College Environmental Affairs Law Review* 23, no. 3 (May 1996): art. 8, 699. My demand letter on behalf of The Nature Conservancy in the Dorset Bat Cave Preserve incident relied on that line of cases.

The decisions in the Lamb Brook litigation: *National Audubon Society v. Hoffman*, 917 F. Supp. 280 (D. Vt. 1995), and *National Audubon Society v. Hoffman*, 132 F. 3d 7 (2nd Cir. 1997).

The Second Circuit precedents on the National Environmental Policy Act, which we used in our memoranda and briefs in Lamb Brook, are *County of Suffolk v. Secretary of Interior*, 562 F. 2d 1368 (2nd Cir. 1977), and *Sierra Club v. U.S. Army Corps of Engineers*, 701 F. 2d 1011 (2nd Cir. 1983).

Kathleen Diehl's assertion that the government's appeal of Judge Murtha's Lamb Brook decision would focus on the meaning of the word "clear-cut," and my comment to the effect that the Forest Service had "shot itself in the foot politically" by filing the appeal, appear in "U.S. Presses to Log in Lamb Brook," *Sunday Rutland Herald and Sunday Times-Argus*, June 30, 1996, D-1.

The nonprofit, unabashedly radical Bread and Puppet Theater is a unique troupe founded by Peter Schumann in 1963 and is based in Glover, Vermont. For many years, Bread and Puppet staged a thrilling pageant (my reaction when I saw it) called the "Domestic Resurrection Circus" in Glover each summer. During these performances, which lasted for several days, some attendee fans camped out on the troupe's farm, but in 1998 one of their number, Joshua Nault, a former Golden Gloves boxer, killed another camper, Michael J. Sarazin, in a fight. After fleeing to France in an effort to join the Foreign Legion, Nault was apprehended and eventually given the surprisingly lenient sentence of two to ten years.

In the wake of this incident, Mr. Schumann canceled the annual Domestic Resurrection Circus, but the group still performs frequently in the United States and abroad. See *Burlington Free Press*, "Man Pleads No Contest in Assault," February 6, 2001, and the theater troupe's website, breadandpuppet.org. I will be forever grateful for Bread and Puppet's help performing at the steps of the court of appeals in New York City on the morning I argued the Lamb Brook case in 1997; its street theater provided a much-needed lift to our legal team and our supporters, and it captured the imagination of the press.

Chapter 17: The Lamb Brook Aftermath

The Society for the Protection of New Hampshire's Forests, which represents itself as a conservation organization, remains a stubborn stalwart in the "working forests" camp of the timber industry and U.S. Forest Service. A section of its website titled "Cutting Trees for Conservation," provides the organization's official view: "Timber harvests are an important component of the Forest Society's commitment to perpetuate the forests of New Hampshire through their wide uses." See https://forestsociety.org/cutting-trees-conservation-storymap.

That, in my opinion, is a classic example of Orwellian Newspeak. Serving at this writing on the board of trustees of the Society for the Protection of New Hampshire Forests are two long-term former U.S. Forest Service employees. One is that agency's retired local boss, who was the forest supervisor for New Hampshire's White Mountain National Forest for fifteen years. Another trustee is the former president of a timber industry business, Seaboard International Forest Products, Ltd.

The contempt of court case *In Re Duckman* arose out of a criminal defense lawyer Lorin Duckman's refusal to follow a directive of Presiding Judge Helen Toor to consult with his client before moving to withdraw his guilty plea. The decision is reported at 2006 VT 23. Here is the transcript of the exchange between Judge Toor and attorney Duckman, which ends with the judge ordering his detention in the Middlebury court lockup:

> THE COURT: Well Mr. Duckman, hold on. I think you need to consult with your client. I don't think you have the right to now withdraw his plea without consulting him. And I'm sure . . .
>
> MR. DUCKMAN: I think you're interfering with my relationship with him right now, Judge. I'm withdrawing . . .
>
> THE COURT: Well, I'm going to ask you—stop.
>
> MR. DUCKMAN: Okay.
>
> THE COURT: Or I will hold you in contempt of court.
>
> MR. DUCKMAN: I haven't done anything contemptuous.
>
> THE COURT: Stop. Stop. I don't think it is an appropriate thing for a lawyer to withdraw a client's plea without discussing it with the client, the pros and cons, the costs and benefits. You did this once before, I didn't say anything about it. I do not think it's appropriate. I think you need to consult with your client about the risks of going to trial if he does that. If after you have spoken with him, he comes in and tells me he wishes to not go forward, I will accept that, but I need to hear it from him, okay?

MR. DUCKMAN: I think, Judge, what you're doing is interfering with my relationship with my client.

THE COURT: You can . . .

MR. DUCKMAN: I would ask for, I would ask for a continuance right now so I can prepare appropriate papers and perhaps I will come back and ask for a change of venue. But I don't think that I am prepared to proceed.

THE COURT: Well, I'm not going to accept that request. So why don't you go out . . .

MR. DUCKMAN: Well, I'd ask for a continuance.

THE COURT: Go speak with your client.

MR. DUCKMAN: I think it is inappropriate to threaten me with contempt.

THE COURT: Stop. Mr. Duckman, I've told you what to do. Go speak with your client. I will be available in ten minutes once you've talked to him.

MR. DUCKMAN: Judge, I don't think you can tell me to go talk to my client.

THE COURT: Well, I just did.

MR. DUCKMAN: But I'm not going to do it.

THE COURT: In that case you are in contempt of court, put him in there and we'll speak at one o'clock under shackles.

MR. DUCKMAN: Judge, I think I'd like an opportunity to be represented by counsel.

THE COURT: Mr. Duckman, I've just found you in summary contempt by ignoring the Court's orders.

MR. DUCKMAN: It may well be an order that the Court shouldn't have given me.

THE COURT: Excuse me. If you continue talking when I am speaking, I will hold you overnight, do you understand. I am holding you until one o'clock. I find that you are in contempt by ignoring my orders. We will see you at one.

Chapter 18: Political Cases

Opponents of the opening of Vermont's only nuclear power plant failed in their effort to stop it, as recorded in a United States Supreme Court case, *Vermont Yankee Nuclear Power Corp. v. Natural Resources Defense Council*, 435 U.S. 519 (1978).

For the website of the plant's perennial grass-roots opponent Citizens Awareness Network, go to www.nukebusters.org. At this writing, Deb Katz remains the organization's executive director.

The best book on the catastrophic failure of the Chernobyl nuclear facility is by Adam Higginbotham, *Midnight in Chernobyl* (2019). The *New York Times Book Review* listed it as one of the ten best books of the year. See the review by Susan Szalai titled "An Enthralling and Terrifying History of the Nuclear Meltdown at Chernobyl," www.nytimes.com/2019/02/06/books/review-midnight-chernobyl-adam-higginbotham.html.

The Tainted Desert: Environmental and Social Ruin in the American West (1998) by Valerie L. Kuletz is a treatise on radioactive detritus and is understandable to readers like me with no engineering background. It examines the dangers of high-level nuclear waste, the impact on public health that its dumping has already caused, as well as the problems associated with proposals for disposal, including at Yucca Mountain in Nevada.

The United States Court of Appeals for the Circuit of District of Columbia has delivered a ringing, scientifically unassailable opinion that should be, but may not be, the death knell of the proposed Yucca Mountain high-level waste depository. See *Nuclear Energy Institute v. EPA*, 373 F. 3d 1251 (D.C. Cir. 2004).

In its per curiam decision, the court rejected as "arbitrary and capricious" the government's proposed "compliance period" for the facility of only 10,000 years. The government adopted this convenient time frame for depository safety despite a National Academy of Sciences (NAS) study finding that the nuclear waste at Yucca will remain dangerous to humans for at least 1 million years. *Nuclear Energy Institute v. EPA*, 373 F. 3d 1251 (D.C. Cir. 2004), at 1270 ff.

Adopting the NAS report, which compelled the court's conclusion that the government's truncated 10,000-year approach is "arbitrary and capricious" (the applicable legal standard, though the court would have been fully justified had it used the word "crazy" instead), the opinion noted that "radioactive waste and its harmful consequences persist for time spans seemingly beyond human comprehension. For example, Iodine-129, one of the radionuclides expected to be buried at Yucca Mountain, has a half-life of seventeen million years. . . . Neptunium-237 also expected to be deposited in Yucca Mountain, has a half-life of over two million years."

The official citations for the negative Supreme Court cases that I was forced to analyze and distinguish from the Vermont Yankee fact pattern when I drafted the motion to dismiss the criminal charges against the anti-nuke demonstrators are *Pruneyard Shopping Center v. Robins*, 447 U.S. 74 (1980), and *International Society for Krishna Consciousness, Inc. v. Lee*, 505 U.S. 672 (1992). The newspaper article setting forth State's Attorney Dan Davis's reasons why he dismissed the Vermont Yankee protest cases is

"Charges Dismissed; Protestors Annoyed," *Brattleboro Reformer*, November 6, 1998, 1.

From the same *Reformer* article is this snippet: "While on the one hand our clients are no longer in jeopardy, I was looking forward to the court and residents of Windham County learning about the safety and health problems at the Vernon plant, Saltonstall said. We had intended to put the nuclear power company on trial."

Rosemarie Jackowski's self-published book *Banned in Vermont* (2010) reproduces at pages 201–251 the entire official transcript of her sentencing hearing in Bennington District Court on October 7, 2004. I reread my Vermont Supreme Court brief in her case, which is archived at the Massachusetts Historical Society. The press coverage that I reviewed includes "Twelve War Foes in Court," *Rutland Herald*, April 22, 2003, B-1; "Supreme Court Hears Protest Case," *Bennington Banner*, September 9, 2005, 1; and "Supreme Court Overturns Protestor's Conviction," *Bennington Banner*, November 23, 2006, 1. Rosemarie's successful appeal is set forth for posterity in the Vermont Reports, *State v. Jackowski*, 2006 VT 119.

Former Red Sox pitcher Bill "Spaceman" Lee unveiled the slogan of his campaign for Vermont governor in a radio interview on May 26, 2016, on the Canadian Broadcasting Company program *"As It Happens*. Lee's comical campaign chat, aimed oddly at Canadians rather than Vermont voters, is at www.cbc.ca/radio/asithappens/as-it-happens-thursday-edition-1.3601462 /bill-spaceman-lee-former-expos-pitcher-announces-candidacy-for-gover nor-of-vermont-1.3601471. Spaceman's campaign rallying cry appears at 6:44 of the interview. I learned of Lee's historic winning game, which he pitched at age 55, from his Wikipedia entry. His equipment for the game, including his homemade bat, is enshrined in the Baseball Hall of Fame in Cooperstown, New York.

Chapter 19: A Precedent-Setting Case for Student Freedom of Speech

The official citations for *Guiles v. Marineau* are 349 F. Supp. 2d 871 (D. Vt. 2004) and 461 F.3d 320 (2nd Cir. 2006). The United States Supreme Court's decision in the "Bong Hits" case is *Morse v. Frederick*, 551 U.S. 393 (2007). The ACLU has posted my legal brief in the *Guiles* case on the web at www .yumpu.com/en/document/view/39418169/second-circuit-appeal-brief-aclu. My brief contains analysis of and citations to all the relevant case law. *Guiles* also has its own Wikipedia page and is mentioned in or is the subject of many law review articles.

Chapter 20: Foiling a Frame-Up

The press coverage of my last jury trial is limited to one article, deep in an inside page in the *Bennington Banner*, February 22, 2013, titled "Man Found Not Guilty of Slashing Attack." The reporter, Keith Whitcomb Jr., quoted me as saying: "This is a case where the client really didn't commit the crime and I was relieved when the jury agreed with that."

Gregory Zullo's ACLU case against Trooper Hatch is covered in "Lawsuit: Trooper Illegally Seized Car," *Rutland Herald*, September 20, 2014, 1; "Was City Resident Profiled?" *Rutland Herald*, June 1, 2018, 1; "High Court Hands Down 'Landmark' Ruling in Case of Alleged Racial Profiling," *VT Digger*, posted online on January 4, 2019, and available at: https://vt digger.org/2019/01/04/high-court-hands-landmark-ruling-case-alleged-ra cial-profiling; and "Settlement in Racial Bias Case," *Rutland Herald*, June 22, 2019, 1. The Vermont Supreme Court case that permitted the Zullo case to go forward, reversing Judge Helen Toor's decision to the contrary, is reported at 2019 VT 1.

Chapter 21: Epilogue: From Lawyer to Water Truck Driver

Humane Borders, the humanitarian organization for which I volunteer as a water-truck driver, has a website that includes a "Death Map for the Tucson Sector" and a searchable database covering the month of January 2000 to the present. It has information on the number of bodies found, with cause of death, age or approximate age, gender, date and place where the body was discovered, and the name of the deceased, if known. See https://humanebor ders.info/app/map.asp.

There is a five-minute, professionally produced video of me on the Humane Borders National Wildlife Refuge water run with fellow volunteers Reverend John and Diane Hoelter, which is available on YouTube at www .youtube.com/watch?v=NxPTRunpC2o.

President Bill Clinton's administration developed and put in place the government's "deterrence through death" immigration policy, which deliberately funnels people desperately seeking safety and freedom onto perilous, killer pathways inside the most remote parts of the brutal Sonora Desert, without sufficient water or food or proper clothing or durable footwear.

The shoes of migrants are what fall apart first, leaving them barefoot. I know this. On almost every water run, I find migrant artifacts, including abandoned footwear, from worn-out women's flats to sneakers with holes and no laces to boots without soles. I have found a tiny baby sock and a green plastic baby spoon, along with empty black water jugs, ripped backpacks, frayed toothbrushes, broken rosaries with scattered beads, dead cell phones, and human leg bones.

These desert crossings are death marches, American-style. In deference to ignorant howls from the uncaring, QAnon-loving, neo-Confederate racists in our midst, no administration has summoned the compassion or commitment to justice to abandon this heartless abuse of vulnerable human beings, whose only "crime" is their undocumented status. We should shelter these refugees and treat them with kindness while their political asylum claims are pending, and we have a legal and ethical responsibility to ensure that their asylum cases are decided fairly and in accordance with international law, not treated with contempt and summarily dismissed by uncaring immigration judges. We must stop sending these innocent people back across the border or to prisons while caging their children in brutal detention facilities on cement floors. If we don't, many more refugees will die trekking across our deserts in search of life and freedom, and America will surely reap a whirlwind.

Index of Names

About the Author

Stephen Lee Saltonstall is a retired lawyer who practiced law for forty years in Massachusetts and Vermont.

Michael Meltsner is Matthews Distinguished Professor and former Dean of the Northeastern University School of Law. As a lawyer for the NAACP Legal Defense and Educational Fund, he was the principal architect of the death penalty abolition movement in the 1960s and 1970s. He is the author of six books, including *Cruel and Unusual: The Supreme Court and Capital Punishment*, *The Making of a Civil Rights Lawyer*, and *Mosaic: Who Paid for the Bullet?*